CLAYTON ESHLEMAN
ANTIPHONAL SWING
·SELECTED PROSE·
·1 9 6 2 / 1 9 8 7·

EDITED BY CARYL ESHLEMAN
INTRODUCTION BY PAUL CHRISTENSEN

McPHERSON & COMPANY

Published by McPherson & Company, Post Office Box 1126, Kingston, New York 12401. Publication of this book has been assisted by grants from the literature programs of the New York State Council on the Arts and the National Endowment for the Arts, a federal agency. Designed by Bruce R. McPherson. Typeset by Delmas Typesetting. Manufactured in the United States of America.
FIRST EDITION.
1 3 5 7 9 10 8 6 4 2   1989 1990   ∞

Library of Congress Cataloging-in-Publication Data

Eshleman, Clayton.
  Antiphonal swing.

  Bibliography: p.
  Includes index.
  1. Eshleman, Caryl.   II. Title.
PS3555.S5A83   1989   814'.54   88-1550
ISBN 0-914232-94-0

SOME OF THESE PIECES first appeared in the following magazines: *Aula Vallejo* (Córdoba, Argentina), *Sixpack, Fiction International, Atropos* (Montreal), *Tri-Quarterly, Sulfur, Temblor, The Ohio Review, Spring Annual, Uj Iras* (Budapest), *Poetry Flash, Talus* (London), *Caliban, The Translation Review, Exquisite Corpse, Syntaxis* (Tenerife, Spain), *Margins* (London), and *Boundary 2*.

The reviews of Elizabeth Bishop, William Bronk, and Charles Olson were commissioned by the *Los Angeles Times Sunday Book Review*.

Other pieces have appeared in the following books: *Residence on Earth* (translations of Pablo Neruda), 1963; *Coils*, 1973; *The Gull Wall*, 1975; *Hades In Manganese*, 1981; *Antonin Artaud: Four Texts*, 1982; *Fracture*, 1983; *The Name Encanyoned River: Selected Poems 1960–1985*, 1986; and *Lost Body* (translations of Aimé Césaire), 1986.

"A Note on Aimé Césaire" was read at "Brock Peters interprets Aimé Césaire and Marcus Garvey," a theatrical presentation sponsored by the University of California Press, at the California Institute of Technology Athenaeum, in 1983. "Seeds of Narrative in Paleolithic Art" was read, with slides, at the "Forms and Functions of the Narrative" conference at USC, Los Angeles, in 1981; it was presented a second time at the Narrative Literature Conference at the University of Michigan, Ann Arbor, in 1987. "Vallejo and the Indigenous" was read at the "New Latin American Poetry" conference, Durango, Colorado, in 1986. "Proteus, Poetic Experiment, and Apprenticeship" was written at the request of M. L. Rosenthal, and read at his invitation at New York University, fall, 1979. "The Translator's Ego" was originally written for a presentation on translation at Bookworks in San Francisco, February 1986.

Answering choirs—
for Joanne and Peter

CONTENTS

THE GROTESQUE ARCHETYPE

THE STEVENS-ARTAUD RAINBOW

EDITOR'S NOTE

IN MAKING THIS SELECTION, I have tried to keep in mind CE's deepest poetic concerns as well as to choose the best examples of each kind of prose he has done. Because he rewrites his part of interviews, I have decided that they count as prose and are candidates for this book. However, each interviewer seems to start from scratch, often asking questions that have come up before. Especially in these cases, and occasionally with essays, I have sifted through lengthy pieces for the most clarity, cutting out what does not seem to be essential, or what is said more incisively elsewhere. In general, I have tried to protect the inclusiveness of the writing and to leave its complexities intact. I have only included three of the fifty-one book reviews CE published between 1979 and 1986 because they are not part of his chosen perspectives. Nearly all of them were assigned to him. Many early prose pieces were not included because they did not measure up to the later ones.

For those interested in more prose by CE, the Appendix should be of value. While these pieces, in my opinion, are not up to the ones in the book, in many instances they contain elaborations and undercurrents of the "essential" pieces and in those ways add a dimension to the larger picture.

—Caryl Eshleman

AUTHOR'S PREFACE

THE TITLE FOR THIS BOOK comes from the last line of Hart Crane's *The Bridge:* "Whispers antiphonal in azure swing," from which I have extracted "antiphonal swing." Antiphony, or the singing of anthems, involves one side of the choir, or congregation, answering the other side. For me, the swing is between the erotic and the artistic, as well as between prose and poetry.

I comment on my understanding of the erotic and the artistic swing in my conversation with Gyula Kodolanyi. Here, I would like to say a few words about the other aspect. Sometimes, in a single piece, such as "The Gull Wall," "A Kind of Moisture on the Wall," or "Seeds of Narrative in Paleolithic Art," prose under an increasing charge seeks the otherness of poetry. While my use of poetry and prose is not as planned as the haibun/haiku structure of Bashō's hike journals, it was through studying translations of these journals in the early 1960s that I became aware of the extent to which something about a poet's prose itches to transform itself into poetry and, in a less obvious way, something about the poetry seeks an argumentative or explanative base in prose. There is also the matter of rhythm: prose wanting to intensify its gait, poetry wanting to stop and survey the field it performs in.

While this is not true for all poets, for many of us fulfillment is only possible through a rounding out of poetry *and* prose, in which the seed of each, yin/yang fashion, seems to be in the other.

There are chromatic shades of distinction between these two traditional poles, including, in my case, prose-poems (looking around while jogging?), reviews (in contrast to essays), journals and notes, which seem to be right as a spontaneous expression and in that way do not ask to be reworked as poems or essays. "Notes on a Visit to Le Tuc d'Audoubert" is a case in point. While the actual six-hour visit was unexpected (a chance phone call in Foix leading to the invitation), I had been reading about the cave for several years, and had all my hunches and notions in place at the moment eleven of us (in rubber-raft units of two) floated off on the underground Volp River to the cave's interior shore where we would then begin our 800-meter crawling ascent. We emerged at midnight. I slept several hours, awaking in the giddy, image-filled trance that over the years I have learned to trust as an ignition point for a piece of writing. I was so excited, in fact, that the "note" jumped from prose to poetry several times per page. About two-thirds of the way through what is now the finished piece (with the words "image pressure"), my mind went blank and I stopped writing. Upon reaching this point while typing up the "Notes" several months later, the earlier charge returned and everything flowed without revision to the end.

I recall Northrop Frye referred to Blake's *The Marriage of Heaven and Hell* as an "anatomy," suggesting that it was less a dissection than a composite work that included as its "members" many of the forms and strategies of the art of writing. Such a term also evokes the writing that Artaud did after years of disorientation and silence in French insane asylums. The man who described himself in the early 1930s as "not dead, but separated," discovered in 1945 that personal letters, while remaining letters with a distinct correspondent in mind, could also become literary epistles, prose-poems, and even incorporate glossolalia. Artaud's fusion of genres was his way of liberating his cell of separations into an enmassed ignivomous flow.

I don't think that it is a good idea to try to posit a total writing form based on such examples. What is compelling is that at certain points in certain poets' lives, "anatomies" constellate themselves and appear to be contingent upon a mysterious centrifugence of the poet's life, energies, research, visions and ideas. More often than not, however, those of us who write poetry and prose seem to live on a stem that sways between the extremes the terms suggest.

In checking the words "antiphonal" and "anthem" in my 1950 *Webster's International Dictionary,* I was surprised and delighted to find, right after "anthem," "anthema: *Gr. Antiq.* A mimetic dance representing the marriage of Bacchus and Ariadne." Given the material on "the mistress of the labyrinth" and its potential significance for poetry that appears in "Placements II" and "Chapter 7 from *Novices*" in this book, it struck me that the title concept might relate to very ancient creative activities. Could this "mimetic dance" be the Crane Dance that Theseus and Ariadne are said to have danced around a horned altar? Might such weaving in and weaving out be an early form of antiphonal swinging? Answering choirs may represent a bifurcation of meandering movements and may suggest that poetry and prose were originally, and orally, a combined informing and making-up.

Until the late 1970s, prose was very difficult for me to write. Either I wrote it rapidly and later found that what I had was impulsive and not thought through, or I labored over it as I had drily labored over compositions and term papers at Indiana University. "The Gull Wall" essay/poem, with much editorial work by Caryl, took six months to write; I must have done half a dozen versions of "Thinking about Gary Snyder," and finally abandoned it because it seemed less than perfect. Then, in response to my letter complaining about the poor quality of poetry reviewing in the *Los Angeles Times Sunday Book Review,* editor Art Seidenbaum proposed that I write assigned reviews for them. I initially balked at the idea of having to respond to anything they sent me (one is inevitably sent things that one would not choose to read and therefore may appear to be a more critical/negative person in review print than one feels one really is), but then I decided that I might learn something about writing prose under such circumstances. I think that between 1979 and 1986 I learned a "middle way" between the earlier impulsive vs. overworked attempts, and that such a tempering accounts for the relatively large amount of prose that I have written since the early 1980s, much of which I genuinely enjoyed writing.

My wife, Caryl, has edited this collection; I am very pleased with her choices, and even moreso with the way she has lifted the essential material out of longer pieces (especially interviews). It is appropriate to mention here that she has also participated in the reworking of many of these pieces (her role in this respect is detailed in "Dedication," a piece of prose at the end of *The Name Encanyoned River: Selected Poems 1960–1985,* not included here). She has, in short, functioned as an in-house, companion editor (what writer, ideally, could ask for more?) since the early 1970s when it occurred to both of us that what I was seeking to do could be more intricately worked out by her editorial participation at various stages of revision.

All antiphonal movement in writing seems to be contingent upon resolving at least some of the conflict that was tied up in one's becoming a poet in the first place. When I was living in Kyoto in the early 1960s, I typed out two quotes on a single page and tacked it to the bookcase. The first is a notebook entry by Blake, 1793:

> Thou has a lap full of seed,
> And this is a fine country.
> Why dost thou not cast thy seed
> And live in it merrily?

The second was from an essay probably by Giovanni Papini which had appeared in the January 1964 issue of Cid Corman's *origin*, falsely attributed to Picasso. At the point I copied out the following sentence from the essay, it carried the weight of Picasso's signature (the piece was called "A Confession," and it felt like Picasso had quicksanded all of us):

> I came to see that art, as it was understood until 1800, was henceforth finished, on its last legs, doomed, and that so-called artistic activity with all its abundance is only the many-formed manifestation of its agony.

The two quotes formed a vise into which it seemed I had tight-ended myself, a sense of personal potency and a potential career pressing against transpersonal impotency and the absurdity of depending on poetry to enable me to investigate my manhood and the world meaningfully. It now seems, many years later, that much of what I have written in poetry and in prose is a "many-formed" response to issues, meanings and contradictions that the bits of Blake and "Picasso" raised. Blake's assertion was not simply true, nor "Picasso's" statement totally false. Much of the work put into the prose collected here involved getting their "tombs" to change key.

—Clayton Eshleman
Ypsilanti, 1987

INTRODUCTION

IT IS IN THE PROSE ARENA of these thirty-four essays that Clayton Eshleman worked out his own relationship to postmodern poetry. Not only did he learn the ropes of mid-century esthetics and ideology, but put his own hammer to them and reshaped, even reconceived, elemental notions of poetry which Charles Olson, Robert Duncan, Cid Corman, Paul Blackburn and other artists drew from their times.

It was an age of terrifying transformations, at the heart of which was the passing of the old European order. As long-forgotten colonies in Asia and Africa found their freedom and began to voice their independence in the United Nations, the U.S. and Russia, the new empires, fought bitterly for their strategic alliances. The postmodernists watched as the Third World emerged from one form of tyranny (of five centuries) only to pass into another, perhaps the more devastating in its abrupt dismissal of the old folkways. It was in the so-called primitive orders of Third World life that American poets glimpsed alternatives and fresh responses to the dilemmas of their Western heritage. By the late 1950s, when Eshleman entered its ranks, the first wave of the movement was almost played out.

A decade later, America seemed hopelessly trapped in an imperial conflict in Vietnam, as literary vision darkened in response. It is this second wave of the ferment which Eshleman commanded, putting the stamp of his midwestern disposition onto poetry, turning it to a new direction, a satiric grotesque humor, the counter-assault to an overweening national hubris. Eshleman refocused postmodernism and drew its energies to a razor-sharp critique of imperial abuse and aggression against alien cultures, which he set out to prove were no more strange or alien than one's own psyche with its hidden and rejected depths.

*   *   *

The essays in the first section, collectively titled "The Gull-Robe," show Eshleman trying to extricate himself from a weight of illusions, conventions, religious inhibitions on which he had been raised. His principal heroes are thwarters of the social will, rebellious voices like Blake, alone at his smithy shaping a new vision, and Vallejo, even though he had been "mired in Christ." "Gargoyles" is a vision of the Catholic Church as a festering neurosis of repressed libidinous energies, whose monsters are all aspects of deformed emotions exploding off its sides. And in "The Gull Wall" Eshleman dissects his friend Paul Blackburn to find in his poetry a deification of woman that had prevented him from perceiving her physical actuality, and thus from living his own life as a man or as a writer. These positions all have in common the antagonisms of a younger writer of the 1960s, wishing to purge himself of the influences of his parents, region, religion, all of which seemed to rob him of the awareness needed to write an original poetry. What he found in himself he now saw in others, and thus his diagnosis of the ills and misconceptions of poetry ray out from his own self-analysis. The counterweight of these dissections is his belief that redemptive energies lie somewhere in physical experience, in the intricacies and secret life of nature from which humanity had too long severed itself. Like Olson, Eshleman wanted to believe that the earth seen through the eyes of earlier humanity possessed answers or principles that corrected the hypertrophic mentality of Western life. Something had gone wrong in history that had ruptured the relations and integrity of human life; the outside world had broken down and an inward, fantasizing, and mythically unsound vision had swallowed up reality. These opening essays cannot pinpoint the exact cause or the sequence of events by which modernity had reached its emotional dead end, but Eshleman was sure that the way of redemption lay in the remote past, prior to the "fuck-up that historically occurred with Neolithic man." Present-day fears of Apocalypse, he tells us, are "the ultimate extension of artificial Neolithic environment."

In the next section, "Vatic Sores," the purpose is no longer extrication but discrimination, a series of delicate or fundamental distinctions between his own sense of the world and of other American poets, recent or contemporary. In "Thinking About Gary Snyder," Eshleman is looking at a slightly senior figure of postmodernism, a member of the first circle of the movement, in whom he finds much to admire and praise, but whose core vision reclaims the vague mythical past of romantic writers, the principal charge against his poetry. This essay is particularly interesting in Eshleman's development, for it shows him chafing at other versions of origins and sources of poetic consciousness, but without answers of his own. There is only the nagging thought that a better, deeper, more violent or unexpected basis of human awareness lay in the sediments and among the cave walls of early human history. Eshleman appears here on the verge of consolidating a historical argument, a necessary element of his own vision. And vision is uppermost in his mind: the essay begins by observing that "Snyder has a vision, and that in itself makes him interesting." In his review of Charles Olson's *Maximus* sequence, though again mostly a praising of one of the seminal texts of postmodernism, Eshleman finds the basic tenets of the vision questionable: "Future readers will have to decide to what extent the poem's visionary content corresponds to aspects of an actual American world that is supportive of it." This essay appeared eleven years after the Snyder piece but the objections remain much the same—that at heart the vision of both depends on dubious or missing assumptions. In his criticism of Elizabeth Bishop, the point is made that her poetry is "always clever," and yet superficial, "a sinister and thorough lesson in Apollonian poetics: a view from the tower, distanced, sublimated, observational, tidy." Even Ginsberg, in the essay "Vatic Sores," undergoes close and astute scrutiny for his indulgence in self-heroics and image mongering. And in the letter to the *American Poetry Review*, Bishop's best friend, Robert Lowell, the central figure of "confessional poetry," is also accused of an invidious narcissism, an incapacity to see beyond self.

Only William Bronk, Antonin Artaud and the painter Leon Golub possess the honesty and direct perception which Eshleman can trust. All three have in common a desire to reach behind the Christian tradition to something more fundamental and explanatory of the human dilemma. Bronk's harrowing, painful and obsessive poetry makes Eshleman "think of him as a kind of sealed Protestant Artaud." Indeed, "Bronk is the first American poet to fully engage a sense of art that is shadowed by a pervasive sense of invalidness, of inadequacy, and even failure." He possesses a "self-repudiating lucidity," and his poetry shows how we "are encapsulated and remote from each other," that "there is a real world, beyond our knowing." Bronk's vision clearly defines the sphere of meaning that exists for most of us, but which has no connection to the actual reality of things outside it. Eshleman demonstrates in this review that he accepts the notion that most of what is taken to be culture depends upon this sphere of illusions and vague beliefs, and that few artists recognize the existence of a different realm of actuality lying apart from it. It is this actuality he wishes to seize upon, but which reveals itself to the few whose discordant visions have been roundly rejected as madness, eccentricity or unpalatable depictions of violence and chaos.

This other reality is primordial nature, the life matrix in which the human organism was once fully integrated. This primal actuality preceded consciousness and was a realm of things without specific or consequent effect; whatever was existed beyond thought or conception, in a dimension of pure events devoid of abstraction. It was this state of pure being from which humanity was exiled at the moment of consciousness. In fleeing from nature, human life discovered the void outside it, and began to furnish its emptiness with the phantasms of its thought. When a mental world had been established, primordial nature was eventually condemned as the pit of darkness, damnation, suffering, a negation of the natural realm that included the physical functions and desires of the human body as well. Thus, when Eshleman turns next to Artaud, he presents him as having reached the edge of that mental sphere of human life to glimpse the reality beyond:

> The friction created by Artaud's unceasing induction and cursing of the physical world is in the service of opening up an underworld out of which a "dark parturition of principles" can be summoned.

The "dark parturition" is of course the Fall, when humanity evolved beyond the mute situation of integrated, organic life. The seals on human exile were fixed with the coming of the Christian era. Eshleman quotes James Hillman thus: "Christ's mission to the underworld was to annul it through his resurrected victory over death. Because of his mission, all Christians were forever exempt from the descent."

Through descent to underworlds, figurative hells of emotion, or the actual hells of political and racial suffering, one faced the reality lying outside the rational dream. In his poetry, descent lay beyond the window at 4705 Boulevard Place, Indianapolis, where the boy Clayton stood

> watching Eden
> how I went to that window as to a kind of lip of life

as a man comes to a place & touches it
wants very naturally to enter
                    ["Sunday Afternoon," *Indiana*, p. 167]

The dream he struggled to "gnaw his way out of" was the "anesthetically clean Presbyterian home where smoking, drinking, swearing and gambling were not permitted, where I was an only child who was not allowed to play with Catholics, Jews, Negroes, children younger or older than I was, children whose parents smoked, drank, etc., and whose mothers wore slacks away from home" (Introduction to *On Mules Sent from Chavin*, 1977). Here was the "grief and soullessness of that midwestern bottleneck" from which he struggled to escape. Years later he wrote in the essay on Leon Golub, "The move toward uniqueness on the part of the artist is to show life . . . without all the filter systems humanity has for eons employed to keep itself from remembering itself and exercising its imaginative faculties at large." In a poem at the end of *Coils*, his guiding spirit tells him, "From this point on, / your work leads on into the earth."

Though "Vatic Sores" may seem at first a casual assortment of Eshleman's reviews of writers and artists, his purpose is to assess American culture, to probe the forces that have impeded, restrained or adulterated the intentions of some of America's leading writers, and to lay the blame for their squeamish or narcissistic indulgences at the door of its major religion, Protestantism. Eshleman gave his succinct view on the matter in a recent interview where he noted,

> Many major European and Latin American poets come out of Catholic backgrounds; very few North American poets do. I suspect that this may be a more significant distinction than whatever [Robert] Bly means by unity and identity. Most of us have a Protestant unconscious, and since Protestantism eliminated purgatory, or limbo, a long time ago, this suggests that we have less access to the pagan world, or to a polytheism than European and Latin American poets with their possibly more rich *and* resistant religious backgrounds. Religiously speaking, they meet more prohibitions than we do, and this in turn stimulates a more aggressive form of transgression.

This comment puts into sharp relief the pattern of authors he has translated, all of whom are from Catholic cultures: Pablo Neruda, César

Vallejo, Antonin Artaud, Aimé Césaire, Michel Deguy, the Czechos-lovakian poet Vladimír Holan. Through them, Eshleman was making a descent to underworlds via translation; seen another way, here was one of the forbidden realms of his childhood, the Catholic culture he was forbid-den to know. Catholicism's dark side was a core of magical thought that had profoundly influenced the arts of Europe and Latin America. Even those who repudiated its dogma and political corruptions were inextrica-bly a part of its visionary outlook, a heritage made up, as Eshleman noted, of pagan and polytheistic thought.

By contrast, American culture was formed from the consequences of the Reformation, in which the self was redefined and shorn of its mystical bonds. In Protestantism, the links backward to the primordial were sealed off, whereas in Catholicism, the iconography and rituals still bore remnants of Neolithic or even Paleolithic ceremony. Though Cathol-icism remained the execrable religion of sexual repression and of corrupt political affiliations to dictators and tyrants, it was, from one point of view, the last living connection to primordial thought. The American writer mirrored the humanistic goals of selfhood of Protestant evolution, and not the dreaded hell-visions of the Catholic world. Indeed, such art tended either toward narcissism, or toward the prejudicial attitudes Eshle-man discerned in Elizabeth Bishop, or toward the inconclusiveness Olson faced at the end of his life. Even Olson seemed trapped in a Christian vision of life when Eshleman noted in his unpublished journal, *Heav-en-Bands,* "Is Olson troubled by Jerusalem? It would seem so in that he participates in the *mystique* of "place"—(as do Irby, Dorn etc.)." Missing in almost all of the writers and artists of "Vatic Sores" is the plunge to the depths of human origin, the desire to know the source from which human identity was torn. Instead, and through the Protestant rationalist vision, the writer in America tried to imagine a fulfillment of purely human interests, a satisfaction of the potential to remain apart from nature.

When Eshleman first traveled in Mexico in the summers of 1957 and 1958, he was struck deeply by the bleak poverty and desperation of rural people, but also by their primitive rituals and primeval existence in the twentieth century. Reality persisted in the continuities of a culture that had not lost its memory of the deep past. *Mexico and North* (1962), Eshleman's first book, a collection of lyrical impressions of Mexico and Taiwan, bore the germ of his later, mature thinking: that the elemental reality eluding American poets lay at hand among these hispanic Catholics of Central America and that the writers who struggled out from under the burdens of poverty and ignorance to write for international audiences possessed a vividness of mind beyond the adulterated imaginations of North American writers. Except for Blake, England is passed over in Eshleman's critical accounts; his literary reckonings track the extensions of Romance cultures and their spread of a porous version of Catholic theology and ceremony—in which the native religions were absorbed into Christian ritual. He despised the theology that had caused such despair and destruction as he found, but in a subtler and undefined way, he was drawn to the mind drenched in its magical arcana; hence his complex relation to Vallejo, a figure pitiable for the Catholic guilt he bore, and essential for the magical transformations of life which his heritage had goaded from him.

In 1974, Eshleman read Mikhail Bakhtin's *Rabelais and His World,* a provocative interpretation of Renaissance satire in which the Russian critic attempted to reconstruct the "history of laughter." The giants and hyperbolic humors of Rabelais' narrator struck Bakhtin as extensions of the forms of mockery to be found in pre-Lenten festivities and other carnival rites of the late Middle Ages. In carnival humor, the burdens of civilization were cast off in the unrestrained antics of men and women disguised as animals, goblins and deformed humans, in a state of lascivious abandon in which prince and commoner romped in the streets as equals. For a day or two each season, the towns of Europe sloughed off hierarchy and artifice to descend to primitive origins once more, to recover from the oppressive rigidities of urban life. Eshleman was immediately struck by the parallel to other forms of primordial descent. But Bakhtin also pointed out that Rabelais marked the end of true carnival laughter, that a paler form of political satire then took its place. Bakhtin's thesis argues the restorative functions of grotesque mockery, and describes connections between medieval Catholic culture and the remote past. With a little stretching, it is possible to imagine the carnivalistes as pantomiming the grotesque scenes found on cave walls of Upper Paleolithic France, in the honeycomb caverns running beneath some of those very towns. Bakhtin's compelling assumption is that a conduit to the primordial past opened in such events and that a flow of revitalizing energies seemed to push up from the abyss into consciousness. It was that very *frisson* of the pit that Eshleman wants to think is still possible today.

Although Bahktin's history marks its terminus in the early seventeenth century, in Eshleman's view Rabelais' impact is to be found in Vallejo and Artaud; in the paintings of Golub, Francis Bacon, Chaim Soutine; in the music and writings of various contemporaries as an increasingly fragmented aftershock.

It was also in 1974 that Eshleman and his wife, Caryl, made their first trek to the caves of southwestern France, in the Dordogne region below Perigueux, where many specimens of Upper Paleolithic art have been found. The caves preponderate along a corridor of limestone outcroppings that drops precipitously into northern Spain, and thins out into northwestern Germany, with remote extensions into Great Britain, and down through Italy into Sicily. The heart of the cave region follows the Vézère River in the Dordogne and includes such remarkable "galleries" as Les Combarelles, Font-de-Gaume, and Lascaux's "Rotunda," the Sistine Chapel of primordial art. Only Altamira ranks with the mural splendors of Lascaux, but where Altamira represents the Modernist discovery of ancient art, Lascaux, discovered in 1940, belongs to postmodernism and the yearnings of the contemporary mind.

The caves roam the subterranean depths of Catholic Europe, with its caverns and warrens seeming to link up with the catacombs and undercrofts of the Christian era. Bakhtin had already postulated the connection between Rabelais and a Roman past, which glimmered in animal masks and outrageous carnival behavior, but to Eshleman the caves now revealed their influence on the Catholic conception of the "underworld": one rock shelter, an *abri* near Lascaux, is called the "Gorge d'Enfer," for example, and another cave has the name "Gouffre du Diable," the devil's abyss. Cro-Magnon man, named for the cave in which five skeletons were discovered in 1868, had an early defender in Henry Miller, a *Perigourdin* by choice, who once wrote:

> I believe that Cro-Magnon man settled here [in Dordogne] because he was extremely intelligent and had a highly developed sense of beauty. I believe that in him the religious sense was already highly developed and that it flourished here even if he lived like an animal in the depths of the caves.

Actually, Cro-Magnon man did not live in the caves, but used them almost exclusively as temples for worship and magic, making them the first cathedrals of Europe.

These matters begin surfacing in Eshleman's poetry as references to Upper Paleolithic culture, primordial human life, an underworld shimmering with psychological phantasms and clues to mental evolution. It took some time to assemble the allegorical puzzle of the caves, and to fix an interpretation of their myriad possibilities. *The Gull Wall*'s allusions to cave lore cast over them the familiar metaphor of a labyrinth, the Minoan maze, which Eshleman perceived as one of its many permutations. The unconscious now had its precise physical equivalent in the Dordogne and at Altamira. Then, in the summer of 1978, Eshleman read James Hillman's *The Dream and the Underworld,* which established a multitude of correspondences between mental structure and the figurative outline of the abyss.

Connections between the caves and the unconscious occupied the voluminous poetry of 1977, from which four collections emerged, most notably *Grotesca* (dedicated to "Mikhail Bakhtin, whose vision of the 'grotesque' coming up through Rabelais to the Romantics confirmed the work I had done on my own in *Coils*") and *On Mules Sent from Chavin,* both published in England. Nearly all the poems from *Grotesca* found their way into his main collection of that period, *What She Means* (1978), which consolidated his thoughts on the cave hypothesis to that point. In putting himself among the caves, Eshleman could dramatize an event that had been hatching in his work from the very first page of *Mexico & North:* his own transformation by plunging into the abyss. Yet, the latent and bolder theme of rebirth suddenly implanted itself in his descriptions of prehistoric mind. His "plots" had featured recurrent rebirths—through Reich, his lovers, alchemical, astrological and other schema—but the clinching adventure of self-change had eluded him. The caves were the richest of all possibilities: they had birthed *homo sapiens* 35,000 years before, and had found their way into the reprimitivized art of the twentieth century, a winding round to origins. It remained to take oneself into its darkness to be *reborn,* and to dramatize the event in *Hades in Manganese* (1981) and *Fracture* (1983) through a palimpsestic language of allusions, parallels, psychological subplots, historical and scholarly amplifications, personal interludes and allegorical dilations that draw in political issues and cultural enemies. The caves become a womb-door in which the dead spring back to life, including parents, his ur-self in Indianapolis, his son and his first wife, recesses of his blocked consciousness, friends, Paul Blackburn's troubled ghost, the spirit of Vallejo and the legions of artistic apparitions who haunt its mazes. Eshleman has hit upon his mother lode in the caverns, and through it joins a tradition of comic and grotesque art reaching back to early Europe.

In titling this third section of essays "The Grotesque Archetype," Eshleman allies himself with a tradition he defined as "abstract romanticism" in his "Response to Mary Kinzie." Such poetry does away with the regularizing poetic conventions to disencumber the creative process, a mode of execution in which one digs below the surface of thought to the universals buried beneath it. The implicit ideological assumption is that a culture or epoch of thought is only a patina of legitimations imposed upon an immutable core of mind linking all of human life. A particular culture formulates its perspective in superficial terms of roles and self, which other strata of mind erase. The archetypal imagination bears no trace of the racial or social antagonisms raging at the surface of thought.

An archetypal poetry turns on rites of passage, the cycle of human life, the community of living things, a perspective on the organic unity of life. But Eshleman fine-tunes his position by insisting on a "grotesque archetype," in which the primordial background is reasserted in modern sensibility through the disfiguring, conflating pressures of undirected imagination. In diminishing the role of will in self-expression, one backs down into mental recesses where Paleolithic art first took its forms, those "churn-like" agitations of image and dissolve, of animal-human phantasms. Such language emanates from what Jerome Rothenberg once called "the basic imagination," the stratum of collective mentality from which, according to Robert Kelly, one dredges the "deep image," the vehicle of "maximal communicative force." Both poets urged such a use of language in 1960, forming an early, ephemeral, but important sub-movement of postmodern writing which Eshleman had glanced off of with his earliest poetry. Fifteen years later, his own position veered around to those original notions, but with mature insight into their historical necessity, their ethical imperative, which were only hazy outlines when first articulated. Eshleman now makes them the central tenets of a second wave of postmodern thought, and their implications continue to be explored and developed through a network of new journals that includes *Sulfur*, Eshleman's sequel to *Caterpillar* (1967–1973), *Tremblor, Conjunctions*, and others.

As Eshleman is careful to remark in his introduction to *Fracture*, the descent to prehistory was made not "to avoid confronting a present that literally affords no place to stand," but rather "to stand before the deepening shaft of otherness" in order to register "with as much precise subjectivity as possible the global conflict over which I have no control." Like the Romantics before him, Eshleman senses a disappearance of natural life in our time, "an odd bend in the amplitude and awfulness of life," as if "spring [had] gone out of the world." Prehistory is a text, a set of inscriptions decipherable as clues to modern consciousness; hence, we are cautioned not to take too literally these excursions into time. They are, above all, the materials of contemporary vision, elements for which a poet has found use apart from their own importance as artifacts. "I have tried to create the visions of the Fathers of Lascaux as a shaping that had 'us' in mind, an 'us' that we can still find in the art of 17,000 B.C."

The essays of the final group, "The Stevens-Artaud Rainbow," draw attention to Eshleman as writer now, to the situation of the contemporary poet in the light of his intellectual circumstances and traditions, to remind us that all the foregoing thought serves an artistic function first. What emerges from his interview with Gyula Kodolanyi, his critical rebuttal to Mary Kinzie, the polemics surrounding Stevens and Artaud, the dialogue with James Hillman, is an artistic *resilience,* a determination to make clear his intentions *as poet,* to clear the air of murky misjudgments and wrong-headed mystifications. Eshleman takes up the cudgels against a corrupt literacy that sees only its own narcissistic interest in what it praises and condemns. The tradition he defends, we should note, is a "rainbow," something distinct and promising after a great downpour of mystagoguery and obfuscation of human nature. The writers he gathers here are the illuminati of organic human identity, much put upon and abused by establishment partisans. Many of the essays are rescue work, but even the attacks upon his adversaries answer to Eshleman's deeper purpose: to show the malefactors as defending a cult of progress, the destructive humanism of a Protestant culture bent upon making an artificial cosmos outside nature. The battle lines square up on these elemental issues: a band of writers in league with natural life against the prejudicial views of critics like Mary Kinzie. There is a strong Manichean flavor in Eshleman's forensics, perhaps a lingering trait of his mother's Presbyterian ardors. Eshleman thinks in terms of prophets, martyrs and visionaries in a landscape of shattered ideals and wasted hopes, a quixotic landscape of extraordinary dreamers wandering like hermits through the alien cities of the West. The voice once great within us is now "grape shot within us," he notes bitterly, adding that in Antonin Artaud's persecuted life the lantern of understanding was "shattered" in his stomach.

The ideas recorded in these essays are a striking concatenation of the century's major themes and preoccupations; Eshleman began writing at a distant, inland periphery of the postmodern ferment, coming of age just as the movement had begun to abate. Perhaps there was a hidden advantage to this; he could turn its unraveling principles into a new gospel, a redemptive strategy by which to make himself into a poet. As a product of a midwestern burgher life, he had his adversaries arrayed before him, as well as the heroes necessary to his radical conversion into artist. Though he takes very little from the instance of Ezra Pound, he is cut from similar cloth and there is much in common between them, both in historical and literary interests. Like Pound before him, Eshleman has rejected the provinciality of American art and taken his influences from abroad, finding himself more in sympathy with French, Spanish and Latin American writers than with American contemporaries. His descent to the remotest human past has followed the line of reasoning of his Modernist forebearers, a chain of speculative positions leading through Pound, Eliot and Hart Crane, to Williams, Olson and Robert Duncan; through Vallejo, Rimbaud, Rilke and Blake, into the absolute dawn of Paleolithic intelligence.

The essays collected here form one of the voices of the poet's imagination, a coaxing, needling voice challenging him to rethink positions, to gather courage to make a firmer assault on authority and received notions. It is here that Eshleman worries a bone, chastises the timidity of fellow poets, or goads himself to imagine more clearly what he intends with his own poetry. The essays are a workshop, a place where prose serves as an expository guide for the reader as well as the poet. Eshleman's thought is directed toward that door of squeamish evasions, the dark stairs leading down to all manner of fearful memory and experience. His view of redemption requires a plunge into the abyss of origins, not only the murky beginnings of Upper Paleolithic consciousness, but any adult's origins—when sensuous memories of the species were alive briefly and easily obliterated by elders and institutions. Eshleman worked out his own recovery in some of these essays, and carefully constructed a redemptive narrative from Blake to his contemporaries. It was through prose that he could hold up a mirror to his own mind and explain to himself what he was looking for in the caves of the Dordogne, in Vallejo, Artaud and others, and in his own childhood and first marriage. In doing so, he illuminated his own intentions but also the dilemmas and solutions of a whole generation of poets working with him.

—Paul Christensen
Kuala Lumpur, 1987

ANTIPHONAL SWING

THE GULL-ROBE

Terrain of the *Residencias*

I TOOK AS ROCK, as source, volume bound in red leather, a weight with red silk page-mark and gold fish in a compass burned into the cover: not book but N E R U D A spelled as compass-points, a directional, and as such, having no beginning or end.

On the frontispiece, a photograph of a man in his twenties in a dark heavy suit and cloak draping outward to curve in over his crossed thighs. The background is obscure and blends with his clothes. Light relieves the right side and slightly arched eyebrow of the lowered face and eye—a collar, and again, from black sleeves, long hands rest in folds, birds of dusky luminary whiteness I've seen at evening relaxing across the loam swell of waters.

To write of Neruda and his poetry, I must recall the beginning of everything I now consider to be my own.

I hitchhiked to Mexico the summer of 1960, to Chapala, and rented for 3 pesos a day a room from Jimmy George, an American ex-butcher, and his sixteen-year-old mostly-Indian wife. A magenta and sky-blue painted house, strolled through by pigs and turkeys, smelling of coconut soap, cave-dark at night and sadly littered with shard faces broken when Jimmy dug his well in the backyard.

I knew no Spanish and spent most of my time shifting from cantina to cantina, walking along the lake shore watching the water hyacinths multiply entwining the swimmers and surface with their lavender flowers.

"Terrain of the *Residencias*" is a hitherto unpublished draft of the Postface to the author's *Residence on Earth:* Translations of Pablo Neruda's Poetry (Amber House Press, San Francisco, 1962).

3

Or sometimes just sitting on the esplanade as it got dark, chewing gritty
dried fish.

One night when the rain had washed out the electricity in my room
and I had become lonely from watching the procession of *rebozos* and old
men in dripping straw, I lit a candle and tried to read some of Neruda's
poems. I didn't do well, so the next morning I ask Jimmy's wife to help
me. And I remember the soft bronze of her face, waist-length pony-black
hair, eyes questioning me in sunlight as the three of us approached each
other for the first time, carefully saying *cielo, tierra, piedra, rojo* . . .
These words were all in the book and I learned them, felt them, because
she would point to something, pick something up, as she pronounced it.
La cosa—how I might work in my own way, become less distant from
those who lived around me. Not to take away; to plant; sky, earth, rock,
bougainvilla . . . We decided to try a whole poem and turned randomly to
"Juntos Nosotros" in the first *Residencia en la Tierra*. She scanned, and
laughed. Why would a man say a woman has a "pecho de pan"? I sure
wanted to tell her. Most of that more actual than written translation was
made for me with gestures, wide eyes, hum of insects, the dance to get
this, that, and goes:

> Now hand in hand you splendidly armor,
> your oar of bone, lilies of nails,
> and my body, my wandering soul, return
> with the strong and faithful of the earth.
> How pure my gaze, the nocturnal power
> descending from eyes dark
> as polished spurs; the sinewed sculpture of my legs
> climbing every morning toward moist stars,
> my mouth of grape flesh, exile and death,
> my arms of a man, tattooed chest
> with its hair a wing of tin,
> white face made for sun depth,
> hair of ritual, black minerals, forehead
> penetrating like a blow, a road; my skin
> of the mature son destined to the fields,
> my eyes of living salt, quick to marry,
> my tongue a soft friend of the mole and the ship,
> bone-white teeth in orderly rows, skin

voiding my forehead of frost
　　　　and the sword revolving
in my eyelids, sheathed in ecstasy, growing
in my chin of stone, my feet of riches—
and you, month of stars, fixed kiss, structure of
a small wing, O beginning of autumn, child,
my follower, love,
your bed is formed by your eyelids' light,
dappled like oxen, and so often
in you the round dove makes his white nest . . .

Sheathed in ecstasy! I was walking down Calle Zaragosa the next night drinking a beer when Guillermo grabbed me, took me to meet an elderly Chilean who had been living in Chapala thirteen years. He had only heard of Neruda, but he happily fished out an old shaggy copy of *National Geographic* that had a picture-essay on Chile and reverently pointed out cities and mountains. In the evenings we spent together that summer, he would relax in the shadows as I stumblingly explained why an image made life for me. In those often quiet exchanges I began to know how certain it was that I came to Neruda in Mexico, not only for my own language, but that Mexico is sur-real in a way that cleared the apparent effects of Surrealistic machinery from the *Residencias,* disordered and unpredictable enough to point up what before had been unrecognizable to me in poetry.

That exchange: thing, man, landscape—all a grain of the poem.

When it rained in Chapala, the downpour was tidal; the earth that had held a shard-hardness minutes before would swim red mud, salmon-colored gullies, high green grass. After a stormy night, gutters would be a swamp of mango-flesh, half-buried bottles, a banquet of torn cloths, flies, melon rinds, and as the sun wrapped Chapala in a tourniquet of fire, earth would again splinter, rocks blister through, glitter, smoking at meridian, blood-stained, ash-brown.

Through the low gobble of the markets, the blare and tinkle of the movie-loudspeaker jolting in the trunk of a 1938 Plymouth across the cobblestones, beyond the meat-stalls opening their wounds to the congress of elbows and sandals, distantly, so as to hardly be perceivable in the present, I would hear the Spanish language, hovering a crimson minor between nail and guitar-steel, delicate as butterfly wings, silent as that particular cantina in Ajijic where, twenty yards from the Buicks and banterings of urchins exchanging phoney pots for more worthless silver, a Tarascan woman crouched on a mantle above the beer-cooler, poised in the triumph of birth for 900 years, her lidless eyes, lipless mouth wide in meditation on the birth and dying of the world.

The *Residencias,* in their celebration of the coarse, their bulk, their charges of light and blood, their swag and their humility, their tumuluses of objects newly discovered, their obsession with sex, death and physical decay, gave an alphabet, a magic of and beyond the Mexican terrain.

It was in these noons that I would see an old man hitchhiking along a road become Neruda's guitar-player dressed in bees, and across io-dine-dark hills his sea-urchins go flying to the heavens, or in the autumnal silence of the street his little girls ajar like doors, and his laugh of hurricaned rice . . .

Early in the evening, when the sky is streaked gangrene and rose, and the rusted goal of bells moan across the lake, I would wind through the entranceway of an unnumbered house a broom slowly moving across the earthen floor, the tongue of death looking for the dead, the needle of death looking for thread . . .

[1962]

A Visionary Note on César Vallejo and William Blake

IN THE MIDDLE of the tremendous ninety-first plate of *Jerusalem,* having overthrown everything outward in worship as a distraction from the human, Blake isolates the following line:

So Los cried at his Anvil in the horrible darkness weeping.

It is an image of terrible power and beauty: the artist as smith in unwavering fidelity to his task, hammering form out of matter that is loaded with midnight, in midnight, with only the sparks and the eternally evasive promise of "becoming" to light his way. The twentieth-century poet begins at this point, or realizes this point, more than those who could, in good faith, believe in God. Yet to be a poet in any way that the naming makes sense is *to* believe in God; to move other men in language requires trust in the moment of creation—without such trust and the substance it gives, poetry is a shell, a parlor game, a manifestation of modern man lost in the streets and cities of his desire. There is this Peruvian, César Vallejo, who seems to drag out of the Andes and pass Blake at his anvil as Christ is being imported to South America; in the glances that they exchange is the suffering of Neolithic man and the knowledge that poetry as art is dead. There is only the human to be expressed. But Vallejo is mired in Christ and there is a heaviness that seems congenital that he can only understand in Marx, or believe that Marx can lift. I am saying that after Vallejo, the jig's up: man must attend

---

This "Note" has not been previously published in English; a Spanish version appeared in *Aula Vallejo* (Cordoba, Argentina, 1967). Originally, it was written to be read at the Celebration of the Humanity of César Vallejo, University of Cordoba, July 1967.

to his suffering as something prior to any meaningful utterance:

> *To pull away! To stay! To return! To part! The whole social*
> *mechanism fits in these words.*

At the base of which is Blake's watery tongue of flame, revolving in all directions at once, anchored; not in one direction alone taking off. Our heads, arms, the tops of tuberous stalks; we are buried up to our chests; we want to go; we murder because we don't know what we do; I murder you not knowing what to do; the eyes avert, one looks off, the other, in shame, cast down; Vallejo is full of pain, he is dying in his pod; who will come and pull him out? Unbury his chest? Roll out his golden peas?

> *What curses & harpoons I'll hurl if I die*
> *in my pod; I'll offer up in sacred banana leaves*
> *my five subaltern little bones,*
> *and in the glance, the glance itself!*

In those lines a little boy is holding up his hand to shield himself from his father. But too only his father can release him. My accuser is my defender (Vallejo on his deathbed, quoted by his widow, Georgette: *Whatever may be the cause I have to defend before God, beyond death I have a defender: God*). Who accuses me defends me: Masochism. I am helpless, waiting for the release to come without:

> *Alkaline fuck-up I keep saying,*
> *nearer than garlic, over the syrup sense,*
> *deeper in, very more, the rusts,*
> *on going the water and on coming the wave.*
> *Alkaline fuck-up*
> *too, a wild one, in the colossal staging of the sky.*

These wild, wild lines, O the man trying to trap it, the fuck-up in the very nature of things, it is nearer than garlic, it runs deeper in the rusts, on going it is the water, on coming the wave—the clouds! the clouds! in the very framework of nature: a fuck-up.

> *Getting all of it, cyma*
> *and all of it, in the crying sense of this voice,*
> *I make myself suffer, I extract sadly*
> *at night my fingernails;*

then I have nothing and talk alone,
I revise my half-years and,
in order to stuff my vertebra, I touch myself.

Cyma in which the wave is frozen, Vallejo on the ground looking up every evolutionary pillar (*at the end of scaled nature and of the massed sparrow*), seeing the wave frozen in structure, which is in his structure, in his voice; he, man, pushed to the point beyond which he cannot go. And it falls back on him, crying as a sixth sense, the self-torture for being locked in his pod, outside of which the world is phantom—he desires to desire, he is overcome by a feeling of wanting to love—there is nothing outside because the locked pod takes everything, a parasite living upon itself—to get out, he would pull out his fingernails, again and again the gesture is to make some gesture, to get out.

For one truly does have nothing when one is living off oneself, this beautiful Vallejo in touch as any man has ever been, the vibration, the antennae of his lines, the mind-body a total complex, coming on you, his poems, collapsing in your arms, the full take and sway of a man—but prior, prior, a fuck-up, facing which he can only revise his half-years (like comb his hair), and so hungry, O God the hunger in that last line, so hungry that *to fill his belly is just to touch himself!*

One feels the hand drop. I had felt, on first reading the poem, that a release was intimated in the last line via masturbation, but now I don't feel that such an act cleared into the consciousness of the man. That is, there is an intimation of physical touch (by which we always make a circle whether we touch our toe or left elbow with right hand; the supreme circle which we can never make, to suck ourselves off, i.e., devour ourselves alive, be all "tail hole")—there *is* touch, but the network of the Vallejo body is so jammed and blocked, it is just a touch, almost like a priest touching a small boy's head. *This happened,* Vallejo says, *between two eyelids; I quivered in my pod, furious, alkaline.* A funny jump, from inserted penis to foetus, a funny mechanistic jump, something he wasn't told as a little boy; as a foetus, he tells us, he was furious, and alkaline, or bitter, the taste of ashes in the mouth, a bitterness in the framework. "This" happened in a vaginal wink, suddenly he was here.

Without orgasm, one's semen *is* bitter and there is no orgasm in Vallejo, no release, no loosening. The musculature of his poems: tight as a drum. Thus he looks to Marx, certainly more believable to an intelligent man after he had been beaten for thirty years than Christ—to Marx, more sophisticated pop, to come and redeem him. I am not making light of Vallejo when I say this. The reason he believed as he did and wrote the way he did is not at all literary; it is a result of the way he felt, and while he is forceful, he is seldom direct. The difference between Vallejo and some hack is that, although disguised, he did tell the truth about the way he felt and to the best of his abilities kept his eyes open (as did Antonin Artaud, who is more shattered, less coherent). Vallejo resembles van Gogh in that he was desperately intent on not deceiving himself to the extent that he would stay with pain if that was what he felt, and not compartmentalize it and move off.

Art is no more real than a monkey wrench, and that is why Blake says that during the Apocalypse, Creation too will be burnt up—for Creation, Blake argues, is Error too. To create is to continue a fuck-up that historically occurred with Neolithic man. The guilt of creation is mitigated somewhat in proportion to the extent of release in making love. The more one's organism can be stirred (loving is now the most direct contact we have with nature, though it was probably not always this way), somehow the more one is lived; or the more I am willing to die the more I am lived.

The poet must always believe that there are a few things a hell of a lot more important than poetry. If he does not, he makes literature and serves what Jack Spicer called "The English Department of the Spirit." The most important thing in the world for man to do is to alleviate suffering and the most important thing for him to be, ecologically speaking, is a grape in the cluster of his species. On the one hand, Blake knew that to be natural was to be in nature, but, on the other hand, as soon as he saw a man standing in the woods, he had to get him out; which is to say Blake was uncomfortable in his own skin. Nature was delusion for Blake, or Vala, a veil, and a beautiful woman was equated with a beautiful flower, in contrast to man who is mystically (and divisively) linked to a state before the Fall.

Therefore, the thing is to get out of this world, to envision an Apocalypse. An extreme state of uncomfortableness, to say the least, and for propagating it Blake is only partly to blame, for one of his finest insights into the falsity of most art was to see the falsity in the equation "Woman's Love is Sin." At the same time, Blake associated the Fall with feminine seduction.

We can now see that Apocalypse is the ultimate extension of artificial Neolithic environment, the hundred-megaton bomb. That is the madness in Blake—that the man who saw that the *lineaments of gratified desire* were what men in women, and women in men, required could at the same time hold in mind the world in flames, and not be able to see through the Christian Nihilism in such imagery. In Blake, love and fury are so close it makes one's hair stand on end. Like Wilhelm Reich, he saw through man, and like Reich too, he went off by not keeping his eye on man *as* he saw through him.

Some of the humanity in the poetry of Vallejo can be put this way: When you read him, you are always stuck with man and you never get off into any solution. Christ, or solutions, has already come, sniffed and gone in Vallejo—however, he is not completely solution-free, for while he appears to have thought through violent revolution, Marx, or the murder of the rich, is always just around the corner, a kind of ghost that may be held in place by the poet's oppressive Catholic upbringing. Like Blake, he saw through most of the Christian screens; unlike Blake (thanks to Darwin?), he stayed with man on earth. To be human means to be here with all our feelings, and Vallejo was so human in that he told us how he hurt, because hurting, aching, anxiety and fear were at the core of his Indian existence. If each of us could tell a few people in our lives exactly and fully how we feel, men might embrace and weep and drop their guns. Vallejo knew he wanted to help, and that to want to help everyone also meant to help the killer kill. He let that through.

[1967]

The Gull Wall

IN THE AUTUMN OF 1960, after I had spent a summer in Mexico writing what I felt were my first real poems, Paul Blackburn and I had lunch at a place in New York City he refers to in his own poetry as "the bakery." At the end of lunch I showed him some of my poems, and after reading "A Very Old Woman" he looked up at me with a big grin on his face and with some superlative exclamation blew me a kiss. By doing so at just the right time he confirmed the fact that I had, on my own, at least got up on my feet. A few years ago, reading one of Robin Blaser's poems, I came across the lines: "the poet's kiss / given   caught *like a love- / adept*   on my lips." He was speaking of an actual kiss, and it made me think of what Blackburn gave me, which was a covenant given by an already-confirmed poet to another non-confirmed one. By confirming me when he did I felt Paul had given me in an ancient and noble way a "charge," the Poet's Kiss, which would only be realized when in some original way it was returned. In 1964, in my poem "Niemonjima," I worked one of Paul's central images, the gull, and transformed it into the Gull-robe:

> And it was only the robe that drove him on,
> a vision of the inland sea, which is called the Gull-robe,
> gorgeous, of white feathers emblazoned with stars & moons,
> the lovely garment every loved woman wears, of midnight-
> blue & silks, in which a light streams for all who ride

A slightly different form of this essay appeared in *Sixpack,* #7/8, the "Paul Blackburn Issue," and in *Boundary 2*. In its present form it appeared in *The Gull Wall* (Black Sparrow Press, Los Angeles, 1975).

away into the darkness carrying the torches of imaginative
love, the softness & precision of loved desire.

A great deal of the meaning Paul Blackburn has for me, his life as
well as his poetry, is involved with the role he played in my becoming a
poet, and this is especially touching to me because during those years he
was beginning to lose grip on his own life and writing. From 1962 to
1964 my first wife, Barbara, and I lived in Kyoto, Japan. I had published
my first book of poems before moving there and the poems in it were
written while I was either a student, on vacation in Mexico, or teaching.
Upon moving to Kyoto, I found myself for the first time cut loose from
any job or study routine to depend on; I was suddenly on my own, I had
24 hours to face and fill, and for most of these two years I was tied up in
the frustrations from my past that I thought I had evaded by becoming a
poet. I was reaching the point when I would either accept my own life as
my material, or reject my life, and continue to imitate other poets. This is
the point at which what is previously amorphous in a young poet's work
begins to appear either original or "academic"—where he begins to doubt
the meaningfulness of his first influences. Since I chose the first alternative, I began to feel lost, a feeling which lasted for a number of years.

Originality at that time meant little more than taking my own life to
task; the writing that resulted seemed to mean less than what I would have
written had I continued to imitate others. I understand something about
this now, I understand that apprenticework, in the sense that I am speaking of it, has a great deal to do with letting the heldback dam of one's past
break through one's mouth with all its roil, its stones and silt, and that this
act itself, taking years perhaps, is only the first stage of approaching an
art of poetry, for as the dam gives way the novice must continually create
out of what is struggling through him as well as keep the past itself in
motion. It is the "creating out of" that is felt as a terrible friction, almost
blockage to the longed-for flow, especially if the destruction of the dam is
sudden.

During those years in Kyoto I would sit for hours before the typewriter, sometimes just staring at the first line I had written trying to figure
out how to make it yield poetry, or at other times typing the line out over
and over, varying it, repeating it, trying to dislodge it from my own
common-sense world of the past which I was still holding on to, not only
because I was sacred of losing all moorings; but because I was working

with the past, I was to a certain extent stuck with the way my mind in the past had functioned. Paul and I wrote each other about every two weeks during those years and every six months or so exchanged tapes. Our correspondence was not strictly about poetry—it was basically about what we were seeing and doing and feeling. It was real sustenance for me because a friendship was being created and I was finding out that not only did I need to find my identity but that my identity was manifold.

In late October, 1963, Paul sent me a new tape which I took over to a man who had a tape recorder. I remember sitting in an empty tatami room by a large window which looked out onto a backyard filled with junk. It was cold gray out and had begun to snow. Paul's voice, filled with images of brick walls and nearly deserted streets, of men huddling by little trash fires in gutters, his peculiar vision of New York City which integrates the literary life with the viewpoint of someone on the Bowery, began to worm into my feeling for my life as it never had before. I was just opening up to seeing a world inclusive of outcasts that Paul identified with.

For I too had been watching outcast leather-workers in Kyoto who seemed to live in the street as well as the migratory construction workers who were building a highway down in the cut below where I lived. They worked all night long, keeping an oil-drum fire going, and I was very moved watching them standing around their fire with their yellow helmets and dark blue wool puttees. At that moment there was no distance between Paul's poems and the junk-filled backyard, the cold in my hands, and the endless repetition I felt watching the tape slowly turn. But it was also a specific repetition, it was not just life repeating itself, but repetition becoming a state of mind through Paul's poetry and his voicing of it—he read some *Rituals* that day, which made me think for the first time, what is a ritual, is it any more than repetition, doing something the way my father had done it, and if so, where is the warmth in that? Something about the way Paul was looking at things found a place in me, but it was a place I was trying to destroy by making poetry. What a dense web of ambivalence was being woven between the two of us that late snowy afternoon—I was being bound into the act of a voice which seemed to consume my defenses against poetry. At the end of the tape it was nearly dark and the snow had turned the junk into little castle-like hills—there was only a faint streak of rose-colored sun left in the light. At this point Paul read a poem whose title I do not remember, I remember only two images in the piece: the first was a vision of a group of primitive men standing around in a circle jacking off into the flukes of a dying fire, and the second came moments later: Paul cried out, "O Leviticus, Oil for the Lamps!"

All the negation in my own life was suddenly present, but it was present to me, a gift—Paul spoke of my negation so that I no longer had to wear it but could begin to work with it as an object. The circle of primitive men became a circle of young Indiana men, pledges to the Phi Delta Theta social fraternity at Indiana University in 1953: I was one of them, and we had been shouted down from the dormitory late one night, ordered to strip, and then bend over holding hands making a circle around the double fireplace which hissed and crackled while "the actives" played *Slaughter on 10th Avenue* at full volume (the fraternity was located at the corner of Jordan and 10th Street), and beat us bloody with long wood paddles. In 1963 I was faced in the act of finding poetry with this impotence in my own makeup—what anguish must have been buried in me that I would have allowed myself to be so abused! There must have been something, some ceremony perhaps, which never took place during my puberty, I thought, which, had it taken place, would have released me from boyhood into manhood—but what could that mean in my present life? I had been reading about an Australian sub-incision ceremony which climaxed a puberty initiation, where the boy was held down spread-eagled over the back of a kneeling man and his urethra split with a sharp rock. Would it have been better had something in my boyhood been bled out of me? It was not simply my manhood that I sought—manhood was too easily just the world of grown-ups. I sought the persimmon tree in the Okumura backyard, I wanted to be in contact with it. Blackburn got through to me that there was something which I experienced as being inside me that had to get out for the contact to exist. He made me aware of this not as one who had succeeded in getting whatever it was out, but as one who had failed and whose cry was uttered as a result of having failed.

It was dark when I left where I was and started back to the house of Okumura. At the point I passed the Senryuji Gate, which led in to the Ancient Imperial Burial Grounds, there was a long flight of wide stone steps which led into Imagumano, my neighborhood. I started to descend and immediately recalled an accident I had seen a couple of years before, the legs of a Japanese school-girl extending out from under the rear axle of a bus. When I witnessed this I had a desire to roll the bus off her. Now the axle became a turnstile and as I approached the bottom of the steps I imagined that I was heading into death, but the death I was heading into was so singular it immediately became absurd—I was suddenly aware that I could not resolve Paul's misery nor could I resolve the death of the school-girl, and that my attempts to do so before were ridiculous. I had been living my life as if it were a life that could be solved from day to day, first I would do this, then get out of it, then that, get out of it, etc., and as long as I had done that I lived with an awful anxiety but pretended there was no fear in my life. But no, that girl's death impinged upon me and it impinged in the living body of Paul Blackburn, and I could not keep Blackburn's sense of life away from me, I was not singular, what I was was not what I had identified myself to be—I reached the end of the steps, I got down to the turnstile I had felt I was descending to, my crib with only *one* being inside, and I was free of its singularity, wonderfully free of the absurdity of my life and within it.

The gull is more than a central image in Blackburn's poetry: it is the presence of the creation itself, the confirmation that Blackburn allows himself—when a gull or a flock appear in a poem there is hope as well as all that the phrase "the creation" suggests—I would almost say that the gull is the presence of God in Blackburn's body of writing, but that would be making a connection he only alluded to in the opening section of what for several years (1963 to summer 1967) he considered to be his masterwork, *The Selection of Heaven,* a 25-page poem he was unable to complete:

> GOD,   that it did happen,
> that loose now, that
> early confirmation
>   of birds, the texture set in
>   words,   1945,
>
> A Staten Island beach in early October
> here in more than flesh and brick,
> 9th Street,   March 1963.   . . .
>
> This grey .   soft .   overcast .   not-quite-rainy day,
> that I can

swim my mind in it, swim it in overcast, the sun
tries, and there they are, the birds, my gulls
circle over a street to the North.

At about the same time that he wrote these lines in March, 1963, Paul enclosed a photo of a gull standing on a rock in a letter to me, and wrote under the picture: *Dear Clay, Never look a gull in the eye, love Paul.* That admonition really puzzled me, because even then I knew that among all other things Paul Blackburn loved to look and watch—some of his finest poems have a basic fulcrum of Paul sitting someplace, like on a street-bench or in a park, and watching what is going on around him, presumably writing the poem in a notebook while it is occurring before his eyes. Anyway, I didn't then pick up the literary connection to the line which comes from the poem called *The Purse-seine,* written in 1960:

we cannot look one another in the eye,
                              that frightens, easier to face
the carapace of monster crabs along the beach   .   The empty
shell of death was always easier to gaze upon
than to look into the eyes of the beautiful killer   .   Never
                              look a gull in the eye.

The "we" includes the woman the poet is with, and thus by implication both she and the gull are held for a moment in the phrase "the beautiful killer." I think that, deeply, for Paul Blackburn woman *was* the beautiful killer, and that since he insisted on always searching for and being with a woman, his failure to overcome that feeling explains much of his failure to develop as a poet and to live longer as a man.

But before I enter into these problems I want to make a few assertions so that the problems themselves can be seen in the proper context. Blackburn is one of the half-dozen finest American poets of his generation. The body of writing that he left us and the generations to come is much larger and much more impressive than what is now publicly and thus as his *image* available. He wrote first-rate poetry at several periods in his life and his finest poetry in the fifties when he lived in Spain, and this work carries on into the early sixties when he lived in New York City. His gifts were various: he had an acute ear and eye that together enabled him to lay a poem out on the page in an utterly unique way—a Blackburn poem is recognizable about four feet away, one can spot it by its shape, the way the lines extend and break, run for full stanzas or bunch in neat units at any place on the page, often in short-lined quatrains. His ability to stop the poem the moment the poem itself stops is uncanny (e.g., *Hot Afternoons Have Been in West 15th Street*). In Blackburn's poetry one always feels that the quatrain has not quite yet been abandoned, it appears, floats out, fragments, dissolves, is felt in two- and three-line units or is *sensed* at times through inner-rhyming: one will occasionally *hear* quatrains when on the page none are visible. In other words, the verse never becomes free, gets free of that traditional cohesive—I would even say *communal*—urge, while at the same time it is open enough to accommodate emotional glide (I almost said "drive" but Blackburn is generally not a driving poet—he more naturally enjoys gliding, veering and banking, or suddenly dropping to a fused position—for just a moment—like his gulls). In many ways, he is the Buddhist path between Robert Creeley and Charles Olson.

As for his content, his best poems warm the reader with a sense of a generous, compassionate and patient humanity, wry and foolish at times, bleak and helpless at others. While there are few revelations of being in Blackburn's poetry, he does get, given the situation he is addressing, a great deal of what it felt like into the composition he is conceiving; he does not approach the poem (as does Gary Snyder for example) having thought its subject through—his poems most often begin with an impulse, a partial perception or sounding, and pick their way out from there. His strongest and most successful poetry is contingent upon a kind of distance that he creates when he is alone, i.e., unobserved somewhere, not directly involved in the action he is watching, e.g., observing Paul Carroll being tossed a white sun-burned body by breakers at Bañalbufar (*Affinities II*) or watching common people fill and leave stone benches at dusk on a busy street in Barcelona in the lovely *Plaza Reál with Palmtrees*. While his writing is free of dogma, there is an implied stance suggesting a way of being. One feels this most in his attitude toward women and sex—toward Romance. The source for this, in a literary sense, is the early-medieval Troubadour tradition, which he knew and suffered thoroughly. He spent more than twenty years translating this poetry, and when it is published in book form I believe it will not only be definitive but will never again be equaled in the American language.

One reason that Paul Blackburn translated the Troubadours is that Ezra Pound complained that here was a great body of poetry to be brought to bear on American poetry which no one had really even attempted. Pound's attitude certainly must have been Blackburn's original incentive. However, such an incentive needed a powerful fuel to sustain this project over two decades, and the fact that Blackburn never completed the *Troubadour* translation, or I should say, the fact that he completed it again and again, keeping it alive, revising and adjusting it, suggests that it kept an obsession in him alive, kept it churning. Central to this obsession is the idealization of woman as expressed by the Troubadours—a view in which woman is a grand icy queen of heaven the poet sings for, a queen who will never be lived with, *period,* an untouchable in a much higher social station than the poet himself, who may reward him with her hand to kiss or with a benevolent glance (there are several tremendous burlesques of this maddening situation in the Troubadour poetry Blackburn translated, notably Guillem Comte de Peitau's *Farai un vers pos mi sonelh,* but these pieces hardly dent the idealization). I can imagine how in twelfth-century Europe such an attitude might have had a great deal to do with the evolution of consciousness, adoration of spring and burgeoning being more and more associated with human love, and of course regardless of what it meant to the lives of those concerned, it produced a genuine body of art.

To consider why such an attitude was attractive to Paul Blackburn is complicated. I don't think he himself knew—for like nearly all men of his age he was sexually cracked in a number of directions and the parts never fit together. On one hand, he was a very warm and sensual man who loved cats and food and wine in a way much more European-Catholic than American-Puritanic, and in this sense he lacked typical American hangups regarding hygiene and order; he was messy (his desk was always covered with strata of unfinished letters, translations and poems) but not dirty, or I should say I always had a good natural feeling about the world in his presence. On the other hand, I had the feeling that for Paul sensuality and sexuality did not flow together—I always had the impression that he allowed the woman he lived with to rot on the vine. He had serious problems about his identity regarding men and women, and he expressed this conflict in a rare self-confrontational passage in *The Selection of Heaven:*

Tell me what else this shoulder might serve for
please, I want to live beyond that

please, the drive back 300 miles
please, the ground is cold, there is
please, no other life, please,
please there IS that
difference, say it
might have been a man but
now, no care, who
could care? it was that dif-
      (small dif-)
   erence be-
tween the man who filled was
more a child . You can
turn your back
or I can turn my back—
      it is a child
unborn, it is our being
all our being
man and wife, or else the rest
of life is Jack the
life is back, is fact, is black, is
rope enuf, is no rope, is the ripper
   is the ripper
   is the ripper
is the child, un-
born perhaps,
     and sucking.

  An idealization of woman in our time has roots in a man never
having got enough of his mother and consequently never finding / allowing a woman to equal / surpass her image. I know that Paul's mother left
his father when he was quite young and, with Paul, lived with another
woman for most of the rest of her life. Paul's mother was the poet Frances
Frost and while he wrote very little about her I know that she was very
powerfully in him (he once sent me a photo of himself at five years old
clutching the handle of a Mickey Mouse cane; his mother was standing
behind him, dressed in black, with both of her hands placed firmly on
Paul's shoulders—her eyes were extraordinarily intense and looked
straight through you). In his poetry, at least, his primal affection is for his

maternal grandfather, about whom he wrote a great graveside poem that is the sixteenth section of *The Selection of Heaven*. He had a disastrous first marriage; after fighting for years he and Freddie broke up, and to get a divorce in New York then Paul had to pay her a ton of money, which he did not have. It required him to work for four years as an editor in publishing houses as well as an eight-hour-a-day professional translator. If my sense of him is accurate, by the time he married a second time, shortly after the beginning of *The Selection of Heaven,* he was losing grip on his life and numb to really living with whom he did live with. When Sara left him the summer of 1967 he was utterly shattered, and in drunk despair made a few attempts to hurt, or possibly kill, himself. The fall of 1967 he returned to Europe, having finally received a Guggenheim Fellowship, where he met his third wife, Joan, who was much younger than he and from a similar Irish-Catholic-American background; Paul lived with her and their son Carlos until he died in the autumn of 1971. I think they were deeply happy together, and I am certain that having a son meant a great deal to Paul—but he met Joan too late, he was too far into a downward spin, his body was too rundown from years of steady drinking and smoking. He died of cancer of the esophagus, and my impression was that the life-negative root I felt in him as early as 1963 was as much involved with this as anything else.

Most people who are artists, though, are not so because they have solved great human problems or even the daily minutiae, but because of the particular way they feel these problems and minutiae are unsolvable in their own lives. It is not even a matter of simply feeling deeply, for there are many, many people who feel deeply and suffer the world thoroughly who never have anything to do with art. No, it takes a particular set of imbalances, incredible stresses in some directions with unusual absences in others, faults, burning explosive deposits and areas of glacial motion that create the energy stresses that volcano under an art. It is not possible to say what is THE artistic conflict (or for that matter, the artistic glory) because each artist is a product of his upbringing, a crucible of his times, as well as a creator of his own vision. True, I can say that a thorough reading of Paul Blackburn's lesser poems reveals him as a man haunted by sex-in-the-head who viewed women as sexual-relief possibilities, but as soon as I point this out I am also aware that his so-called failures are part of the reason he is compelling, and fragments such as got through to me and burned me against my own stem on the 1963 tape he sent to Kyoto may be the very things that count. Perhaps it is fair to say that he did not explore his obsessions far enough, that he was defeated by the very vulnerability that allowed him to let in and assimilate his world. When I look at photos of Paul taken in the early fifties he looks amazingly compact and focused, and in spite of what happened to him this plumb-line was present until the end. He was a very non-competitive man living in the fifties and sixties in the most competitive art center in the world—he absorbed too much—many people took advantage of his mea-ger defenses, his own generation of poets lacked respect for him—it may be that he was simply too frail to withstand the world he chose to live in, yet when I say that I must also recognize at the very base of what I know of his being a kind of meaninglessness, a failure to know what he was about, to compete, in other words, through asserting his ideas and making them felt in those he was in contact with. It is easy to be sentimental here—surely many people watched Paul Blackburn lug his fifty-pound tape-recorder up 2nd Avenue to the St. Marks Church to record poetry readings once or twice a week for seven or eight years, and many, not just a few, but many poets alive today are beholden to him for a basic artistic kindness, for readings yes, and for advice, but more humanly for a kind of comradeship that very few poets are willing to give. HE WAS AN ANGEL working for no profit or big reputation gain to keep alive a community of poetry in New York City—he stayed with the poets instead of the critics and publishers and he paid for it. In fact, those who let him down the most were often those he felt the closest to. I remember the formation of the Poetry Project at St. Mark's Church around 1967 when suddenly money became available mainly because a poetry program had been built up through Paul's unpaid efforts. The Church, by which I mean the minister and some local poets, decided to establish paid readings as well as a paid director, a poet who would be paid $15,000 a year for doing officially what Paul had done before informally. It was obvious to a lot of people that Paul was the natural choice for the position, but it was not given to him. I recount this episode mainly for its aftermath: Paul continued to serve, continued to tape readings, to read and help arrange readings. I think he continued because in a dogged and pathetic way he was like the old employee replaced by the machine who insists on contin-uing his work even if in a mock role. Paul lacked the anger to tell the whole gang to go fuck themselves and take his energy and intelligence elsewhere. This kind of mole-insistence is very interesting, and the more

I think about it the more it reveals about Paul. When one paid him a visit, often, after being cordially met at the door one was turned into a listener for what Paul wanted to play among recent tapes or what he felt the visitor should hear. At times it felt as if he was teaching something, like helping one to get over a prejudice about someone else's poetry—as for me, I never really knew what was up—certainly there must have been a reason to listen to so-and-so for an hour before being able to have a conversation—or was that just something Paul put *me* through?

One thing I have had to struggle with in writing this is that I must not explain his meaninglessness, must not give it a mythic quality, for when I think of his death I think of an absence that was never explained in his life. It is possible to say any life is meaningless or meaningful, of course, depending upon the good or ill will with which one approaches that life—but I speak of extruding particularities with Blackburn—the anecdotes he enjoyed telling that became more and more without conclusion or point as he grew older and less in control. I have imagined his relationship to his gull as one of retreating into the gull's head to sit and be by himself, for it was contact with others that was much of his trouble, contact—to not have to stay in contact, to avert his eyes, to tell the story or put on the tape to derail for a moment the other so Paul would not have to feel he had to make sense of his own life—I see him enter the gull's head and pick up little things in his hands to look at and puzzle over, like childhood toys he had almost forgotten—there he is safe, no one can betray or not betray him in this place—then he becomes anxious after a while and crawls back through the gull's eye into the presence of others.

I went over to Sparky's pen
where the little turds were steaming with joy, I picked them up
and placed them on the out-stretched Gull-robe. After I had a pile
I began to mold them into a gull shape, then I wrapped it in
the robe and dug a hole, burying the Corpse of Gull-robe
by my childhood place of secret joy.
As I completed my task a figure loomed at garage edge,
Weren't you supposed to clean the eaves trough this
afternoon, it said,
I smiled, ok,
a ladder was in my hands

I was 9 feet off the ground, Clayton was standing under me,
          the despair in his face, checking me out for evil,
concerned if I was doing a cud job, was I swallowing my cud, was
I doing a cud or was I spitting out the influence, was I swallowing
the cudfluence or was I manufacturing my own salts?
          As he stared at me I transferred myself to 12 years old
and through this transference maintained the vector of his stare
through the eaves trough into the interior of the white garage. Here
is the place I understood Blackburn is to transform himself. I kneaded
the energy from Clayton's eyes, made out the white garage interior,
in the rear was Sparky's inside pen, so she'd be warm in winter,
above the pen the shelf where storm windows were stacked,
building out from this shelf was a false garage ceiling Clayton
had constructed, to pile boards and garden tools on—the ridgepole
and false ceiling made a hazardous little house at its peak
four feet high, an attic of sorts, enormous
wonder of my puberty body up there on a hot summer day
interlocked with urine
                    Attis
                         saw, here I now crouched, unzipped,
a vine institched with tiny skulls spilled out
plums, persimmons, grapefruit, I transferred
outside the white garage again and got more energy from Clayton's
          eyes
pumpkins, pears, an outbranch of apples,
the strengthened false ceiling now abounded in vegetation,
I transferred to a wall, picked off the grass stained hedge shears,
began to sever the fruits from my vine, hanging them on pegs and tool
          nails,
transferred down to Sparky's pen, scooped up her puppies
drawing the birth-glisten from their blind bodies
I built tensile webs; now the walls went into transformation, spider
guardians began to scuttle
in and out of the vegetal wall, this circulation developed for a week,
the following Saturday I opened the right-hand garage door onto a
jungle! A place Clayton had never seen—I left the cavern and started
          forth,

Blackburn's presence was now everywhere, about a mile from the
    cavern
I could see the blue Mediterranean waters, out on the beach in solitude
a figure was seated on a little wood chair at a table writing,
as I approached it turned and watched me, its beak closed, its eyes
beady, unmoving, at the base of its feathered neck were human
    shoulders,
from the freckles I knew, yes, and from its short muscular build—
Can you speak, I said,
    the creature nodded yes then shook its beak no,

                    it sat at Blackburn's kitchen table on one
of his kitchen chairs,
                    I walked over to see what he had written,

*In a way, it's hard to know that I know you anymore. Deep, OKay,
yes, forever, etc. But you've learned & grown & changed so much in
the last couple years it IS hard to know. Things do get thru in poems,
to & from both of us, I guess, that are not discussed in letters. Then
long time when I do not feel like letters or any other contact, that
problem. And the whole problem of experience, the sharing of it,
giving it to someone, or wholly.*

I've returned the Gull-robe, I said,
    and fashioned a place for you, for when it gets cold out here,
would you like to see it?
                    The Gullpaul stood up and began to walk
    back with me, along the path he took my hand,
and we walked hand in hand to the Cavern of Self

I have to leave you here, I said—
as you gave me your life
that moment in Kyoto 1963
when I was nearly dead with despair,
so I have created
a place for you wrought
from the most intense moment of my puberty—
this is not how I thought it would end,
but the weight of the sadness of death is

in me, even facing you here—
I had thought to put a bar in along the right-hand wall
but that meant comfort, and the place I leave you
is shelter yet terrible, is formed of my spirit
which you helped form, yet dark with Clayton's eyes
transformed into spider guardians,
Use this place, or abandon it,

    he entered it, his back lost in the echoing struggle

[1973–1974]

[from]
The *Sixpack* Interview

PIERRE JORIS: Now that *Caterpillar* is finished, can you at this point judge what that work has accomplished—on two levels: outward, for the people who read it, and second, how do you see *Caterpillar* in relation to your own work?

ESHLEMAN: For six years, *Caterpillar* kept an image of original and vital poetry before the public, and one aspect of this vitality has to do with American body; I believe that it is only as the body emerges as a force in our poetry will the stranglehold of academic pseudo-poetry be overthrown to the extent that what is original and vital will not have to take a backseat. This is one sense of what was being accomplished by *Caterpillar* while it was being done. As for myself, the magazine was born in the lull between two big work periods and certainly I used *Caterpillar* to get fuller contact with what was going on in poetry. It probably helped, the editing that is, to loosen up my poetry and at the same time the act of judgment regarding the work of others made me look more closely at what I was writing. I printed something of my own in each issue, not merely to see it in print, but to read it in the context of my judgment about other poetries. When I pick up a magazine and do not find any of the editor's work in it, I wonder what can he or she do relative to what he or she selects. There is a gap, for me, if the individual effort is not there in the context of judging others.

This interview took place in Paris, fall, 1973. It was rewritten in 1974, and appeared in *Sixpack* #9, 1975.

JORIS: How open were you to other, different work—letting it influence you; and to what extent were you consciously trying to influence, shape contemporary poetry?

ESHLEMAN: I never settled on a decision as to the form poetry should take—at times I would find more "poetry" in someone's journals than in his intended-to-be poetry, and all this sighting was contingent upon my own poetic evolution. I began *Caterpillar* in a time of war, personal as well as social, and the first issue has so much preoccupation with social issues that the man who hired me a couple years later at the California Institute of the Arts, and who had only read the first issue of the magazine, Maurice Stein, hired me as a political revolutionary who just happened to be doing a magazine at the time! When he and I actually met, he seemed disappointed, because by that time I had got the Viet Nam War in place and was building something instead of protesting and tearing down. But I did want to influence contemporary poetry in that I wanted only to print work that was serious, that took life seriously, and was honest. I was never interested in *Caterpillar* becoming a definable "group" magazine.

JORIS: How did you go about balancing the two functions of poet and editor, respectively? Did you have any trouble, in that they might have impinged on each other?

ESHLEMAN: Editing is an exercise in judgment: Can one see strength in something that has no "name" pasted on it? For me, this is the positive meaning of the word "tradition"—to keep one's attentions so alive that the best can be discerned while it is being done. One way to address the difference between the world of the English Department where most attitudes toward poetry are formed, and the world of my contemporaries, people whom I printed in *Caterpillar,* is that English Departments engender, in the name of tradition, a dependence on a body of criticism to read a poem—to such an extent that the act of reading is replaced by a kind of career analysis. . . .

JORIS: What about the Norman O. Brown piece in the first issue?

ESHLEMAN: I printed Brown's lecture because it was a lively piece of thinking, and because its argument, that the real response to a work of art is not criticism but another work of art, appealed to me. The thing is, it's not a matter of sensibilities *vs.* politics—the political is more the outer aspect of sensibility. If you love something you want to see it *living* in the human world. Or put it this way: Politics is the visibility of an act. If the act has substance, if it has an artful, an imaginative aspect, then it makes sense to encourage it and attempt to place it among others. Political gesture in the world of art becomes empty when it is not backing something imaginative, when it is merely furthering a career, helping someone make a career merely in the name of art. . . .

JORIS: Earlier, you had said you didn't really see yourself as an editor or as a translator. You have done a lot of work in translation, though, and I wonder how that has influenced your own work.

ESHLEMAN: On looking into the poetry of César Vallejo, it was as if all translation was before me. I thought I knew some Spanish. I did not know Vallejo's Spanish. It was the combination of sheer difficulty in his language, a convoluted strained syntax, and its mesh with a voice attempting to articulate sensations, that lacked historical foundation; and in the center of that I felt a double, as if, were I to articulate my person right then, "he" would speak in such a way to cross in and out of Vallejo's utterance, shadow it, mesh with it, vary, etc., but cross at seminal junctures; not that I was he, not that Vallejo was speaking my poem, but that Vallejo if tapped in American language would accompany me, a sinister brother, muttering and shaking his gourd in my ear. . . .

Vallejo's form is bound up with his formalness; he is always in a fairly clean black suit, his shoes, while scuffed, have been polished—he's just polished them himself before he left his and Georgette's apartment in Montparnasse—he walks over to the most reasonable cafe with a view, orders a beer, which he sips slowly throughout the morning, composing and revising. While he is not at all Bohemian, he hasn't had a full meal for several days, simply because there is no work available for a Peruvian Communist writer in Paris in 1937—and all the Latin-Americans with any money at all are no longer around. These poems have been sifting in him for more than a decade, and by this autumn morning in 1937 he is at dregs, weighted sufficiently to write calmly, at times quite simply, these things that in my own more adolescent roiliness, in 1962, spoke like nightmare and dream utterings. If Vallejo had slipped out of his suit when he was realizing the "Poemas humanos," I see him like a picked mushroom dissolving into a blackish horrible-smelling muck—I mean the balance that allows utterance at all is that tenuous in "Poemas humanos." Louis Zukofsky responded to something I'm suggesting here when we were walking together through Union Square a Sunday afternoon in the fall of 1966 and I asked him if he had read any of my Vallejo translations. Zukofsky started shaking his head in a troubled way, and said "Yes, yes . . . but sick, too sick, too sick to write . . ." For me that sickness is the poison in the mushroom that if digested and stayed with, changes miraculously, it seems, into its contrary vision—that physical revulsion haunts itself so probingly through Vallejo, that it alchemically becomes a broth, a nourishment that stayed me.

JORIS: The only poet besides Vallejo you are strongly involved with, in the context of translation, is Antonin Artaud. At this time, Artaud appears to be a very powerful figure for you—especially the Artaud "le mômo" persona—in what I would like to call the imaginative/imaginary congress or dialogue which the poet holds with some artists who seem especially relevant to him. Could you comment on this involvement?

ESHLEMAN: My involvement with Artaud is more literary in origin than that with Vallejo. Like Vallejo, he is very difficult, an interesting challenge to translate. . . . In late Artaud poetry, Rodez and after, there is a conflict with the body that interests me; concentration camp body as primary and the book as consequence. After Artaud, in European poetry, a neutral zone takes over into which are collapsed the poles of affirmation and negation. Artaud and Paul Celan are the only two European poets I know of who have written great poetry after the Second World War, and in their individual ways both are the fruit of the annihilation of the "human form divine." In Celan there is no anger left, his voice is bodiless, a ghost-voice, without the contour of believed-in experience. Artaud, on the other hand, fought heroically for his anger and—how can I say it—he won his anger, he fought for his anger with his anger, to the very end he remained incensed that the function of the judgment of God, as rendered by mankind, had been to sever the human body from its root connection, its "cogollo" tie, to the earth, and present it to Artaud as a kind of snapping spiritual skeleton, sex-crazed, religion-crazed, materialism-crazed—in pieces, in other words, and it is in confronting that that, he, Artaud, is these pieces, mental pieces, as well as a root capable of sensing still buried powers. Artaud, to my mind, wins his battle. It is quite easy, fashionable, to use Artaud's wrath and paranoia against him and thereby get out of the firehose pressure in which mankind today stands and which Artaud himself signifies. Artaud is part of what any poetry must accommodate to be relevant. Ultimately, I see Artaud standing for imaginative integrity—and he is not merely an underground hero but, like the painter Francis Bacon, an artist in the grand manner.

JORIS: The dialogue I mentioned before seems to me to happen in two ways in your work: in translating key works by those authors, and, more recently, in those new and very startling portrait poems you are writing.* Do you see these two modes as being related?

ESHLEMAN: If translating is a way of bringing other poetries into focus, then the kind of "portraits" I have been doing are a bringing of such focuses over into poetry. That is, it is one thing to translate an Artaud poem and another thing, or another kind of translation—a more difficult kind of translation—to do a portrait of Artaud in which all I know of Artaud is material I am shaping to say how I see him, not as face or bust as is often done in painting, but as an image, as the body of his imagination, which will be a critique, a cutting out of that which I do not see as essential to Artaud, and a manner in which my life material can be set aside to concentrate on his. An *enactment* of Artaud, in other words. Not that I have always followed all of these ideas in my portraits—for example, the one I did of Artaud begins with Artaud as a newspaper-wrapped bundle of meat tossed from a newspaper delivery truck looking up at me, a ten-year-old as I come to the corner of Boulevard Place and 49th Street in Indianapolis for my paper-route. In the Artaud Portrait, I use myself to a small extent to bank the poem off of.

JORIS: Concerning your work up to, and including *Coils,* could you comment on the following:
    What do you consider the source-energy of your work?

---

*Joris refers to the "portraits" of such figures as Van Gogh, Artaud, Paul Celan, Charlie Parker, and Hart Crane, in *The Gull Wall,* 1975.

Could you elaborate on the difference between sexual energy and progenitive energy?

How the spider-image of woman functions in your work as a liberating force—or the Aztec goddess.

ESHLEMAN: I think my source is desire to translate what I consider to be important of what has impinged on me into imaginative constructions so that I can continue to learn from them. Another answer: Real source is never known. When one identifies something as the source, one risks removing the power from it. I recall something Robert Kelly either wrote to me or said to me in the early 1960s, when he felt that I should discover my parents in the backyard grass rather than as figures roasting hotdogs: "Source can never become subject without flawing the poem."

Sexual energy is the cosmic tunnel I am in, which I generally feel most immediately as my body—it is, as Yvonne Rainer said of her body, "my enduring reality"; I suddenly recall it was Marilyn Monroe who, when asked what she considered to be the most erogenous zone, answered: "the mind!"—so the two seem to stand in a relationship that the yin/yang diagram depicts.

I have chosen Blake to loom, to be the giant figure on my night-path, from whom I am to take strength but also whom I must overwhelm, when I am strong enough, if I want to be the father of my own poetry! This is a very complex matter and I have just started in the past few years to think about it. It relates to your question in regard to "source." Blake as source-material, as the widest and most wild, least domesticated, imagination I am aware of.

Yet there are progenitors in art that one does not choose. All twentieth-century American poets stand in varying degrees in the shade of Whitman's mighty oak—and many, many American poets have not chosen Whitman at all, but he is there. I intuit that when I come to grips with Blake, if I can and do, then I will learn something very important about Whitman. One has to be very careful how one expresses oneself about this matter of progenitor or it sounds like cheap, literary competition.

The spider in *Coils* is primarily an image of the self—not an image of woman. Women are no more nor less poisonous than men, if anything less, and anyway the last thing I want to do in *Coils* is to continue to sponsor that stupid carry-over of natural ferocity as an image of woman.

Joris: You once said to me, "No art comes out of a common denominator," that to be an artist and make great art involves the *extra*-ordinary. This could be read as a sort of elitist position, and above the law of the common people. . . .

Eshleman: Oh I didn't mean anything by that remark other than that it is individual difference which counts and is remembered by the world. Why is Hart Crane's poetry more memorable than Conrad Aiken's? For one reason, because it contains itself against the horizon, there is less bleed in a Crane poem than in an Aiken.

Joris: I would like to go straight to the last lines of *Coils,* lines that open upon a future:

> Yorunomado closed the left half of my book.
> From this point on, he said,
> Your work leads on into the earth.

I would like for you to talk about the directions your work is going now—into the *earth*?

Eshleman: I am fully in a labyrinth of, and not of, my own making—I've gained entry, fought my way into a center. I am faced with "earth" as my own mask to continue to penetrate the second half of life which, as I read it, is a fuller more dense working than the first. Apprenticeship will be over if I can develop without the aids associated with the help of less-than-progenitor—the closer one comes to one's progenitor the more harrowing thought becomes, for as one moves into progenitor the way becomes steeper, more is risked, and progenitor is earth, or to express it in visionary terms, is more and more Covering Cherub, for Paradise is to work at full risk in the relative freedom of control and wildness. One complex shadowing that emerges at this point is what does one do once the reason one became an artist in the first place is resolved.

One thing is very certain at this point: what brought me here will *not* take me hence. (That line, based on "what brought me here will take me hence," is from a poem of Cid Corman's in which he is envisioning himself as an adolescent faced with potential maturity—Corman in his poem is hitchhiking, a kid seeking to leave his youth, move away from home, etc., wanting to be on his own.) Well, I am on my own now, and what brought *me* here is a wave of frustrated adolescent energy that is now rolling tide on sand. . . . For a moment let's pretend I am Ulysses in the thirteenth book of the *Odyssey,* mother is at an end, man stands on the dryness of a masculinity, seeking the definitive articulation—but that too fades, it is only useful for an instant; for the charge at the center of the labyrinth is, in alchemical terms, to win the combat of one's two natures, and if that is done, then one is given or takes the thread that leads out, so that one does not wander for the rest of one's life; for that is what the wandering or failure to develop becomes, to wander for the rest of one's life in the very labyrinth one broke into when breaking into imaginative utterance. At this juncture it is easy to over-assert or under-assert "individual difference." If you under-assert it, you start trying to worm back to the youth you are biologically beyond—you become interested in, say, violent revolution, you assert suddenly the all-importance of social change. Or, if you over-assert your situation, you tremendously value heaven, you become a critic defending the territory you have gained and by doing so you signify that you are in stasis. "Going on into the earth" for my poetry means, on a literal level as a move, a re-positioning, the coming to Europe and seeking out the prehistoric painted caves in the belief that there is a light and intelligence there that I am to penetrate, a new sort of den, *not* the lair I was dropped in. I think I have a foundation, in that in *Coils* I have resolved the relation between gratification and transformation—such is the fulcrum off which I can move now.

[1973–1974]

Gargoyles

THE GREAT CATHEDRALS SOAR to the sky, they rush upward laden with saints, with porches with all the geometrical abstractions we have come to associate with being tied again, or re-ligion, re-bound back into a barrow that mounts itself, lives in the form of a cross and still is earth-bound, pinned to the earth in the shape of the millions coming in to pray, to wager, to kneel, to consider, and this human presence is fumed into the very structure of the work, and it would consolidate and disappear, not only in stone but in the ghosts who stand by the door today collecting contribution, or pass back and forth in the cross's center, on earth, performing a ritual which involves more suffering, the worshippers' hands tied into oath and observance, than it does joy. Yet the life of all people who have carried stone as well as given themselves over to a vision of sin and redemption is figured in the sudden burstings from the stone towers, as if the repressed sex upon which all religion rests were to be present at the same time that it is choked. From the highest towers, traditional centers of the most holy, they fly, I should say sprout, the souls of the damned, they squeeze and press outward from the trunk of establishment, open-mouthed, their backs split, howling rainwater, or even with a drizzle their muzzles are adrip with the bulge pressed out to the point that religion and what will never be bound exist in league. They swarm like bees or angry barracudas out of the idea of building; often they are actually two figures, one mounted or carrying the other, a priest carrying

"Gargoyles" was first published in an issue of *Fiction International* (guest-edited by Diane Wakoski), and reprinted in *The Gull Wall* (Black Sparrow Press, Santa Barbara, 1975).

a woman whose skirt hoisted reveals her buttocks which become the hole of the gargoyle, life drips from her anus, life drips and drips from the outpost of meaning—they are winged and they are snake, they are crouched and heavily clawed, they are variation, refusal of the cathedral itself to ever be complete, the life of cathedral, the meaning of edifice, that it burst, French-ticklered, bean-sprouted, from its own crown.

[1973]

[from]
The Atropos Interview

What's the average gestation time for a poem? Is there one?

"Gestation time" is not simply a conscious matter; one carries unresolved experiences around for years before they dream their way into symbolic structures through which one can become aware of them and what they might mean. For example, I was in a social fraternity the first three years I was in college, and I suffered terribly the first year when as a pledge I was daily humiliated and beaten with long wood paddles. I had nightmares for years about the fraternity and in 1968 even went back to Bloomington, Indiana, and lived in the present-day Phi Delta Theta house for two weeks to re-observe it and try to find a way to write about it. When I returned to New York City, I wrote a 50-page poem called "The Lay of Phi Delta Theta," sections of which were printed—but I didn't like the piece finally and put it aside. I continued to have nightmares about the fraternity. Then in 1975 I went back to all my material and realized that a few things I had put down could be used. I was reading *Helter Skelter,* the book on the Manson gang, at the time and thinking a lot about rites of passage and initiation. I worked hard for several weeks, during which time I overcame my own hurt and was able to work with the fraternity at a certain distance. Once "Still-life, with Fraternity" was complete, the Phi Delta Theta experience ceased to appear in dreams.

Do you revise much?

I used to revise a lot in the early 1960s when I was trying to find my own ground in poetry. The poem then felt like an endless doorknob I was

37

polishing and never getting perfectly shiny. Then I went into Reichian therapy and changed the way I lived sexually. I found that this had an effect on how I wrote: I lost interest in "polishing" and began a new poem when the one I was working on didn't seem to be going right. That was a release—but a superficial one, I found out. I don't now much like what I wrote between 1966 and 1970. It seems superficial, dashed through, with too much an aura of a physical excitement that remained outside of it. Around 1970 I began to revise again, and still do—a lot. But I revise in such a way as to constantly allow the poem to go off in other directions than what a single draft indicates. I started working on "Portrait of Francis Bacon" knowing only that I wanted to do something off his paintings. I finally got a poem that satisfied me—with around 350 worksheets behind it.

Many of your poems are concerned with male/female relationships. They seem to contain Tantric and neo-Tantric nuances and symbology. In "Collage to the Body Electric" you deal with Tantra overtly. In "Brief Hymn to the Body Electric" you deal with it suggestively. What significance has it for you in your personal life, and within the parameters of your poetry?

When religion opens its doors to sexuality, watch out. Every adventuresome soul is excited about the possibility, seemingly always just around the corner, of a fusion of the sexual and the spiritual. So the basic concepts of Tantric sexuality look very good indeed. However, the people who speak of the concepts never tell you exactly what Tantric sexuality entails physically. The only book I have found that does is Kenneth Grant's *Aleister Crowley and the Hidden God,* and it is probably just one view, to a certain extent conditioned by other philosophies that Crowley drew on. However, Grant is very precise about a few things. He explains that Tantric discipline sees woman as a pylon, or gate, through which cosmic power can be inducted. The man seeking this power brings the woman to the edge of climax and then pulls out and imbibes the moisture on her vagina which at this point is thought of as a mystical elixir. As a practice, this strikes me as a vicious form of male chauvinism, about as charming as Chinese foot-binding. I am not at all opposed to the idea of a man drawing strength from a woman's vagina, but I feel it must be mutual, that the woman is just as much subject as is the man, and that knowing when to let go, and going with letting go, is essential for "the lineaments of gratified desire," Blake's extraordinary phrase. Tantric sexuality is hung up on the modern fear of losing control while fucking. It suggests that transcendence occurs for the man alone and only if he robs his partner in that crucial moment of her own release. Reichian sexuality, like that which we find at times in Blake, affirms that mutual sexual gratification is the cornerstone of imaginative work, that transcendence occurs as antiphonal to sexual happiness.

You may ask what all of this has to do with poetry. Well, I have thought through it in my poetry and pondered some of the systems and images associated with release and constraint in the lower body. Near the end of his life, in some of his most searing poetry, Antonin Artaud accused God of murdering him in his Muladhara Chakra. As often with Artaud, the insight is brilliant and slightly misplaced. It is not God who is murdering man there; it is anyone murdering anyone there when control is asserted at the very moment physical being is crying out for release.

Are you familiar with the poetry of Robert Graves, Muse-poet? Or his The White Goddess? *Many of your poems seem to pay homage to her.*

I read part of *The White Goddess* while deciphering several of Paul Blackburn's poems that have women's names encoded in them. Blackburn used Graves's tree-alphabet to covertly honor and curse a few of the muse figures in his life. I guess I never finished Graves's book because I am not very sympathetic with the idea that a muse or goddess, let alone a white one, is in back of all genuine poetry. All of that finally seems like just another way to bury specific woman in safe, generalizing archetypes. It is no more the job of women to serve as men's muses than it is for men to serve as women's muses. That is such a limiting way to experience the earth. In *Coils* I created a few of my own archetypal figures (taking a lead from Blake), but they are my own mental formations and not replacements for the role certain women have played in my life. I've tried to make that clear by letting specific women, on a first-name basis, come into *Coils* also. So I am distressed that you think many of my poems pay homage to Graves's white goddess. I have never intended anything of the sort.

What inspired your poem entitled "Sugar"?

Listening to Caryl talk about some aspects of her childhood at the home of Oreste Pucciani and Rudi Gernreich one evening, aspects which I had not known about, made me realize just how different her life as a child had been from mine. The next day I asked her to repeat what she had said, and began to conceive the poem once I saw that "sugar" was the connective or motif that tied a number of her experiences together. Around four P.M. the same day I sat down and wrote, with no pauses or changes, to the line at the end of the third-to-last stanza, "Caryl Reiter whose childhood I am in love with." At that point I recalled my last visit with my father, several days before he died, and how at one point he reached out and began to tickle my shirt-button and go "kitchikitchikoo." My feeling of love for Caryl's invisible childhood had led me to realize that my father had always thought of me as an infant, and because I was in a charitable mood I found this very touching, rather than pathetic. So I wrote the episode into the poem. The thing that fascinates me about writing "Sugar" is that in the midst of pondering Caryl's struggle against her parents' craziness I felt, for the first time while writing, compassion for my father.

You have a new collection being published by Black Sparrow Press. Can you tell us something about it?

Caryl and I spent several months in the French Dordogne in the spring of 1974 visiting the painted Upper Paleolithic caves. One of the things that impressed us the most about them is the way in which figures and signs are superimposed upon each other, suggesting that in the minds of the drawers no fixed boundaries or center existed. In Les Combarelles, for example, the cave itself is a series of hairpin curves which are covered by thousands of intersecting forms and near-forms. While we were in the Dordogne, we met Alexander Marshack who is doing research on the cave art using portable microscopes and infrared photography to see more than the naked eye is capable of. Marshack showed us a photo of an inscribed ox-rib from an Acheulian dig near Bordeaux. At around 350,000 BC, according to Marshack, a hominid appears to have made a slash in the bone (referred to as a "core meander") and then to have placed the cutting instrument on this first slash and slashed to the side (creating what is referred to as a "branch meander"). In my opinion, whoever did this was creating history (thinking of it in the Olson-derived sense of *istorin,* "to find out for oneself," in which I would stress "out," to find out, or exit, for the self).

Taking a lead from the caves and the terms used to describe ancient slash marks, I began, around 1975, to try to find a way to "meander" in my poetry, but also to keep a "core" at work within the meandering. "Core" and "meander" suggest "center" and "periphery" to me, and I recalled that Wilhelm Reich had observed that there is a functional antithesis between the two, that the life process takes place in a constant alternation of expansion and contraction. Biologically speaking, the parasympathetic represents the direction of expansion, "out of the self—toward the world," pleasure and joy; the sympathetic, on the other hand, represents the direction of contraction, "away from the world—back into the self," sorrow and pain and, ironically, inspiration. Imaginatively speaking, the antithesis evokes "I" and "other."

It seems to me that the attempt to get rid of the "I" is as crippling as the attempt to get rid of the "other." Both are points of dynamic interchange and it is only when one is fixed and made central (as has been the rule with Western Man for several thousand years), that the flux of contrariety is halted and opposites appear. In the poetry of *What She Means*, the new Black Sparrow book, I am seeking a focused movement forward, through material that stays open to lateral entry. As the focus proceeds, it is turned, or meandered, by what enters it from the side, filling and weighting the loomlike motion. I *mean* "focus," for what I am describing is not in any way "automatic writing" or that canard "free association." I use my poetry to think with, but want my thought to be open to its own spider-alphabet, to twist, dissolve, whatever, out of my own experience, which means that background and childhood continue, as agents in composition, taking on different meanings, as opposed to disappearing, as I age.

It is interesting to me that in the past few years two of the three peers I feel closest to (Jerome Rothenberg being the other) have, on their own, spoken of and made use of terms similar to "meander." In conversation with Charles Stein and George Quasha (published in the Kelly issue of *Vort*), Robert Kelly spoke at length of "ta'wil," a Sufi term that has been translated as "the exegesis that leads the soul back to its truth." At one point, he said: "And when I say that the poem is ta'wil of the first line, I mean very specifically that a line comes, a statement comes, carrying its own measure with it, its own length, and I have to find what that means, by finding it in the energy to go to the next line, and in that energy to go forward. Now in *The Loom*, that specifically becomes, for the most obvious time in my work, the Recital. The Recital emerges. The narrative develops." In the opening piece in *The Man Who Shook Hands* (Doubleday, 1978), Diane Wakoski exclaims: "digression/ a structure/ thank you Olson, thank you Creeley/ digression, a form of music, for music is that movement which we follow, that sound which we recognize not because it says anything but because it is motion which suspends motion, which does not ask for dialogue or response—digression which leads me to that serious proposition, that understanding of poetry, of talk, of the speech that comes from all of our lips, those words we call poetry, or dialogue, or digression, or discussion—can they pass into music?—and makes me ask if to speak seriously is not the most serious form of making love?"

It strikes me that the common push of all three terms, Diane's bread-and-butter "digression," my archeology-based "meander," and Robert's esoteric "ta'wil," is to make use of as much material as possible in the process of composition, opening up contact points between narrative and soliloquacious acts and, most of all, allowing the poem to generate its own movement in peristaltic manner, wherein contraction/expansion, which we associate with biological activity (the way a snake moves), becomes, in the poem, meaning/non-meaning. Meaning is a contraction in the sense that it is a closure, while non-meaning is an expansion in as much as it desires to mean. A more elaborate discussion of where these three terms lead would engage poetries which from other viewpoints appear quite different, such as the poetry of Larry Eigner, John Ashbery, Louis Zukofsky and Robert Duncan. I think there is something in the air now that these terms are circulating through, and it may have to do with what seems to be around the bend of both Western *and* Eastern culture: the Pleistocene, the engagement of a vision that looks beyond racial and ethnic difference to a sense of man and woman, human and creative for at least 75,000 years. I know that this is more than just my preoccupation. Both archeology and anthropology are increasingly eliminating the traditional view of not only the primitive as stupid, or "simple," but also Neanderthal as cretinous gorilla. Poetry must not only accommodate such speculation but must be willing to turn with it.

[1979]

Terrestrial

ORGASM FLASHES, an unprintable pattern I have glimpsed then lost. Small cysts like parachutes, or albino testes, grapes to the seeker. The earliest chakra, the Muladhara Bridge, is the place in our bodies to confront the image of a woman bundled into herself at the rise of the bridge between nature and being. The outside is faceless. Another kind of face. Ape face. Shit face. The other is an invitation. What I am not is benign, of my kind, since my kind, basically kine, floods back immediately into the unknown. To love the upside down of ourselves. My father broke out of his own "rest home" several times to seek his (dead) wife. Stole his own car keys, drove and drove. He was found once 185 miles north of Indianapolis, out of gas in someone's driveway. Dusk, near-skeleton sitting in car. "I am looking for Gladys." Did he see her? Did they see him? His clothes were crawling with her, but that was no good. He wanted to be with his wife, his other, in chamber—and had she appeared, with hippo head, coming around from the back of that house, with legs he had known, walking with my mother's walk, would he have accepted "her"? Suppose she had appeared as scorpion. "We don't understand, mister, but there has been a scorpion on the back porch all day, flexing. Is this perhaps what you are looking for?" My father takes the creature and smashes it to his face, turns to me, ferociously saying: "As I never knew you, you never knew me." Fair enough, I respond, but go with the image . . . We are now in Mexico. My father's face is a mask, wood onto which a

"Terrestrial" originally appeared in *Sulfur* #5, 1982; it was reprinted in *Fracture* (Black Sparrow Press, Santa Barbara, California, 1983).

43

scorpion is clenched, a scorpion is fornicating my father's face! About
time! Flexing over his nose, as if to dip into a nostril, as if to contact the
first man! As if to break my father's scrotum, to scatter the male nature of
everything I touch. My poor father in Oldsmobile, shrunken lizard drift-
ing wifeless non-death, head stuck out—only a scorpion could cap him!
My father? But about whom, really, am I speaking? My other? And now
butterflies are descending, with shears, they are whistling away the flesh,
so that progenitor is sheer excrescence. So that what I am is excreting and
growing. So that there is volume in the Oldsmobile, vast volume, so that
progenitor is monkey behind, and none of this is bloody. I have kissed my
father's skull and found a monkey vulva, and kissing the vulva I have
tasted cave, for the first time the real taste of cave! Octopus cave crossing
a savanna, its beak interior containing a monkey queen, around her,
milling young monkeys, around them, agitated "guardians," in swirl, a
cave octopus, disappears, in my father's face, so that father is no longer
total, but amphibian, a ghost staring through reeds, and there is the burial
grounds of English Literature, Wordsworth balancing the norias, in Kali
form, like an amusement park ride, with fiery cauldrons on each arm,
dipping and loosing his molten sparks. How dense the father still is. Can I
make him diaphanous? Can I ride him through to the veil? And again this
counterwish: You should be making him denser if you ever want to reach
that lode in which language eats through the wall of beginning to speak.
Wall I seek an inner burial that is alive with the resonance of death. Wall I
seek the intelligence of the combining of my father's actual bones with
the terrestrial intelligence investigating his genetic marrow. Wall I want a
union that has nothing to do with unity or one or solution. Wall I want to
be in your texture as one layer of the words perplexing my distance from
the sorrow of individuation, for there is no such thing as the individual,
nor is there any such thing as the collective. There are motions, with steel
spring fingers, careful collectings as well as jeeps bursting, tiny, among
the ferns, in a spacious nowhere in which your eyes Caryl are stars and I
grind my fists into my sockets to unleash the puny molten spells of bright
gold swimming into the migraine centers of El Salvador.

Vision that life is benign, pronounce yourself, outside of paradise, outside of symbolism. Dear brothers, is it not time we treated our monkeys
to a salad that is outside our wiles to be men? A salad in which rocks
which are alive could be listened Beethovenly to, so that our digital

diapers could be felt as mountains, that we might burrow through our earliest turd and open out a freshness in which all beings are friends, all beings, even these right now using us as jungle gyms. For the inner terrestrial in our garden must be greeted, and how I wither as I say this, for if others do not, what chance the tender American? Simple political horror of the five feet around me, bull's-eye each of us are in the particles of any political contract—while in the animal coalmine we are all mammal locked, eye to eye, muscle to muscle, a gravel shifting of centuries we pretend to have no knowledge of. This poetry is an attempt to think through the last glaciation, to restore memory of that which erected us. For there is a two-beat fuse ticking in life as we know it now:

1) our natal demon was to unpack from the animal to be born out of animal, as if animal was womb, and we who recall possibly an earlier birth seek like shell-shocked chicks to stand free of the hair in which we were closet and cloth

2) once free, detached from our pipeline to other worlds, there is nothing to do but commit suicide. We are now in the process of killing ourselves off because we do not know how to reconnect to all of the otherness that has become our enemy.

The glass wagon boats of the dead occasionally break through my fabric—or my skin, but I am not afraid, since I am nothing here but a voice a tongue on the end of a pirate diving plank a spatula pressed down onto the tonsil of an older need to place stone to stone in speech to accommodate these diced eyes these seers as they break blisters, disease, as they shine in boils, dead thronged bridge, carnival in which the millions before us, inhabiting our bodies, instruct the father to know that she has no face and that his love for her is intact in my rotting shoulders. I cannot embrace him, but I can let his desire trickle through language so that anyone willing to contemplate what I say will take on the shadow of a former self and understand why his suit pockets were not filled with Woolf rocks, but chunks of salami, what the two of them called "mother's salami." His desire to feed dead Gladys meshes with my appetite for fracture like teeth into food made of teeth, the tooth food doing the chewing.

[1982]

VATIC SORES

Thinking About Gary Snyder

THE MOST HELPFUL THING one contemporary can do for another is to read him and then say how he feels about what he has read. It is not a matter of complaining about what is not in someone's work—any poet or writer can be found wanting in particular ways. In the present case, I have been reading Gary Snyder since 1960, a book at a time, always finding material that I agreed with and disagreed with. Now, with the publication of *Manzanita** I feel the impulse to address certain basic images his work evokes for me.

Snyder has a vision, and that in itself makes him interesting. In fact, since it is an achieved vision, a result of his "fishing in obstinate isles" of many cultures & differing ages, and since he more and more appears to practice what he preaches, he deserves our basic gratitude. Snyder's vision, to say it as directly as possible, is the perception that everything is alive. I know he speaks of the circumstances of the vision somewhere in his published work but I can't locate the source. I believe it was this vision that led him into Buddhism and poetry, and his life work since then has been to seek confirmation of the vision in his daily life and chores as well as in history and myth so as to mobilize it into a poetic argument which ideally would enable the vision to be felt in any unit of meaning in anything he writes. Rather than struggle for an elaboration of the vision in terms of his own psychology or, more grandly, his own Self, Snyder has almost from the beginning looked outward—to such an extent, I might

---

*Snyder, Gary. *Manzanita*, 30 pages (Four Seasons, Bolinas, California, 1972). This essay has not been previously published.

say, that the emphasis of the vision appears to be more on what most people mean by the word Nature than on Self. While this is ultimately a questionable distinction, it is in looking at Snyder's poetry a functional one. Snyder has spent many years in disciplined meditation and it is probable that much of what most poets use their poetry for Snyder worked through in meditation. Perhaps one meaning of doing meditation is to work through one's problems and understand one's own life to such an extent that one can shift off ego and give oneself vitally to the outer world, to work for man having solved the nature of one's own soul. However, I have just made a distinction here that I do not believe in, but it is a distinction that Snyder's viewpoint leads one to make. While he does not argue it, I feel it is implicit in what he chooses to honor as material and what he chooses to avoid. The distinction is that there is an inner and an outer world, an inner nature and an outer nature, man and wilderness etc. While Snyder's viewpoint is not dualistic in a mechanical way, nor is it really rational (as his mentor Pound can be thought of as rational, that is, irrationally rational), there appear to be problems in it that one can signal as dualistic, though to identify them as dualistic would not seem quite right.

Snyder's poetic argument goes something like this: everything is alive, man deer bush and rock; everything exists in a great circuit of interdependence, everything because of being alive has a soul, fish as well as man. Because everything is holy and because man (for some reason) more than fish is aware, it seems, because of this, man has a special job in the universe; he is to be a kind of enlightened custodian; it is his job to keep the great circuit intact and flowing, to protect its energy so that it continues to feed (and feed on) itself. Man must do this not only for fish and deer but for man himself (and here the poet as shaman/healer comes in, an integral force in the scheme); he does this through ritual imitation of what he sees beyond his own hands and through a worked-for state of mind, a reverence for life, by which he respects what he kills by eating it and what he cannot eat he introjects as clothing, pouches and craft, etc., that is, he is not a sportsman. Snyder accepts killing (he takes a stand against Macrobiotics which tries to avoid killing through making up a diet of essentially grains) as long as it is for subsistence; he writes in *Earth House Hold* (p. 120):

Hunting magic is designed to bring the game to you—the creature who has heard your song, witnessed your sincerity, and out of compassion comes within your range.

It is not clear what Snyder means by "out of compassion"; the phrase could be a covering for avoiding the unpleasant fact of slaughter, and that the "food-chain," while a beautiful thought looked at as a phenomena, is tooth in throat, cries & abandoned baby animals, etc., when viewed in operation. Nevertheless, Snyder has a point in urging that all of an animal be used; ritual, animal-games and animal-naming exist, he tells us, to keep the "power" of the animal "within" the hunter. Snyder calls this "the power within," and since he believes singing (and/or poetry) is the proof of this "power within" it is an important aspect of his poetic argument. William Blake writes that Albion (mankind) "fell" when he allowed his vision to separate from him, and began to see it as an outward creation, with a will of its own (what most people call Nature, Blake refers to as "The Female Will"). It seems to me that both Snyder and Blake are evoking a powerful human desire in their attempts to understand what makes man "whole" and what is the cause of most men being at such a distance from where the seer believes mankind could actually live. For if the power is not kept within, it is generally viewed as being without, and as without, a threat, and something to control/contain, almost as a forest fire is "contained." Snyder always makes his points very quietly, with almost no drama:

The ex acid-heads from the cities
Converted to Hari Krishna or Yogananda,
Do penance with shiney
Dopey eyes, and quit eating meat.
In the forests of North America,
The land of Coyote and Eagle,
They dream of India, of
    forever blissful sexless highs.
And sleep in oil-heated
Geodesic domes, that
Were stuck like warts
In the woods.

And the Coyote singing
   is shut away
   for they fear
   the call
   of the wild

(Manzanita, pp. 24–25)

If Blake and Snyder seem similar in their desire for the keeping of power within, they appear considerably different in their elaboration of the power. For Blake, a state of power within can only be achieved by all of mankind and the only indication that such a power even exists comes from the imaginations of visionaries; mankind, since the first man, has lived at the Limit of Contraction and the Limit of Opacity. In Blake's view, man in Nature (man as we prehistorically and historically know him) is "a worm of sixty winters." Snyder, on the other hand, asserts that the great interdependent circuit, or "the mythological present," not only has been lived on earth by man as we know man now, but that it is likewise not the exception but the rule; whenever evil or suffering appear in Snyder's poetry, they never appear intermingled with "the mythological present" but as forces that seem to exist by virtue of the fact that Western Man has chosen to live outside them, i.e., to neglect "the power within." Evil seems to come about when faith is broken with the circuit, when the circuit's blood is spilled outside of proper ritual, and while Snyder writes in his "Hymn to The Goddess San Francisco in Paradise" that "there is higher than nature in city," he seems to loathe the machines (and their fuel as well) that appear to be necessary for city-building:

A bulldozer grinding and slobbering
Sideslipping and belching on top of
The skinned-up bodies of still-live bushes
In the pay of a man
From town.

(Manzanita, p. 21)

What one man perceives another man is not going to perceive, and thus what for one will be simply true, for another will only exist as a matter of faith, i.e., to wish it were true. For me, Snyder's vision that everything is alive runs a spectrum; at one end I agree emphatically—at the other end I would say Hardly, or so dead that to call it "alive" would mean a misrepresentation of the aliveness at the other end. Can I use the word "alive" about both my wife and a pebble and convey anything meaningful? Again, when Snyder asserts that all living beings have souls, I run into the same kind of problem: I can feel the soul of a cow in its eyes, but I cannot feel the soul of a lobster in its eyes. This does not therefore mean I am indifferent to the maltreatment of beings whose souls I cannot feel, but it probably does mean that since I do not experience lobster soul I would not feel I had to write a poem about a lobster if I ate one, or had to wear the lobster's claws around my neck. I am not sure where such differences lead, whether they would ultimately lead to two incompatible universes or not. Also unlike Snyder I do not feel that primitive peoples are any more noble than any other people; my reading in anthropology leads me to believe that most primitive people are terribly haunted by the extent to which they are at the mercy of the elements, and that they spend most of their lives impotently trying to appease the elements and constructing complicated and rational relation-systems among themselves which tie them so up in knots that what I honor as individual responsibility and liberation hardly exist. I bring this up here not to debate the relative humanity of ourselves *vs.* people we identify as primitives, but because, as I hope to further point out, the foundations of Snyder's poetic argument are established on a primitive bias—in fact, the importance Snyder places on ritual and sacrifice suggests a profound yearning on his part for a way of life that would deny him his present life.

In the present book I feel that the evolution of Snyder's daily life over the past eight or ten years has had a lot to do with the sharpening conflict of vision *vs.* the opponents of the vision. It appears as if early and meaningful experiences in his life took place when he was out in the woods, as a logger and as a look-out. When I first met him in the early 1960s he was settled in Kyoto, on the outskirts of the city in a rented house, presumably there because it put him close to his monestary and his teacher. Then in the mid 1960s he met and married his third wife, and after spending a little time at a commune on a Japanese island Snyder and his wife returned to the USA, bought land in the California Sierra and have built a homestead there, where they presently live. The impact of his recent marriage and the building of his own home in the Sierra seem to me to have had a very profound effect on the man: Before his union with Masa there was not much sense of woman in his poetry; she was there in the early work but pretty abstract, hardly a sexual being. The most impressive thing about *Regarding Wave* (New Directions, 1970) is the mesh of much of his earlier feeling for Nature with a feeling for the human body; there are several poems in *Regarding Wave* called "songs" that indeed speak of a power within, and make for some of the most impressive American poetry of the past decade. In *Manzanita* there is only one poem, really, that deals with the sensual and sexual life, but it is a strong one and is called "The Bath." Rather than continue to develop this "flank" of his poetry Snyder seems to be turning more to the implications of the sound of jets in the sky passing over his home, the vulgarity of the local American steakhouses and the presence of bulldozers which I imagine he can see as he moves through his day. In a superficial way the bulldozers are coming in stronger because there are more and more of them and because Snyder now owns property on a mountain that they are slowly chewing into. In a more important way, the bulldozers represent an increasing threat to Snyder's vision and poetic argument. I think this should be fairly obvious, since unless I have distorted Snyder's viewpoint there is not much room for civilization, at least as we know it now, in it. As the tension of vision and potential destruction of the vision grows more acute there may come a point, a crisis, in which Snyder will either have to revise his vision so as to introject (and symbolically "eat") his opponents and thus maintain an equilibrium with them, or do actual combat with them in defense of the vision as it is. *Manzanita* is an exciting book because of the aura of danger and crisis constantly at its edges. This book should be read in the company of a poem I am surprised Snyder excluded from it, "Little Dead Kids Butts" (*Caterpillar* #17), in which opponents of his vision (in muted symbolic Viet Nam GI garb) are directly and ferociously addressed:

> We can live with death, meat, and blood
> So if you come near my children
> With "orders"
> Your "orders" your
> Limp-cock shitting-tongue
> Trigger-finger "orders"
>
> I'll kill you
> Soldier
>
> And dress out your meat.

There is a powerful and convincing sense of indignation in this poem, and the piece especially interests me, because in it, for the first time in Snyder's poetry, I feel an emotional reservoir being tapped.

The more I think about Snyder's vision, the more it seems not only endangered but badly riddled, to such an extent that it is more of a memory or a dream than a vision. A dream because the terms by which the vision is delineated have a decreasing bearing in reality and thus appear more and more referential to a dreamed or invented past. True, the vision has not entirely left the realm of the living, and I would imagine that Snyder's present daily life keeps him in touch, perhaps now more in touch than ever before, with living members of his vision. While it never becomes a matter he deals with, I feel that his stress on the beauty in Nature has a lot of pain under it. Yet, as some have said, his sense of beauty in Nature cannot just be passed off as Snyder's prettying-up of Nature. As usual, if we look closely at what Snyder writes we find thought, even if we might not, after taking thought ourselves, agree with him. Snyder accentuates beauty in Nature because Nature has been greatly maligned by man, and such malignment arrests the way man views himself. WASP body-hate is utterly enmeshed with the sterilization and perfuming of the sensual. Snyder's feeling for beauty comes less from adoration of a separate will, a Blakean "Vala" so to speak, than it does from seeing an animal from an animal's point of view. There is a difference here, and it is worth pointing out:

> Thus I could be devastated and athirst with longing
> for a lovely mare or lioness, or lady mouse,
> in seeing the beauty from THERE
> shining through her, some toss of the whiskers
> or grace-full wave of the tail
>
> (*Manzanita*, page 30)

Another criticism of Snyder I have heard often voiced is that he preaches a lot of Buddhistic crap to the young. I think this criticism must come from a lack of understanding exactly what use Snyder makes of his Buddhism. I will have more to say about his "religious sensibility" at the end of this essay, but now I want to argue that the man uses his Buddhism in an extremely decent way; he says its meaning lies in meditative discipline, which is hard work, and which does not argue dogma—but rather can lead to greater awareness and sensitivity to all life. Of course most young people wouldn't spend any real time at all working with meditation and, instead, allow Snyder a kind of culture-star status when they go to hear him read his poetry. I can understand this, to a certain extent, because of Snyder's bearing, his clarity on issues he chooses to publicly address—people unfortunately want to worship him for these attributes.

*

There is no wilderness left in America; thus it is very questionable that any man-group and animal-group could be said to exist in an interdependent circuit of being. Instead of wilderness, we have forest preserves and national parks. If you discovered a "deer" in one of my poems, you would have to deal with it as allusion or symbol, i.e., there are no deer in my life. Like most Americans I have no first-hand experience with deer, in fact it is best to say I don't know anything about them. From reading Snyder's poetry I imagine he does shoot, skin and eat deer; in one of the poems in *Manzanita* ("The Dead By The Side Of The Road") we are presented with the sad and moving image of Snyder and his friends trying to make use of animal-bodies and bird-bodies they find at the side of the road. Snyder writes:

Her wings for dance fans

and I feel the hope, his hope for mending a tear in the circuit. But does Snyder then dance with the Red-tailed Hawk feathers? We are not told. If he doesn't, then the making of a dance fan would seem an incomplete gesture, a ritual not fully carried out. The point is that Snyder does not have the kind of relationship with the fauna around him as the seventeenth-century American Indian appears to have had, in which the buffalo appears to have been genuine flesh of God, literally keeping certain Indian tribes alive. And that literal dependence is for me, necessary to give a vision such as Snyder's a root in the actual world.

Not only does Snyder not live like the American Indians that increasingly haunt his imagination, but he can hardly even pay homage to them. He writes that he would like "to help my land/with a burn. a hot clean/burn," for

then
it would be more

like,

when it belonged to the Indians

Before.

The tone feeling of these lines is elegaic; it is despair that is being registered more than even the hope of a rite of participation, at least at Kitkitdizze, where Snyder lives. I would like to suggest that Snyder belongs much more to a Romantic tradition in poetry than the *surface* itself suggests. At this point in his career his state of mind reminds me oddly of Hart Crane's when Crane was struggling with "The Bridge." The Romantic begins with a vision, which we could almost call his "innocence" and then attempting to make it stick, to find substance in present time to give the vision validity, is stopped cold by what is going on in front of him, the so-called world of "experience." Crane struggled with this all the way through "The Bridge," and the feebleness of the sections he wrote last for his epic can partially be attributed to Crane's being gnawed at from within by the notion that America was a shithole that didn't even deserve the poem! Crane and Snyder both offer an example of what the Romantic does as he increasingly is eroded by "experience"; in "The Bridge" the single most impressive piece of writing is the section entitled "The Dance" where for a few pages Crane openly lies to himself ("Lie to us," he cries to his poet/shaman/self, "dance us back the tribal morn!"), and creates a fantastic vision of integrated moment in the past which is exactly a dramatic version of Snyder's "mythological present." The Romantic maneuver is that since the vision exists in mind it must have existed as actuality sometime, and thus the redeeming anchoring of the vision in the actual world is "remembered" or "dreamed." Like Crane, Snyder looks to the American Indian for the most recent confirmation in actuality of his vision, but he is much more doctrinaire about it than Crane was, and it looms much larger as a credibility factor in his poetry. In *Earth House Hold* (pp. 117–118) he wrote:

> At this point some might be tempted to say that the primitive's real life is no different from anybody else's. I think this is not so. To live in the "mythological present" in close relation to nature and in basic but disciplined body/mind states suggests a wider-ranging imagination and a closer subjective knowledge of one's own physical properties than is usually available to

men living (as they themselves describe it) impotently and inadequately in "history"—their mind-content programmed, and their caressing of nature complicated by the extensions and abstractions which elaborate tools are. A hand pushing a button may wield great power, but that hand will never learn what a hand can do. Unused capacities go sour.

An entire book could be written on the shadows and complications of Snyder's thought and language in this paragraph. We would have to explore what he means by "imagination" and "knowledge of one's own physical properties," as well as question him as to why someone living in history could be fairly described as "impotent" or why "historical" man's "mind-content" can be considered more "programmed" than primitive man's, and why a car is any more abstract than a stone. Instead of going into all of that, I would prefer, for now, to point the reader at the first sentence in the paragraph that follows:

Poetry must sing or speak from authentic experience.

I would maintain that Snyder is speaking of things outside the ken of his own experience in the paragraph quoted, and that the reason why the "songs" in *Regarding Wave* are power songs is because they are coming directly from his own experience. Snyder and I can both talk with anthropologists or read books about people who live in New Guinea or on the Trobriand Islands and we can both struggle with the meaning of what Mead and Malinowski, for example, are saying about the people they are observing. However, we have to admit from the start that we are getting the Manus and Trobriand Islanders through the bodies of Mead and Malinowski, and that the personal lives and values of the anthropologists have everything to do with what they see and express. I think anyone is pressing the limits of truth pretty far by saying they have any authentic experience of anything they read about in a book; in fact, as grim as it seems, I feel I know nothing about the Manus and the Trobriand Islanders having read several books on both peoples. Yet Snyder either does not feel this way at all, or is willing to stand in considerable contradiction, for on the basis of his reading (as well as sheer intuition and feeling) there is a powerful undercurrent in his poetry that life was once upon a time a hell of a lot better on earth than it is now.

[1972–1973]

Doing *Caterpillar*

THE MAIN REASON I BEGAN *Caterpillar* in the fall of 1967 is because I did not feel that poets like Robert Duncan, Diane Wakoski, Jerome Rothenberg, Frank Samperi, Cid Corman, Louis Zukofsky and Paul Blackburn had a dependable and generous magazine outlet for their writing. I hoped that these poets, along with perhaps a dozen more, would become regular contributors to the magazine and that around this "core" I could bring in eight to sixteen pages of art reproductions per issue as well as writing by younger and lesser known poets. I saw a poetry magazine as a granary of sorts, where writing could be stored until it was to be consumed or consummated in a book, a mid-point between its inception and its ultimate form. I also hoped that by getting the magazine out regularly, readers would be able to follow the development of regular contributors' writing. Looking back, I think it is possible to do this in the cases of Robert Kelly, Thomas Meyer, Kenneth Irby and Gary Snyder.

The quality of translating was much on my mind, so I adapted Zukofsky's *A Test of Poetry* to "A Test of Translation" and did the first two "Tests" myself, on Vallejo and Montale. My idea was to set differing versions of a poem side by side and, with a minimal amount of comment, encourage the reader to measure them as articulations of the original poem. Behind this was a sense that we needed to know exactly what had been done in the past as much as we needed new translations. Poets like Sappho, Basho and Catullus have been translated so much that we cease to question the accuracy of the translations.

This essay, in a more extended form, first appeared in the *Tri-Quarterly* issue on "little magazines," 1976.

I also wanted to bring things that were not poetry per se to bear on poetry. I experimented with Macrobiotic cooking for a year and in #3/4 edited down Georges Ohsawa's *The Book of Judgment* to four pages and set it before a long poem by Theodore Enslin. In #5 there was a Scientology lecture, in #7 and #10 passages from the writings of Wilhelm Reich and in #13 a statement by Billy McCune, a convicted rapist. The McMaster lecture on Scientology looked suspicious almost as soon as #5 was out. Putting it in *Caterpillar,* in a context with thoughtful writing, made its slovenliness evident to me even though it had not been evident when I was sitting in the Scientology offices on 32nd Street.

I learned from Cid Corman's *origin* that it was not only a matter of lasting for several years and appearing at least quarterly, but of making a magazine of real use to the contributors. *Poetry* (Chicago), during Henry Rago's editorship, seems to me to be a good example of a serious, eclectic magazine in which you might very well find a poem by James Wright facing a poem by Charles Olson. Yet, though Rago printed me several times, I never felt any connection to the magazine. When I was living in Kyoto and seeing Corman weekly (in 1962–1964, when he was editing his "second series" of *origin*), I found that Cid was deeply involved with everything he published, that he maintained a taut correspondence with some of his authors and that in turn some of his regular contributors could count on being "featured" at some point, when perhaps half of an issue would be given over not only to their poetry, but to some of their correspondence. It seemed to me that *origin* had a central and severe limitation—that of the unvarying 64-page format—and that this limitation not only affected how much Cid could print of any one person but also tended to prescribe a certain kind of poetry to be written. While Corman began with Olson and printed sections from the beginning of the very long *Maximus* sequence, and at the beginning of the "second series" printed a little of Zukofsky's *A, origin* was primarily a magazine for "the short poem" (which Corman himself has always written) in which the "self" has been omitted or resolved, and is not seen as a processual part of the struggle/unfolding in the poem itself.

Corman made his attitude clear to me in San Francisco, summer 1959, when he was planning his "second series." He told me that he wanted to present an alternative to "sick" poetry, and that he did not intend to publish such writers as Ginsberg, Burroughs and McClure. What Corman seemed to oppose was anything that smacked of "confession," subject matter which included drugs and any detailed attention to homosexuality or heterosexuality. While these elements do not necessarily make a poem strong or weak, they have turned out to be elements in a gradual enlarging and deepening of grounds to be dealt with in the poem. In seeking to "exercise [our] faculties at large," as Robert Duncan stated in regard to the writing in his *The Opening of the Field,* many of us have attempted to eliminate the censorial mind in us which does not consider certain things to be "proper" to poetry. By 1969, it was clear that Corman also included personal and historical mythology, even when used as part of the poem's visible energies, in his evolving concept of "sick" poetry (see his review of *Maximus IV V VI* in Caterpillar #8/9). William Bronk, along with Corman-as-translator, became the central figure of the "third series" of *origin,* and Olson, who at first represented the opposite pole of Corman's editorial tension, disappeared.

The tension in Hart Crane's *The Bridge* is that of a mustang haunted by a dream in which it is a sonnet and, like Chuang-tze's butterfly, not knowing whether it is a sonnet dreaming that it is a mustang. It seems to me that 1945 is the point when, to update two lines of Vallejo, "the winds changed atmospheric needles and the tombs changed key in our chests." There was something in the air felt by Charlie Parker and Jackson Pollock as well as by Charles Olson as soon as the concentration camps were liberated; whatever it was, it was connected to a much more complex *and* complicated sense of "self," and the poetry that has been open to this phenomenon is processual, longer and more difficult than much pre-Second World War American poetry. Crane's dilemma could also be stated as that of a poet with a plan for a long poem, where certain procedures are to take place which don't seem to work once the poem is underway, and thus the plans, as they did to a certain degree in Williams' *Paterson,* become at odds with the veer the poem is taking. With *Caterpillar,* I wanted a magazine that was open-ended, where the contributions that expectedly or unexpectedly came in determined the nature of a given issue.

The word "caterpillar," as a special word, was given to me by Will Petersen on a Kyoto street corner in 1963, when he quoted Blake's couplet "The Catterpiller on the Leaf / Repeats to thee thy Mothers grief" (without telling me it was by Blake), and then leapt aboard a trolley. The statement amazed me, and upon discovering it was by Blake, I bought his *Complete Writings* and began to struggle through them. I also brought caterpillars into our house and tried to raise them in a shoebox filled with mulberry leaves. Reading Reich in 1966 I came across a drawing he had made stressing the peristaltic movement basic to all living forms:

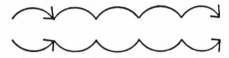

In looking at photos of Viet Namese war victims, I saw a burned baby who looked like a "black caterpillar" and when I edited a series of books in 1966–1967 before starting the magazine, I used one of these "black caterpillars" on the colophon page. I was also aware of the caterpillar "tractor" used in earth moving as well as tearing down old houses, so by the time I was ready to do the magazine, "caterpillar" seemed sufficiently complex to use as a name.

In the summer of 1967 I wrote to around twenty people, telling them my plans and inviting them to send whatever writings they wanted. Most responded, although there were several disappointments. Since I was in New York City and had visited him several times in the past year, I called Zukofsky up on the phone. How is it to be printed? he asked. Photo-offset, I answered, and almost before the words were out of my mouth I heard him sigh. Well, send me a list of who is going to be in the first issue and then I will make up my mind, he said. I sent him a tentative list (Duncan, Blackburn, Sorrentino, N.O. Brown, Leon Golub, Snyder, Wakoski and his ex-student Samperi, among others). A few days later, I received a postcard from Celia Zukofsky that Louis had decided not to send anything. When I told Robert Creeley my plans, he seemed only irritated and told me that if I did not have a group of poets it made no sense to start a magazine. That was it, as far as he was concerned. I borrowed an old *El Corno Emplumado* mailing list from Margaret Randall that had seven hundred names and addresses on it, wrote up a two-page statement on *Caterpillar,* mailed it out and received around a hundred fifty one-year subscriptions. The timing was right. I copied each name and address in a huge ledger that I found in a hardware store on Canal Street.

I had $1000 in the bank and a teaching job at NYU that paid $6000 a year. For the first issue I went to a printing broker and put the entire production in his hands. He told me that 1000 copies of a 140-page issue could be typed, printed and bound, including stock, for around $700.

After the first issue, I bought the old used IBM typewriter that I still have and typed each issue myself. When it was time for the produced issue to be delivered, odd delays started taking place. At one point, the broker promised me at least 100 copies on a Friday afternoon, so I invited some friends over to celebrate that Saturday night. The copies were not delivered and I was so ashamed that I put a note on the door at 36 Greene Street saying that the party was off and walked over to the Hudson River.

The issue, carelessly produced, appeared a couple months late and with it I received a bill for $1400. When I refused to pay, the broker took me to court. I went in alone and told the judge what had happened. The broker had a lawyer who kept repeating that the magazine had been perfectly produced and that since unforeseen costs had come about, I should have to pay the difference. The judge picked up the specimen copy and saw for himself what it looked like. He then picked up a copy of the Bible and literally tossed it into the lawyer's lap, saying, "This is a perfectly produced book." I thought I had won—and in a way I had. The judge ruled in the broker's favor, but only allowed him $200 over his original estimate.

Two days before #2 was to be delivered, I only had several hundred dollars to my name and no idea how I was going to pay for it. That evening I was invited up to Adrienne Rich's apartment to read some poems to her creative writing class. I got a lift back downtown from one of her students and told her my plight as we rode along. She immediately offered to loan me the money for the printing bill and wrote out a check.

Once #1 was out, I asked Andy Brown, the owner of the Gotham Book Mart, if he knew anyone who might be interested in buying *Caterpillar* manuscripts and correspondence. He suggested that I talk with Ted Grieder, the Special Collections Librarian at NYU. I did, and lucked out. Grieder offered me $1700 for the first year's materials and a little more for the second and third years. This helped out a lot—and if I had only kept the magazine small, and the press run down to 1000 copies per issue, along with what subscriptions brought in plus the dribble of income from bookstores, the magazine might have broken even issue by issue. But with the seventh issue the number of pages jumped from 160 to 256, and I upped the press run to 3500 copies. This was a real mistake.

After #6 was published, Michael Hoffman of The Book Organization decided that his salesmen could sell *Caterpillar* along with the magazine and book titles from *Aperture, Jargon* and *Something Else,* etc. All of a sudden, *Caterpillar* entered that no man's land between the "little magazine" and cultural monthlies that can hold their own on newsstands. The idea did not work at all, but instead of dropping it, I approached Eastern News Distributors who, on the basis of modest success with *The Paris Review,* agreed to take on *Caterpillar.*

Number 8/9 sold quite well, but by the time I did #15/16, a 304-page issue that was priced at $3.50—not so much today but overpriced at the time—the bottom fell out. Only 700 copies were sold and most of the other 2300 were destroyed (only covers were returned, torn off the unsold copies and mailed back, at my expense, to the distributor, to prove the issues had not been sold). At this point I was nearly $10,000 in debt, and if my parents had not died and left me a little money, #15/16 would have been the last issue. As it was, I paid off the printing bill and cut the size of the issue as well as the press run down. At 1200 copies, averaging 160 pages per issue, the last four issues made a slight profit, and I paid all contributors either $15 or $25, depending on the issue.

When I think back to the period covering issues #7 through #13, I can't recall how I kept myself and the magazine going. After #5, I quit my teaching job at NYU and, until I moved to California and Cal Arts in 1970, I had no salary. I lived off tiny royalties from my own books, off of readings, and sold a lot of my personal correspondence to Grieder. If it were not for Grieder (and my Greene Street landlady, Anna Donovan, who kept my rent at $85 a month), it is doubtful that *Caterpillar* would have got beyond #5 or #6. During this period, *Caterpillar* received two small grants of $300 and $400 from The National Translation Center, and two grants from The Coordinating Council of Literary Magazines totaling $2500.

So a new thing that I got involved in at this time was raising money. In New York, this meant following up any lead and wasting a lot of time visiting people in their offices and going to cocktail parties. Occasionally I got as much as $100, and once Harold Wit gave the magazine $900. I told Wit that I was going to see if I might have better luck on the west coast the summer of 1968; he suggested that I look up an old friend of his whom I will refer to as BK.

After arriving in Los Angeles, I called BK at his Wilshire Boulevard office—he was a stock broker—and made an appointment to talk with him the next moring at nine A.M. I waited half an hour, and when no one showed up, I asked a janitor if he knew BK. He did, and told me that he might be having breakfast in Nibblers at the corner. With my little stack of *Caterpillars* I went in. There were lots of men eating breakfast so I picked one out and asked him if he was BK. He was. He had forgotten, he said, that I was coming over; wouldn't I sit down and have some breakfast with him?

In five minutes I felt that he had no interest in "little magazines" and that I was wasting my time. Out of the blue he asked me what I thought about LSD. I thought he was trying to find out something about me and was probably like most people of his profession at that time against drugs. I told him I had taken LSD twice and that while I had had interesting experiences I did not think it had anything to do with the creative process as I understood it. (I made that attitude up for BK's benefit, but it is what I actually believe today.) He said that he disagreed, and it came out that he had been turned on to acid by a hooker a few months before, and was now experimenting with all sorts of things, in all sorts of combinations. Somehow in talking about LSD, I mentioned that I was in Reichian therapy, and that interested him too. He said, let's go back to my office and talk there. We did, and he canceled all of his morning appointments while we sat in his office talking, undisturbed, until noon.

At a certain point, he interrupted what I was saying to ask me how much money I needed. Like the LSD question, it came out of the blue. I thought, if I ask for too much he won't give me anything and if I ask for a pittance and get it I will be a fool for not asking for more. So I shot for something in between: $10,000 I said. He said, ok, I'll give you half of that, but you must first raise the other $5000 from someone else. Then he said: And be sure I get a tax write-off. Oh sure, I said, stunned. Was this guy for real?

The next thing I knew he was inviting me over to his house, so I followed his car in the one I had rented. When he showed me around, I saw that he had a small uninteresting painting by almost every twentieth-century master. After a brief tour of the house we sat down at a coffee table in an alcove off the livingroom, and he offered me a joint out of an elegant wooden box in the same way I imagine that you would offer someone a Cuban cigar. I got high instantly. He then pushed what looked like a fat ornate sugar bowl toward me, took off the lid and asked me if I had ever tried "that." There must have been a half pound of cocaine in it, a drug I knew nothing about. We sniffed some, and his daughter walked in, reminding him that he was supposed to go shopping and buy some new clothes for a trip to Europe the family was taking the following week. At this point, he decided we should take off, get some lunch and then go shopping. I waited out front while he went out back to get another car to drive. He backed out in what looked like a Stutz Bearcat but that may have been a hallucination. It *was* a convertible, and we drove around the peaceful leaf-mottled streets of Beverly Hills stoned out of our minds. Somehow he found a Santa Monica Boulevard pizza restaurant he liked. I only remember eating an enormous amount of a "house special" on a rickety white metal table outside, next to the parking lot.

Then we drove to Fred Segals for BK to buy clothes. I was standing in a daze by the inside of the door when he came over and said, go ahead! buy yourself some pants! I wandered over to the $12 corduroy rack and BK came rushing over exclaiming, hey, get yourself something nice! So I found the leather rack and picked out a gorgeous pair of dark blue leather pants that cost $85. BK paid for our things off a fat roll of hundred-dollar bills. He had not found everything that he wanted, so we went to a second Fred Segals and my head started getting funny. Without quite knowing what I was doing, I walked in, picked out a $115 dark blue leather coat and told the clerk that BK would pay for it. As soon as I did this I about fainted. Had I blown everything? Was anything at all going to come of this? Was it all a set-up for him to put the make on me? BK found what he wanted, paid for everything without batting an eyelash and drove me back to his house. He said that he had enjoyed our day together and that as soon as I raised the first $5000 to let him know.

By the time I got back to New York, things got a little clearer. BK's offer was a fluke and it was not going to be easy to match it. I needed the $5000 he had promised desperately, so I wrote him, claimed that I had raised the match, and asked him for what he had promised. Two weeks later, a check for $2000 arrived. When I tried to call him, he was always out and never returned my calls. His secretary finally informed me that I would not get the other $3000 until BK was shown proof that I had actually raised the first $5000. I had an idea: I called up a wealthy friend, told him my predicament and borrowed $5000 from him. He sent it to The Coordinating Council of Literary Magazines as a *Caterpillar* dona- tion; as soon as it was in, I asked the CCLM to write a letter to BK stating that the amount had been raised. They did, and weeks passed without the $3000. So I then called up a friend who lived in Berkeley and told her I would pay her way down to Los Angeles if she would try to pry that

$3000 out of BK. She made the trip and was successful; the $3000 came and I paid back the borrowed $5000.

The upshot of all of this was more complicated than getting the money in the first place. Since the leather suit was the only terrific looking thing I owned, I wore it everywhere, especially to the Gotham Book Mart four P.M. literary parties. Rumors began to circulate that I was getting rich off *Caterpillar*. If I had been down and out, a junkie or horribly unhappy, I imagine that people would have let matters pass. But relatively speaking I was healthy and had bounced into the city in 1966 and in a year had an impressive magazine going. It is hard to imagine the rancor that is shoveled from person to person in NYC unless you have lived there and had some of it dumped on you.

The New York printer of *Caterpillar* was David Miller, who probably still manages a large photo-offset business on West 19th Street. David was one of the generous people who made *Caterpillar* possible; he carried me for several years when I was unable to pay more than 30 to 40% of a bill when an issue arrived. I found David in a curious way. When I was teaching English as a Second Language at NYU in 1968, there was an attractive French woman in one of my classes with whom I would occasionally have coffee after class. One afternoon, we were sitting in "The Peacock" on West 4th Street, and I was on the verge of inviting her to my loft. But a red light kept passing through me. I didn't understand why, but I went along with it and we ended up parting outside the coffee shop. A week later, she dropped out of my class without explanation. A month after this, I got a phone call from a man who said he was her husband's brother. He claimed that she had tried to kill herself after she had dropped out of school and that he had found out that she was having an affair with me right before this happened. He said that he thought she might have said some things to me that he or her husband did not know, and since he was trying to help her, he wondered if he might come over and talk with me about her.

I said ok. As soon as the man walked into my loft I was pretty sure that he was not the brother but the man himself. He was very upset and looked as if he might be violent. I told him what had actually happened—including my intentions before I changed my mind that day—and then suggested that he was the woman's husband. He admitted that he was and told me that his wife had talked about me with a lot of interest and that he assumed we had been involved. He also said that he was

planning on taking me apart as soon as he was sure. We talked for quite a
while, and soon it was clear that he was a miserable guy who had probably ruined the marriage himself. Now his wife was back in France with
her family and he was trying to lure her back. He said that she had tried to
kill herself three times since he had known her. We parted on friendly
terms, and he started calling me two or three times a week, always joking
that his shrink was on vacation and that I was the only person he could
talk to. He was a paper salesman and knew printers all over Manhattan,
so after many hours of phone calls, when he asked me if there was
something he could do for me in return, I suggested that he might introduce me to an honest and dependable printer who would print *Caterpillar*
for only a 10% mark-up over costs. That is how I found Miller.

A word about *Caterpillar*'s subtitle—"A Gathering of the Tribes"
—which was dropped with #11. My impulse to gather poetic tribes,
deriving from the spirit of coming together that permeated the 1960s,
came out of my desire to do a magazine with a single point of view *and* a
magazine that was also eclectic. Some part of me wanted to believe that
by publishing poets as different as, say, Gerrit Lansing, Cid Corman,
Diane Wakoski and Jack Hirschman, and including writing and music by
musicians Philip Corner and James Tenney, as well as essays by Norman
O. Brown and the filmmaker Stan Brakhage, etc., a symbolic "gathering"
could take place (and in 1967, that phrase still had a little zest to it). And
maybe it did. The falsity in the phrase lies in the fact that I did not solicit
work from the Ashbery tribe, the Lowell tribe, or the Bly tribe, and I
would have had to do so to make the phrase really stick.

My greatest pleasure in doing *Caterpillar* was in the preparation of
the manuscript for the printer. I held off typing up an issue until the last
minute and then did it non-stop over two or three days, so that the
material would coalesce in my mind as typist-reader. Once everything
was typed, I paper-clipped individual manuscripts together and spread
them out fan-wise around me on the loft floor along with the art work.
Then I would start picking up two or three contributions together and see
how they "set" next to each other—what piece would be best to open an
issue with? To close it? There was a potential rhythm to each issue, which
assumed the kind of reader who would read it from beginning to end, and
with a 256-page issue, such a reading was unlikely. Still, it was a stimulating challenge to get all of that work together in such a way that it
cohered and made an image out of its separate parts.

[from] A Letter to American Poetry Review

Dear Editors:

I enjoyed Marjorie Perloff's "column" on Lowell and Berryman in the May–June APR [1983], and it made me think about some things I'd like to comment on:

I wonder about the "unendurable sufferings" (top of second column, p. 32), especially in the light, or the darkness I should say, of the European backdrop, for such a strong term might identify concentration camp victims. One of the sores that her essay opens up is to what extent the so-called "suffering" of Berryman and Lowell was self-induced short-circuitings, a conscious making of oneself sick, or crazy (in contrast to insane) out of a need to fuel the poem, or aura the life, as if they had nothing, or not enough, to go on relative to other experiences and sources, so that being nutty, cruel, and living life as a psychological binge, provided form and content as well as identity. I think it is crucial to make a distinction between the madness and writing of Artaud, say, and the madness and writing of Lowell; writing-wise, it is the difference between "Skunk Hour" and "Artaud le mômo"; in the former, all we learn of Lowell's predicament is that his mind's not right—whatever that means (it seems to mean, in the poem's context, that his madness is demonstrated by wanting to watch young people fuck in parked cars); in the latter, Artaud at least attempts to get at the core of his, and man's,

---

This letter was sent to the *American Poetry Review* and rejected for publication because, in editor Arthur Vogelsang's words, "it allowed Lowell and Berryman to be beat over the head rather than discussed or evaluated." It was published in *Sulfur* #8, 1983.

69

terror and works with the demons (suppôts) who were apparently created
in what he calls "the Bardo of electro-shock." There is something stingy
and trivial in the way Lowell engages whatever is eating at him—he
seems to have no context for it outside of describing literal circumstances—and in that way he remains a Protestant and, I feel, is not really
penetrated by the source materials ("history, philosophy, religion, anthropology") that Perloff says he and Berryman "devoured." I think she is
closer to the truth when she notes how disconnected Lowell and Berryman were to "the great art movements" of their times. Not only did
Lowell not go to visit Jasper Johns, say, but the "devouring" of whatever
was read, or viewed, did not seem to take hold as an "otherness," or
assert itself as material, in his writing. Again, the contrast with Artaud is
striking: for all of his self-possession, Artaud actually made the quite
difficult *journey* (not trip) to the Tarahumara Indians of Mexico and not
only wrote ethnographically valid prose about what he saw there, but
used the experience to amplify and resonate his own condition.

What I am trying to get at is that the other edge of the Protestant
blade that played havoc with the souls of Lowell and Berryman is a kind
of psychological Narcissism—and not the Greek myth in which the figure
loses himself in his *image,* but a form in which the image is refused and
the figure insists upon himself, not as image, but as the literal truth of his
suffering.

Such blades seem to lock together in the following way: The figure
never really goes mad, nor does madness really enter his writing. He
drives himself to the brink via booze and insomnia, i.e., misbehaves,
breaks his wife's nose, etc., is institutionalized briefly, dries out, etc.
Since such a cycle is neither visionary nor really damned, neither is the
writing. Lowell, for example (for the cycle itself is not simply Lowell's),
is more interested in describing, rather briefly, the inmates in his asylum
than in concentrating on why he is there. If something cannot be described, it will not be addressed—or a metaphor will be used to titillate
and at the same time screen off the psychic condition: "Each one of us
holds a locked razor." Any unwary reader will find himself empathizing
with Lowell's condition without being told anything about it. . . .

[1983]

Elizabeth Bishop

THE COMPLETE POEMS contains all of Elizabeth Bishop's poems, 108 to be exact, written over a period of fifty-seven years. In addition, there are twenty-six translations from the Portuguese, French and Spanish. While she undoubtedly did not simply write two poems a year, the small production over a long lifetime of writing raises a number of questions that probably only a critical biography can answer. Did she write many other poems that she did not consider good enough for publication? Are there thousands of pages of worksheets for the 108? Or did she simply not write much?

Based on the evidence in this book, I would guess that only the latter question can be answered affirmatively, for the personality of the work argues an upper-middle-class life of travel and leisure-time in which scenes and events would occasionally crystalize into deft metaphorical observations. She must have also spent a good deal of time working out meter and rhyme, for the emphasis of all her writing is on the scrupulous, completed thing, cleansed, as it were, of all the *scoriae* of birth and development.

At her best she sounds like this:

At low tide like this how sheer the water is.
White, crumbling ribs of marl protrude and glare
and the boats are dry, the pilings dry as matches.

A review of Elizabeth Bishop's *The Complete Poems 1927–1979* (Farrar Straus Giroux, New York, 1983), published in the *Los Angeles Times Sunday Book Review*, April 17, 1984.

> Absorbing, rather than being absorbed,
> the water in the bight doesn't wet anything,
> the color of the gas flame turned as low as possible.
> One can smell it turning to gas; if one were Baudelaire
> one could probably hear it turning to marimba music.
> The little ocher dredge at work off the end of the dock
> already plays the dry perfectly off-beat claves.
>
> from *The Bight*

At her worst, like this:

> In your next letter I wish you'd say
> where you are going and what you are doing;
> how are the plays, and after the plays
> what other pleasures you're pursuing:
>
> taking cabs in the middle of the night,
> driving as if to save your soul
> where the road goes round and round the park
> and the meter glares like a moral owl,
>
> from *Letter to N.Y.*

Most of the time, doggerel and exact observation blend into decorative patterns like this:

> On the unbreathing sides of hills
> they play, a specklike girl and boy,
> alone, but near a specklike house.
> The sun's suspended eye
> blinks casually, and then they wade
> gigantic waves of light and shade.
> A dancing yellow spot, a pup,
> attends them. Clouds are piling up;
>
> from *Squatter's Children*

The rhyme sing-songs the writing back to a childlike mood in which the actualities of Brazilian "squatter's children" disappear, i.e., Bishop's children are out of *National Geographic,* not the world of the film *Pixote.* Such a stanza, while very well written, reflects the absence of the "other," in any credible personal, historical or political sense, that pervades nearly all of her poetry. I stress the word "credible," for black and

Indian maids, children and gardeners, *are* the subjects of poems upon which her reputation—which is considerable—is based. But the writing itself—tidy, punctilious and always clever—presents these people as mischievous, exotic diminutions of the colonial mind. Occasionally, a grim truth leaks between her lines. I ask the reader to reflect on the following from "Manuelzinho," her portrait of an Indian gardener:

> Or, briskly, you come to settle
> what we call our "accounts,"
> with two old copybooks,
> one with flowers on the cover,
> the other with a camel.
> Immediate confusion.
> You've left out the decimal points.
> Your columns stagger,
> honeycombed with zeros.
> You whisper conspiratorially;
> the numbers mount to millions.
> Account books? They are Dream Books.
> In the kitchen we dream together
> how the meek shall inherit the earth—
> or several acres of mine.

The fact is that the numbers *would* amount to millions if Manuelzinho and the thousands of other Indian gardeners were to be paid fair back wages by their "masters." Once that is recognized, the last four lines fill with savage irony, but not one Bishop herself is presenting—as Blake did in "The Little Black Boy"—as a compassionate understanding.

This sort of mentality permeates Bishop's writing whether she is in Brazil, Nova Scotia or New York City, and it is a sad and vexing limitation, for she is capable of observing the natural world precisely *and* imaginatively. In the same gardener poem, she can write:

> Between us float a few
> big, soft, pale-blue,
> sluggish fireflies,
> the jellyfish of the air . . .

While a kind of Argus-eyed observation is always present, occasionally Bishop attempts to stretch the poem into a more demanding context, to engage a personality that she considers her equal. One example is her "transformation" of Pablo Neruda's "Alberto Rojas Jiménez Viene Volando" into "Invitation to Miss Marianne Moore" (which, given her influence on Robert Lowell, may be the stimulation for the latter's *Imitations*). In Bishop's hands, however, Neruda's powerful elegy, filled with canceled eyes, raining marrow and guitar-players dressed in bees (which visually evokes the world of Marc Chagall), becomes an Edward Gorey-like fantasia, of Moore in a holding pattern over Manhattan, "with heaven knows how many angels all riding / on the broad black brim of your hat." This is a masterful example of the "academic" poem, in which an earlier more powerful work is diluted and reified.

Another more ambitious attempt to confront a peer is the much anthologized "Visits to St. Elizabeths," apparently based on visits Bishop made to Ezra Pound, incarcerated as a lunatic there. I say "apparently," as neither Pound's name, nor any details or reflections based on being with him, appear in the poem. Each stanza increasingly fills with descriptions of an insane sailor wearing a watch, and a "Jew in a newspaper hat" dancing and weeping about the ward. Pound appears in the penultimate line of each stanza as a "man," qualified by adjectives that initially present him as "tragic," "talkative" and "honored" (does she mean that ironically?), but shift into an increasingly negative cast of "cranky," "cruel," "tedious" and finally "wretched" as the poem progresses. I think that those who have anthologized and honored this poem have done so out of a sincere belief that it is a compassionate portrayal of that very convoluted man. To my reading, it is a vaguely camouflaged, mean attack on Pound that refuses to argue any of its adjectival assertions. In the last line of each stanza, Bishop repeats that this "man . . . lies in the house of Bedlam." Since a verdict of insanity saved Pound probably from a death penalty for treason, the word "lies" implicitly accuses Pound of lying about his condition. Well, this may be so. My point is that in the poem's context, Bishop concludes that Pound can be summed up as a wretched liar.

All in all, this is the kind of poetry that has, over the years, determined the standards for publication in *The New Yorker,* and is currently the spirit presiding over the child of *The New Yorker,* the *American Poetry Review*. It is a verse that aspires to decorate the reader's consciousness in much the same way that, to quote Robert Kelly, "the furniture displayed in *The New Yorker* would decorate the reader's home." It has enormous appeal to those who prefer to dismiss Pound as a perverse pedant and still believe that the poem is a well-"behaved" clavicord, an object in a spotless salon, in which detailed knowledge of a subject is honored as long as the subject poses for the poem and is presented *correctly*. Elizabeth Bishop's poetry is a sinister and thorough lesson in Apollonian poetics: a view from the tower, distanced, sublimated, observational, tidy.

William Bronk

EVEN A CONSCIENTIOUS READER of contemporary poetry may know little about William Bronk. At the beginning of his *William Bronk: An Essay* (Truck Press, 1976)—the only extended work I know of on Bronk—Cid Corman offers a brief picture of the poet's life: "He was born in 1918 in Hudson Falls, New York . . . and has lived there—in the same attractive rambling wooden house—mostly alone—having never been married—virtually all his life—apart from excursions to Central and South America and elsewhere. He is a tall handsome gentleman. His modest income derives from a small coal and lumber company he inherited from his father."

Life Supports is made up of eleven hard-to-find collections, the earliest dating back to 1949. The single finest is *To Praise The Music* (Elizabeth, 1972). All in all, they span thirty-two years, nearly a lifetime's work. This is an utterly compelling, harrowing and masterfully written body of poetry. Its publication is a major literary event.

Bronk's poetry has the haunting monolithicity of Giacometti's portraits, and the elegance and pain of Beethoven's late Quartets—as if played by skeletons using their own bones for instruments. His American literary precursor is Wallace Stevens, but his mature writing (from 1964 on) is completely his own. He is obsessive in somewhat the same way that Antonin Artaud is—in fact, one might think of him as a kind of sealed, Protestant Artaud.

A review of William Bronk's *Life Supports: New and Collected Poems* (North Point, San Francisco, 1981), published in *The Los Angeles Times Sunday Book Review,* November 15, 1981.

He is the first American poet to fully engage a sense of art that is shadowed by a pervasive sense of invalidness, of inadequacy and even failure. Yet he does not offer self-pity in lieu of affirmation:

> I refuse. I will not
> be less than I am to be more human, or less
> than human may be to seem to be more than I am.
> I want as the world wants. I am the world.

His poetry is about all those things of which we have concepts but which we find nonexistent or unapproachable. It is philosophic in nature and, at a glance, icy. However, because of its self-repudiating lucidity, and its relentless attempt to construct a sensible meaninglessness, one is drawn into its hollow fugal chambers. It is a poetry that turns on statement, in which the words often feel like weighted, worn, ancient coins.

To Bronk, not even deaths or deep disasters have shape or reality. We are encapsulated and remote from each other, and interchangeable if not identical though we may appear different in different light (he is never suspended from disbelief). Although we may coincide with reality, it is a coincidence in which we remain, nevertheless, apart. What happens to us is not what happens. There is a real world, beyond our knowing; we know nothing of the world and will never know. All we say is metaphor which asserts at once our unknowing and our need to state in some language what we don't know:

> We are not
> fulfilled. We cannot hope to be. No,
> we are held somewhere in the void of whole despair,
> enraptured, and only there does the world endure.

His ignorance is childlike as well as tested, a child's wonder transformed through experience not into bitterness or cleverness but—and how rare—into solace:

> We cling like animal young to the flanks of the world
> to show our belonging; but to be at ease here
> in mastery, were to make too light of the world
> as if it were less than it is: the unmasterable.

I have reservations about certain aspects of Bronk's poetry and want to state them in the context of my essential admiration of it. We never learn to what extent Bronk's own hangups color his "ignorance of reality" (he himself claims that there are no mistakes or faults, thus undercutting even a basis for psychological meaningfulness). When he writes that "good or evil, it doesn't matter what we do" or "Do as you will. It doesn't matter," I smell the ghost of Aleister Crowley, or an attitude that at its blackest point would logically have to equate Hudson Falls with Auschwitz.

Yet Bronk's failure to attach any importance to cultural destruction and his dismissal of history as though it were non-existent, like other aspects of his negativity, find ground in our ghostliness, our immateriality, how we are hardly here at all, and in an empty vastness. Such thought connects to a series of essays (*The New World*, Elizabeth, 1974) based on the poet's visits to Incan and Mayan ruins (as one might guess, Bronk is most at home amidst stripped-bare temples). His prose on Copan, Tikal and Palenque, is extraordinary and serves not only as a stunning backdrop against which to read his poetry, but as perhaps the most accessible entrance to his worldless world:

> One of the strongest impressions that we have is that under the mask and metaphor something is there though it is not perhaps man that is there. There is something which is. Nothing else matters. Copan is a liberation. It is all gone, emptied away. To see it is to see ourselves gone, to see us freed from the weight of our world and its limitations. . . . We are happy at Copan to witness our own destruction and how we survive it. If something may be said to happen, what happens to us is not what happens. . . . We are delivered from our continuous failures and frustrations. Perhaps more importantly, we are delivered from our self-limited successes, the awful banalities of the good life. Joy and desire surround us without our doing, without our understanding. The world or what we term the world, that medium in which we find ourselves, and indeed whatever of it we set apart and term selves, is not related to what we make of it and not dependent on what we make of it and not dependent on what me make of the world or make of ourselves. It is not in the least altered, nor is our basic nature altered, by any cosmology or culture or individual character

we may devise, or by the failure or destruction of any of these, as all of them fail. If they seem for a time to succeed, they blind us as though they were real; and it is by our most drastic failures that we may perhaps catch glimpses of something real, of something which is. It merits our whole mind. . . .

Charles Olson

CHARLES OLSON'S *The Maximus Poems,* out of print for several years in its original three volumes, has now been published for the first time in a single volume. The poem itself is 655 pages long. Olson (1910–1970) worked on it for the last twenty years of his life, and it is the fruit of his lifetime effort as a poet, scholar and teacher to construct a poetry and poetics large enough to embed man once again in the world. It is probably the most ambitious poem ever written by an American.

Olson believed that the West was coming to the end of a great cycle of dispersion in space, identity and syntax, that began around 3500 years ago with the defeat of Troy and the subsequent waves of northwestern migrations. By engaging archaic myths in a context which also included historical facts, he hoped to overwhelm "the End of the West" implicit in *The Cantos,* the epic of his predecessor, Ezra Pound.

Read carefully, which is no easy task, *The Maximus Poems* represents a revolution in the concept of the poet and his relation to his source materials. This review will attempt to suggest what Olson has taken on in this work, some of its features and directions, and to reflect on the extent to which it covers the immense territory of history and the soul that it stakes out as its own.

There has been a growing consensus of opinion over the past one hundred years, by writers as different as D. H. Lawrence and Christopher Hawkes (both of whom influenced Olson), that between 40,000 and 8000

This review of Charles Olson's *The Maximus Poems,* edited by George Butterick (University of California Press, Berkeley, 1983), appeared in the *Los Angeles Times Sunday Book Review,* September 4, 1983.

BC there existed a worldwide science of life. The last Ice Age, or Upper Paleolithic, is not only the period in which the autonomous imagination seems to have been formed (which is the archetypal base for all subsequent creative activity), but a time in which, to reverse one of Heraclitus' aphorisms, people did *not* seem to be estranged from that which was closest to them. The thousands of paintings found in the narrow corridors and recesses of caves in southwestern France and northern Spain suggest that man then lived his life at arm's length, so to speak. He still had a primate gleam in his eyes, and he inscribed his "art," like stigmata, onto nature's living walls (no frames, no glass, no museums, etc).

In such a world it may follow that the person who painted a particular cave was an artist, a sorcerer, a hunter and a recordkeeper, all wrapped up into one. If we think of such a figure as the whole rope, we can then see how the multiple strands have unraveled over the ages into what today are the "departments" of art, history, medicine, psychology, etc. In the twentieth-century industrialized West, the artist has become a single, almost invisible, strand of such a rope. At the moment a young person enters poetry he finds that he has inherited an abstract place involving activities that the vast majority of his society considers unessential, decorative, suspect and even criminal. His place, or cage, is constructed out of a multitude of restrictions, from the periodic sentence to scientific objectivity. In short, he may be forced to acknowledge that society's judgment of him is correct, for his means have denied him his faculties at large.

Most artists—and who can blame them—end up wallpapering the cage in attempts to camouflage it and at least make it comfortable. And most of the few who do not, destroy themselves in misconceived attempts to dismantle it. Occasionally there is an Antonio Gaudi, or a Jackson Pollock or a Charlie Parker who, while being defeated, twist their given conditions into shapes that convey their imaginative rage for the full range of human experience.

Charles Olson is one of these figures, and *The Maximus Poems* is fundamentally the record of his attempt to destroy the specialized, effete artisan, and to create a vision of the poet as a primary thinker capable of responding to the mythic and historical dimensions of time and space in the place in which he finds himself.

Olson's "place" was Gloucester, Massachusetts, and it is the spore out of which the entire work proliferates. While he was born in Worcester, Olson began to visit Gloucester as a child with his parents on summer vacations, and he moved there permanently (for the last thirteen years of his life, with a couple of teaching interruptions) in 1957. As the locale for an epic poem, Gloucester evokes Paterson, New Jersey, the setting for William Carlos Williams' *Paterson*.

Starting in 1950 with a series of poems presented as "letters" to Vincent Ferrini, another poet living in Gloucester, Olson began a multiphasic project that not only concentrated on the nature of the city during the poet's lifetime, but also placed Gloucester in a historical "view" in which its seventeenth-century fishing activities, religious and aboriginal conflicts, maps and community records, were identified as aspects of what the place itself contained. However, there is no story, in the traditional sense, involved. Olson might be said to "open up" Gloucester as a man in an enormous, unknown mansion might attempt to figure out its extent and holdings.

Intuiting that a first-person perspective would be limiting to the project in the long run, Olson created what at first looks like a Greek god, named "Maximus" (the mightiest, or the greatest), through whose transpersonal mouth the epic would be spoken. It happens that there was a second-century AD Greek eclectic philosopher named Maximus (from Tyre, a Phoencian city-state, like Gloucester, slightly off-shore), which gave the Olson Maximus historical depth. However, the new Maximus was more a state of mind than a character like Zeus (late in his life, Olson suggested Maximus was primarily "an inner inherence," that is, the agent through which the work coalesced). And it must immediately be added that Olson, as a reader of Jung, also conceived Maximus as an archetypal "homo maximus," a universal soul in whom the Above and Below of creation, as well as the self of a people, are reunited.

The reader at this point may begin to feel that he is being drawn into a whirlpool of associational sources. This would certainly be the case with the poem itself. Here, instead of enumerating the carefully thought out materials from old Norse, Vedic, Egyptian, Gnostic, Indian and Greek sources that are folded into Maximus' "deep-swirling" dynamic, it might be more useful to ask the reader to imagine the following image:

Picture Olson himself (at 6' 7") standing on Main Street in Gloucester, considering all he knows about the place. As the poem develops, his task will be to slowly press down and out into the earth until, as Maximus, with outstretched arms and driven down legs, he is buried up to his head. His outstretched arms harken back to the Indo-European migration routes (as a film might be shown backwards) that ended in the colonization of the American continent. At the same time he is also a vertical force whose legs are not only entwined with the history under the present, with the founding of Gloucester by the Dorchester Company in 1623, but with the geology of the land mass, formed by continental drift and receding glaciers. At one point, the head, or hill, of an area adjacent to Gloucester, speaks:

> Gravelly Hill says
> leave me be, I am contingent, the end of the world
> is the borders
> of my being
>
> I can even tell you
> where I run out; and you can find
> out. I lie here
> so many feet up
> from the end of an old creek
> which used to run off
> the Otter ponds. There is a bridge
> of old heavy slab stones
> still crossing the creek on
> the 'Back Road' about three rods
> from where I do end northerly, and from my Crown
> you may observe, in fact Jeremiah Millett's
> generous pasture
> which, in fact, is the first 'house'
> (of Dogtown) is a part of the slide of
> my back, to the East: it isn't so decisive
> how one thing does end
> and another begin . . .

The "field" of Maximus is not only a tracing back to its origins, but an attempt to keep the particles of history and migrational flow present as if they were the blood cells of a living, circulating "body." The nearly impossible mission of the work is to allow its materials to circulate freely *and* to cohere, so that at the same time it works against dispersal on as many levels as Maximus can imagine, it is by this very act increasingly permeated by the associational connections of the myths and rituals that

appear to be the remnants of a very archaic science of life. As an operation, the poem is a combined hunting and planting, in which some materials are presented as quoted fragments, while others are reimagined and
"grafted" by Maximus who, halfway through the poem, declares:

> I looked up and saw
> its form
> through everything
> —it is sewn
> in all parts, under
> and over

Besides Maximus and his doubles (Odysseus, Hercules, John
Smith, Ptah, etc.), Gloucester and its doubles (Phoenician Tyre and
Gondwannaland), the other principal presences are the Muse (as a protean
Great Earth Mother), and Maximus' serpent consort (Typhon, an enormous Algonquin water snake, etc.). The overlays become so complex
that, for example, at one point an image of the serpent as a "blue monster
. . . opening an opening big enough for himself" becomes Olson/
Maximus in his letter-carrier uniform inserting his "delivery" in a mail
slot.

To argue the extent to which *The Maximus Poems* succeeds, one is
put in the vexing position of realizing that in certain ways there is nothing
to which it can be compared. Also, Olson died in 1970 while the work
was still in process and, like Pound's *Cantos,* it has an end but no
conclusion (which is true to its ever-all meaning). In the last two hundred
pages (edited with great care by George T. Butterick and Charles Boer),
Olson often appears to allow himself descriptive and egotistical liberties
that the entire work was originally set up to overcome. In a way, Maximus collapses back into Olson who as an ailing man dies into the poem.
Another problem, which should be clear by now, is that the poem takes
on so much that at certain points it seems that anything can happen in it,
and without an acute sense of what can and cannot be included, it may be
argued that the poem loses consciousness (though in its support it must
also be acknowledged that Olson cut out many passages in the mid-fifties
when he felt that it had gotten off course). The sheer amount of information the poem attempts to be responsible for questions the nature of
transformation in the poetic process per se. Lastly, future readers will
have to decide to what extent the poem's visionary content corresponds to

aspects of an actual American world that is supportive of it. Olson's loathing for "the Nation" that bulks larger and larger in the second half of the poem may be felt to undercut the heroism of Maximus and, in varying degrees, to invalidate it.

At this point in time, it does not seem essential to me whether one likes the work or not. What counts is what one can make of it and do with it. For readers who have limited themselves to the writings of the "Confessional" poets of the fifties and sixties, *The Maximus Poems* will seem like a foreign country with foreign languages based on foreign sensibilities. For anyone really curious about what can be done with "the long poem" after Pound's *Cantos* and Williams' *Paterson,* Olson's effort may be so challenging that they will be forced to re-evaluate what poetry can mean in our time.

Given all these difficulties, the *Maximus* reader might want to consult Butterick's *A Guide to the Maximus Poems* (University of California Press, 1978), and Don Byrd's study, *Charles Olson's Maximus* (University of Illinois Press, 1980). Both books are valuable companions for anyone setting off with Maximus "in a box upon the sea."

Out Climbed Artaud

IN ANTONIN ARTAUD'S MATURE POETRY (1945–48), there is a multifoliate binding of attraction/repulsion for virtually all the materials and sensations that the poet is conscious of. The friction created by Artaud's unceasing induction and cursing of the physical world is in the service of opening up an underworld out of which a "dark parturition of principles" can be summoned.

"Christ's mission to the underworld was to annul it through his resurrected victory over death. Because of his mission, all Christians were forever exempt from the descent."[1] Artaud's rage against the "sickly sexuality" of Christ eroticized on the cross is, to my reading, the rage of a powerful imagination against a dualistic world in which the underworld has been Satanized and anesthetized as a source for poetic vision.

Christ is an aspect of the "anchored mind" that Artaud refers to at the beginning of his poetic masterpiece, *Artaud le Mômo,* and the reason that he protests so vehemently against all forms of initiation (other than "initiation off oneself") is that he realizes that they anchor the initiate's mind to established and frozen imaginations.

If the enemy is the anchored mind (and by extension, in this poem, the sexually degraded body and ego), the victor, to the extent that there is one, is the Mômo itself, a presence that Artaud has "made live" in a way parallel to Gérard de Nerval's "beings" which the former poet "saved from the shroud of the Tarots." Furthermore, as Nerval's *Les Chimères*

Originally published as the Introduction to *Antonin Artaud: Four Texts,* translated by the author and Norman Glass (Panjandrum, Los Angeles, 1982).

are "the poems of a hanged man," Artaud's autistic Mômo is the progeny of insanity, incarceration and electro-shock.[2]

Artaud's incarceration from 1937 to 1946 in several insane asylums rhymes with that of a concentration camp victim. He was forcibly detained, his head shaved, his clothes and possessions taken away from him, and fed so little (all his teeth fell out) that he would have starved to death had not his mother herself weekly brought him food. Rather than shipping off a potentially great poet to the Nazi ovens, the French kept this one in a semi-starvation cell with his own excrement for company. Artaud's experiences during this period, rather than totally destroying him, helped turn him into one of the great poets of all time. If one wants to wiggle into the cockpit of French literary history, it is possible to view Artaud, at the end of his career, as Rabelais pulled inside out—slowly—as if over hundreds of years, so that the stretched glands and meat snap, festoon and cobweb the inversion. At the point that *Artaud le Mômo*, in an almost stately way, climbs forth, a tarantulan birth has taken place. The French language, castrated into a court language a few hundred years ago, has been enghosted and burns like a phantom cornucopia in the maw of the Mômo's speech.

The presence of the Mômo pervades all of Artaud's writings, letter-essays as well as poetry, from about 1945 on, or that point at which, having nearly died in electro-shock, he began to converse and write again, making a "return" to the world of literary imagination. Given the circumstances under which the Mômo was created, it is understandable that it is a monstrous presence, but its monstrosity is not simply that of deformity and pain.

Artaud deeply desired to eat the delirium that gave birth to him, so along with layers of European popular and esoteric culture, his Mômo is constructed out of a sense of Tarahumara peyote ritual, of a people who "eat Peyote right out of the soil/while it is being born." The Mômo is at once a delirious inherence as well as a sophisticated critic of all reductions of the whirling dervish of the soul.

In the Notes that follow our translation, we have commented on what the word "mômo" itself suggests. Here I would like to say that its delirium and raillery evoke William Blake's Rintrah, or the just wrath of the Prophet. Blake, without any explanation, identified Rintrah with Merlin, or "immortal imagination." It is thus possible that an archetypal figure of Merlin the Magician, seduced and abandoned by Vivian, trapped, raging under a rock, is present in Artaud's Mômo. If this makes sense it would not only help to explain Artaud's intense ambivalence toward magic, but also his revulsion with feminine sexuality.

Artaud identifies so closely with Nerval because he is convinced that the only poetry that really is poetry comes out of a kamekaze-like confrontation with death. It is only, in this fantasy, the moment that the poet/pilot takes off in an unlandable balsam-nosed plane that something "previous to source," "a magnetic innervation of the heart," can be uttered. I do not think that this is necessarily true, yet I am sympathetic with Artaud's courageous desire to get at the heart of his own derangement (rather than to use his poetry to sweeten it) and recontact death as a depth and vitality in life.

[1981]

---

1. *The Dream and the Underworld,* James Hillman, (New York, 1979), p. 85.
2. All the comments in this Introduction relating to Artaud's life are based on Thomas Maeder's *Antonin Artaud* (Plon, Paris, 1978).

Golub the Axolotl

OVER THE YEARS Leon Golub has been an important example to me of the necessity to do exactly what you want to do as an artist, to take your knocks for it, but at the same time not to become bitter or to confuse the reception of your work with its ultimate worth. It is tough to practice one's vision and to remain receptive to a world that for the most part rejects not only the vision but the life behind it.

Golub's tender armored tenacity, his resistance to any easy assimilation, his insistence on the artist as one who does not filter out the mire of society in his work—these aspects of what I would think of as integrity and solidarity with the genuine human condition—inevitably result, in our society, in a peripheral location. Most artists and writers who take a peripheral position, or who are peripheralized by the art world, seal over at a certain point and begin to cannibalize themselves. There are a couple of points in Golub's artistic evolution where I can feel the work stammering in place, starting to wear a cowl of despair and confusion—but in both cases, stasis became gestation, and he moved ahead. Golub's entire body of work to date has a peristaltic reflexibility of contracted insearch and expressive outreach.

In the early 1980s, Golub's paintings of mercenaries, interrogation and torture, became a subject of great interest in the art world, and the Rutgers University Press monograph,* with a substantial text by Donald Kuspit, is to a certain extent the result of such attention. The optimistic

---

*Donald Kuspit: *Leon Golub, Existential/Activist Painter,* (Rutgers University Press, New Brunswick, 1985). "Golub the Axolotl" appeared in *Temblor* 6, 1987.

part of me takes the attention from the art world and the monograph as a moving and reassuring sign that one can paint like Leon Golub has for thirty-five years and, during one's lifetime, be treated with respect and genuine acclaim. Another part of me believes that only when I can walk into a Bank of America and confront Interrogation II hanging over the bent heads of the tellers, will Golub's art have been truly received. And I don't expect that to happen in either of our lifetimes. In fact, if it did, a whole set of paranoiac speculations would be set in motion, like: Has North American society now assimilated (co-opted) even Golub? The pessimistic part of me says that seeming acceptance by one's enemies is much more undermining than their rejection. Paradoxically, one needs, is even nourished by, rejection on the part of a society that in its actual daily performance denies the self a sense of worth and imaginative fulfillment. So, except for a few people like Donald Kuspit, whose affirmative response to Golub's art is unquestionable, the warring parts of me wonder what the art world's current interest in Golub is about. Nevertheless, I would like to think that there are at least several thousand North Americans on earth today who can receive and respond intelligently to an impassioned, harsh and confrontational art that does not, for a moment, release them from their complicity in their country's imperialistic role in domestic and world politics.

At the beginning, in the mid-1940s, Leon Golub finds himself, with a paint brush in hand, standing before a "liberated" Buchenwald. Unlike most artists of his generation, he did not whitewash this backdrop and begin to work out schematic, abstract diagrams on it—or cover it with a landscape that would make the viewer feel that he was still in a nineteenth-century relationship to nature. The core of Golub's career is in its complex response to annihilation. It is to some extent sounded by two lines by Charles Olson in a poem called "La Préface":

My name is NO RACE   address
Buchenwald   new Altamira cave

Olson's poem was written in 1946, the same year that Golub's "Charnel House" and "Evisceration Chamber"—based on concentration camps—were painted. Olson's presentation of Buchenwald and Altamira, with space rather than a verb between the two nouns, presents the reader with an overwhelming question: What do these nouns have in common? The meaning that I draw from them is that the astonishing ancientness of man's creative impulse, which was discovered in this most inhuman century, may somehow offset total despair. Olson's choice of Altamira is slightly inaccurate for my meaning, as it was discovered in the nineteenth century. However, the bulk of Upper Paleolithic cave art which we are now aware of was discovered between 1900 and 1940, and thus comes back *into time* as mankind nearly passed *out of time*. This seems to represent a staggering synchronicity, and the pairing of the first imaginative constructions with the most recent inhuman destructions argues *contra* Adorno that there *can* be poetry and art after Auschwitz and, most important for both Olson and Golub, it did not have to jettison the mammalian image. Olson went ahead to write a body of poetry that attempted to be responsible for human culture for the past 3000 years. Golub, while not going back as far as Olson, made use of Primitive and Classical art to construct an ontogenetic vision that is at the same time his own artistic birth and evolution. He was not crushed by man's inhumanity nor—as his career magnificently bears out—has he evaded it.

After his initial recognition of the Holocaust, Golub himself seems to have disappeared. He slipped into the water-filled wreckage-laden basement of Western culture and transformed it into a primordial bath, or foetus world. The murky paintings of the early 1950s, with their grotesque quasi-human forms, are entangled with the "Birth" series in such a way that they prefigure the emergent child. In Golub's uteral world, amputated members have a curious finlike appearance, i.e., end-man is beginning-man. And while such creatures seem to be struggling against a "primitive" dissolution, they also seem to be fighting the wind tunnel of Abstract Art. They are thus "edged" with contemporary time as well as being evocations of the artist's immemorial struggle to give birth to himself in his art. Without wanting to push it too far, I would suggest that at every stage of Golub's career there is an active resistance to Abstract "dissolution." For example, the flecklike burn-rubbled interiors of the "Burnt Man" paintings of the early 1960s are in themselves "abstract" and are only restrained from spreading out across the canvas in a particle flow by their bounding Classical outlines.

At the point when an artist is on the verge of creating an image that is uniquely personal and universal, there may be an unbearable tension. Psychologically, it can feel as if one is at the same time engendering oneself and opening a conduit through which the new engendered self can emerge—as image. In the work of the majority of artists and writers, the effort of bringing oneself forth is not represented as subject. Golub's paintings are unique in their time for the extent to which they openly parallel emergent artistic consciousness with a recapitulation of mammalian birth.

I say "mammalian" here instead of "human," because the images of emergence are hybrid: The amoebic tension of parturition is emphasized by the "Sphinx" series, several paintings of which depict "fabulous" two- (or five-) headed beasts that seem to be on the point of division. In "Siamese Sphinx I" (1954), the head placed over the animal's rump seems to be excrementally twisting its way out, while the frontal head grimaces at the viewer as if it were giving birth. In all the paintings of the early and mid-1950s, I feel the struggle of unborn man in a Holocaustal/primordial limbo, which, on an aesthetic level, reads out as a tug-of-war between Nihilism and a yet-to-be-resolved sense of how the human figure might become a vehicle sturdy enough to support a lifelong meditation on man's destiny. The great "Damaged Man" (1955) reveals a furious, gagged, adult foetus in the strait-jacket of a spiky caterpillar body.

This vision of the figure-to-be-born as already possessing a mature body—or to put it another way, the figure in larval state already possessing adult characteristics—is mirrored by Golub's "Philosopher" series of the late 1950s, where massive quiescent adults, the first Golubians clearly out in the world, seem to be mainly reflecting on having just been born. Like the baby's face in "Birth VII," the Philosophers have utterly innocent "infant" eyes. The expression on the baby's face in "Birth VII" seems as old as the expression on "Philosopher I"'s face seems young. As I glance back and forth between the two reproductions of these paintings, the faces momentarily fuse, each the mask, or stone hood, of the other, out of which Leon Golub's just-emerged soul gazes with a pristine, undirected stare.

To reflect on figures in a larval state that already possess adult characteristics is to evoke the Mexican axolotl, a curious amphibian which keeps its gills throughout life and breeds in this larval state. And to think of certain artists, like Golub, as axolotls, brings up the matter of the advantages and disadvantages of prolonged immaturity or, in a phrase that has almost become archaic today, artistic apprenticeship.

Because we cannot imagine our grandchildren living the same kind of life as we do today, old-fashioned apprenticeship has given way to an obsession with immediate "arrival." Originality, which in the past, especially in the East, meant a slight modification on the style of one's master, now means a quick sizing up of the "art situation" and flicking a twist into current trends. In short, the artist today is under pressure to be immediately mature, to not allow his art a childhood.

The most obvious example I know of a prolonged twentieth-century painter apprenticeship is that of Arshile Gorky. Golub's apprenticeship (which might more accurately be described as an artistic neoteny) is less obvious than Gorky's, and more complex, because the ontogenetic element is so pronounced, and because it constantly seems to be shaping stylistic influence for its own purposes. On one hand, Golub is "in time" from the very beginning, from the point at which he paints "Charnel House" in 1946, and there is no time in his body of work when he appears to forget that he is a conflict-ridden twentieth-century man. On the other hand, Golub's paintings do not address historical time until 1969 when in "Napalm I" the rash of red paint smeared across one of the fallen, naked combatants suddenly links the painting to the Viet Nam era. This is to argue that from the early 1950s, when the first axolotl-like forms began to breed in his canvasses, to the Gigantomachies of the late 1960s, Golub was working an image of man (from foetus to adult-in-action) in a frame that resisted man in historical time. It is as if for nearly twenty years (the time it takes a human male to go from birth to manhood) Golub allowed himself to remain immature, to very slowly amass a concentrated biological sense of becoming a man, of approaching manhood as it engages, and is worked over by, post Second-World-War North American society.

The risk in allowing himself an almost molecular development was considerable. While I think there is a handful of paintings from the 1950s and the 1960s that now can be recognized as masterpieces, I am not sure that they would look the way they do today if they lacked the encompassing context of Golub's advances in the 1970s and the 1980s. His insistence on taking his time in a world in which the present seems to be whirling electrically into the future is courageous, for if an artist does take his time and does not "jump on the bandwagon," it may look to the world as if he is not meeting the nuclear reality of today's pace.

Indeed, if the devil is loose in the world, and if the sky is already cracking its pillars, why scurry about for years at the shadowy edge of the spectacle, trying to figure out how to make monsters more viscerally real?

I am sure there are many responses to such a question. In Golub's case, I would propose that while he was painting to his maximum at each stage of his career, he was also calculating the amount of density necessary to solidify his figures in historical time once he de-eternalized (or de-primordialized) them. Furthermore, it seems to me to be more affirmative to paint man as an ugly brute than to not paint him at all, more humanly responsible to show North American mercenaries torturing Third World people than to make a painting that can be hung in a restaurant and blend into the decor and music—a painting which affirms the status quo by refusing explicit political content. The predicament that Golub had to work through in the 1970s seems to go like this: How eliminate the anonymous Classical aspects of the figure (which in the early paintings inevitably look backward, and may be dismissed as too concentrated on the past) and yet anchor historical figures in a context that will not be sucked into the velocity of our age and become a computer chip in the millrace of the instant?

In the mid-1960s, when Golub's Philosophers sprang into action, they discovered what they wanted to do: physically fight. The 120 × 288″ canvas of "Gigantomachy I" is a web of striking, thwarted gods and Titans who cannot be distinguished from each other. The body textures—chalk-white with rust and charcoal-colored sketched-in muscle suggestions—hint that because they have not been burnished forth into social identity such figures are ghosts. The background, without specificity or setting, like nearly all of Golub's backgrounds, is a neither-here-nor-there murky mustard color.

In "Gigantomachy III," the background darkens and at one point seems to soak with blood, as if history is approaching through the back of the canvas (such "blood," in the paintings of the 1980s, becomes a solid bricklike background). While the painting virtually sweats with desire to express and contain male violence, the figures remain phantasmagoric. Their anatomy does not add up—certain feet are like massive, brushlike clubs—and the cause/effect timing seems oddly "off." Here the central kicker is swinging a gigantic foot over a figure who appears to have fallen before the kick. It is hard to tell if this "out of sync" quality is intentional or not. It tends to emphasize the anti-natural mood of the scene and make it more dreamlike than imitative of its source, the Greek Pergamon altar.

By the end of the 1960s, the blood-splashed background of "Gigantomachy III" has been localized as napalm gore in the chest of a fallen combatant who is otherwise as ahistorical as the ambiguous gods/Titans. By 1972, Golub must have realized that his "murals of conflict" were as problematic, relative to the twentieth century, as Picasso's "Guernica" with its old-fashioned weapons and mythological beasts. In "Vietnam I" (1972), the combatants are given black pants and guns, and their ruddy hatch-marked torsos consequently feel flayed. They are firing across a tank-shaped rupture cut out of the canvas itself at a man and a woman. The "gods" are now starting to look like soldiers and the "Titans" like embattled peasants. Golub's art has become a kind of zoom camera depositing fragments of the war "over there" at the viewer's feet, insisting that any aesthetic contemplation be accompanied by confronting America's role in global terror. As Golub moved toward the 1980s, the challenge increasingly became to paint well (not beautifully, but with verve, precision and abrasive particularity) *and* to confront the viewer with the fact that the inspiration behind such work is humanity suffering *now*.

In the 1980s, the groups of soldiers and peasants have metamorphized into mercenaries and victims. Golub has moved these figures forward, as if on wide-screen TV, with the feet of both interrogators and the tortured eliminated, thus by implication standing, or hanging, in our own space. Because the mercs are dressed as we are, in fact smiling at us as they go about their "work," the "DMZ" between an Asiatic "there" and a North America "here" has been eliminated. The mercs are grinning at us because they know the "news" is part of our daily entertainment, and because they believe that we can be entertained by the pain they are inflicting on others.

Viewed as a whole, Golub's work to date, as Kuspit's monograph makes evident, seems to be built on phases that increase in tension before recycling into a new phase. To put it in one sentence: It is as if the propeller-foeti amoebically divide and birth themselves into large block-wall-like "philosophical" babies, who slump and pose as burnt or destroyed men and then, discovering that they can act, begin to smash their way into history, creating a route into our awareness that leads from Rome via Viet Nam to El Salvador. Golub's most difficult and crucial advance seems to me to be the move from "Vietnam II" (1973) to "Mercenaries I" (1979). I know that this was a very difficult period for him. He mentions in one interview that he nearly stopped painting at this time.

On a superficial level, it appears that the breakthrough into the "Mercenaries" and "White Squads" was contingent on having allowed newspaper photos to become naturalistically dominant in the "heads of state" portraits (1976–77). However, I think this move was dependent upon a more complicated one which meant cutting himself off from the Classical and Primitive "compost" that had nurtured his work up to this time. Such compost was permeated not only with the affirmative elements in Golub's long apprenticeship, but with that vague sense of timelessness, or primordial connection that many artists yearn to maintain as an active component in their work. If Golub's shaping of the "Mercenaries" series had failed, he would have been exchanging an art that through its resonance at least connected him to great art of the past for an illustrational, message-oriented, political one. Most artists and writers are put in this position at least once or twice in their careers, and most opt for ambiguity because, for one reason, it is just too frightening to stake one's neck on a single theme or subject in an age without a central story or myth.

For every great or unique artist there are thousands of intelligent, highly sensitive artists who, as Blake put it, "keep the divine vision in a time of trouble," and are thus part of the evolving poem/painting of the world that involves the imagination and fate of each of us in each other, including those of the past and those of the future. There is an eternal pathos in creative activity because the vast majority of artworks quickly become fertilizer which, in turn, stimulates new shoots which, in turn, also join that earth. While every artist in some way desires his art to outlive him, most stay very close to the image compost that enabled a seed to take root in the first place and, in that way, predetermine their development. Great art may be a demonstration in a single shoot, as it were, of the depth and the complexity of the compost itself. Unique art, on the other hand, may add to the stalk a bloom of a peculiar color or tinge that had not been seen or grasped before, stating in effect that the compost is lacking in something that this art is *adding on its own*. Such art almost inevitably appears to be incoherent or ugly until, in time, enough of it is absorbed by the compost to become part of artistic nurture. One of the unending ironies of art is that the more an individual artist desires immortality the more he will be magnetized by the imaginations of those who have come before him, and probably co-opted by their awesome quicksand. The move toward uniqueness on the part of an artist can appear to involve jettisoning art itself in an attempt to show life without artifice, psychology, established and occult religions, the initiations of others, etc., that is, without all the filter systems humanity has for eons employed to keep itself from remembering itself and exercising its imaginative faculties at large. Were these filter systems to totally disappear, would it be the end of art, or would art truly become the mental gymnastics of paradise?

In the paintings of the 1980s, Golub has eliminated the combat frenzy of the paintings done in the 1960s and the 1970s and, by matching his own peripherality with peripheral subjects, has come to terms with his own position in today's art world. I believe that one of the things that he had to confront was that the "heads of state" portraits were an instructive dead-end. In this respect, I think that W. H. Auden was on to something when he wrote in an essay entitled "The Poet and the City": "It is extremely difficult today [1962] to use public figures as themes for poetry because the good or evil they do depends less upon their characters and intentions than upon the quantity of impersonal force at their disposal." While the "heads" enabled Golub to focus on media images, they seemed to be too far removed from his own social "station" as an artist at the periphery of both the art scene and North American power to advance the energy of his complex vision.

To move from Pinochet to a tacky merc (forgetting the head of state and concentrating on the guy who does his dirty work) was an acute and astonishing adjustment. Mercenaries, like Golub himself, may be seen as peripheral figures, a kind of Hermic trash, scuttling back and forth between military elitism and civilian desperation for work. If the figure of the peripheral artist evokes the Dostoevsky "creature between the floorboards," the mercenary intensifies the connotations of such a figure into a livid focus: The mercenary is not only marginal man, but marginal man without politics, willing to kill or torture anyone for a price. He is like the medieval masterless Japanese samurai, known as the "ronin," or "wave-man," a warrior tramp with day-to-day allegiances who goes with the flow.

At the same time, far from being a TV dot pattern who can snuff thousands by signing an order, the merc, like most North Americans, makes a few hundred dollars a week, can be fired at whim, and has no real significance. While he is "over there," he is very close to most of us here, if for no other reason than like most American workers, his is a lifetime of meaningless labor. In the technological world, workers are laborers, for they feel no personal pride in what they do, and are not responsible for what they make. This, of course, does not make them killers, but if one thinks about American society today—from the consciousness level of Saturday at midnight in the typical local bar, to wife, child and animal abuse, and all the land mines of violence to others and to the self across which millions move on a nightly, daily basis—if one looks unromantically and unflinchingly at how people actually treat one another in our "great society," the mercs not only blend in and are absorbed as part of the machinery of violence, but they typify a certain kind of cruel pointlessness which every North American soul bears as a scummy watermark.

Golub's mercs often stop work for a moment and turn to acknowledge our fascination with what they do, as if they were chefs in a see-into kitchen, and we were the well-heeled clientele, eager to not only dine but to watch our cuisine being prepared. For these mercs *are* making something for us, are they not? They are whipping the out-of-line into line, crushing the testicles of a rebel who has refused to make his daily contribution to the "American dream." In Golub's corrosive clarity, it is one Satanic ball, from interrogation and torture in the afternoon to horsing around with whores and booze at night. Work and play, torture inciting sex, sex inciting torture. In these paintings, Golub has once and for all boiled the fat and anonymity out of his Gigantomachies. There are no gods—only these lordless henchmen. As for the Titans, they have become unidentified suffering flesh, the power of the earth as manifested in a human being strung up and pummeled because he lacks the correct identification card.

Baudelaire wrote, "Caricature is a double thing; it is both drawing and idea—the drawing violent, the idea caustic and veiled." Leon Golub's mercenaries, the violent carriers of caustic and veiled North American hostility toward "the other," would seem to meet Baudelaire's definition, but they extend the ground of caricature too. They fuse the grotesque with the documentary (we sense the verisimilitude of the news photo moving like a Procrustean frame behind them), and Satanic laughter with winks and friendly fuck-yous. In "Mercenary V," the squatting white holding his revolver to the forehead of a black in raised push-up position turns to look at us, as if posing for us, and raises his left hand in a kind of pointless open salute and wave. I am not sure if he has just waved or is about to give me the finger—and his leer and half-mast eyes are so out of focus that I cannot tell if he is making a face at me or anticipating my applause when and if he "blows that nigger's brains out."

While the Mercenaries have social identity, like the Classically inspired warriors, they are anonymous. By placing them in a limbo between caricature and representation, Golub has contained the nature of the mercenary, a being whose identity is clear yet unrevealed. The ambiguous gesture of "Mercenary V"'s left hand is repeated by body as well as hand gestures in groups of figures in other paintings. The "out of sync" aspects of "Gigantomachy III" have become orchestrated into a functional motif to prevent these paintings from slipping into cartoon-like caricature or photographic representation.

In this regard, the masterpiece of the series is "Interrogation II" where three mercenaries are involved in torturing a naked, tied-up and seated, hooded victim. Golub has painted the torturers so that they appear to be more interested, for the moment, in our response to them than in their "work" itself. The two mercs to the right of the tortured man are grinning at us (one is black, the other white; Golub is careful to leave no single social strata unimplicated)—in fact, they look as if we had just yelled at them, Hi, Benny! Hi, Will!—what are you guys *up to?* The third merc, let's call him Frenchie (he has plastered back hair, a pencil moustache, and a neck scarf tucked inside his blue short-sleeved workshirt) is a little suspicious of Benny and Will. Are they getting too much attention from us? He holds up his left hand in a slightly effeminate pose with cigarette (one can smoke *and* torture at the same time), and with his right hand, in a rather wooden, puzzling gesture, seems to be on the verge of grabbing the front of the hooded man's face—but the gesture is more baffling than it is precise, as is Benny's hand gestures, for while he is turned toward us, grinning, he is also slightly advancing toward the tortured man, with his hands held forward, thumbs raised, but the gesture, like Frenchie's, is baffling—and curiously *still.* In contrast to the slashing action of the Gigantomachies, these mercs seem as if they were rehearsing a play, or as if they are at play, like big kids on stage, where they just happen (by unavoidable implication) to be torturing someone. All six hands of the three torturers are as much involved in a mudric sign language as in manhandling the hooded victim.

To see the mercs as actors turning to us, a composite director, for a confirmation that they are accurately portraying the roles to which they have been assigned (or as in my previous example, to see the action as that of merc/chefs and viewer/clientele), is to emphasize the interplay that Golub establishes between image and audience, an interplay that is rich with psychological entrances and exits—lubricious, intransigent, and condemnational. This space between caricature and representation is one we all share. All of us move in an unfathomable and unclosable gap between our image of ourselves and the way we fear we appear to others. We are definitely real, we think, but we are never sure that our appearance to others is what we see in the mirror. It is as if we wander around in a peristaltic aura, which shakes with the gray jelly of father and Dagwood as well as of soul and man. Golub's mercs are like worms slithering around in the interstices of our baffling and pathetic self-regard. Their smiles go into our eyes with the same subtle and voracious glee with which they offer their zippered fly-covered hardon to a whore or their boot tip to the forehead of a crawling man.

[November 1985, Los Angeles]

Vatic Sores

WHAT DOES ONE MAKE of a book, more than 800 pages long, representing thirty-seven years of poetry, with the Buddha's footprint on the cover—a cover in red, gold and black, as Germanic as it is Tantric? Allen Ginsberg's *Collected Poems 1947–1980* is one of the most "packaged" books I have seen. The notes include photos of friends and lovers, detailed explanations of political events mentioned in the poems, as well as the apparatus of individual volumes (dedications, epigrams, introductions, etc.). The eighty-page Appendix is a kind of scrapbook tour through the Ginsberg "family"—the selected peers with whom he has traveled in squadron, shaping and sealing his image, over the years.

*

The first poem in the book, "In Society" (1947) strikes several tones and themes that will be elaborated throughout Ginsberg's career: A dream meal turns out to be human meat, a sandwich whose main "ingredient" is a dirty asshole. In the second stanza, an unidentified "princess" appears and rejects the poet, who screams at her: "Why you shit-faced fool!", projecting the remains of his meal onto her. The poem ends by telling us that the poet's "messianic voice" finally inspires *and* dominates the whole room. Thus, flesh is filth, but brought into the poem it evokes a core of hysterical power. Outburst is messianic. While the self is dependent upon

This essay originally appeared in *The Ohio Review,* autumn, 1987.

101

the society that hedges and torments it, the self is also capable of over-whelming society—the poet is a priest who can stop war and neutralize plutonium.

*

Most of the early poems are either Williamsesque "exercises" with carefully observed scenes, or abstract, self-conscious attempts to find a way into the use of such words as Heaven, Lord, Eternity and Soul. "Paterson," written in 1949, edges beyond these limitations and is, in an oblique way, a kind of first draft for "Howl." The most interesting "fig-ure" in Ginsberg's early poems is "the Shrouded Stranger," a murky composite of Death and macabre adventure, ultimately the "ghost" of his mother, for this "stranger" wears a white shroud as well as a darkened one (in his Preface, Ginsberg notes that his next book will be called *White Shroud* and is "a dream epilogue to 'Kaddish'"). Inside the veils of the shroud is Ginsberg's "dark woods," or limbo, a threshold he crosses in "The Green Automobile" (1953). Like "Paterson," it is groundwork for "Howl," a mapping out of a wild journey through imaginative as well as American landscape realms. The key stanza, regarding the work to come, is the following:

> Neal, we'll be real heroes now
>> in a war between our cocks and time:
>> let's be the angels of the world's desire
>>> and take the world to bed with us before we die.

The cock is Ginsberg's kingpin (or pinned king, as it were), and through his body of work takes on a kind of menhir-like stature. Symbolic aspects of the cock aside, such inflation carries the burden of making one's poetry so important that it may become genuinely important to oneself in a country that does not regard poetry as essential to human development. It is as if the door to the North American unconscious is so dense and bolted that the size and projection of the battering-ram is bound to look out of proportion. In this sense, Ginsberg's inflated sense of mission, of self, of the importance of his feelings, etc., is an understand-able and at times moving part of his program to create a poetry capable of engaging North American reality. The antipodes in Ginsberg's poetry are, on one hand, the Williams world of "no ideas but in things" (which for Ginsberg means an unending attention to the hell of the materialistic North American landscape), and, on the other, the Shelleyean world of lofty, immortal yearnings. In his best writing, Ginsberg fuses these incompatible directions into a voicing that is his own; the coalescing agent appears to be the assertion of the humanity of his homosexual sensibility. To be obsessed with a Shelleyean heaven and a Williamsesque hell (the "thingness" of North America shaped by the labor suffered into it) is to drag a massive dualistic cross into one's work. My reading of Ginsberg leads me to believe that its resolution or failure of resolution occupies a great deal of his struggle to blast himself into the deadened white households of North American life and awaken Protestant-drugged sleepers.

*

Whitman arches like a phantom over the entire enterprise. The problem Ginsberg inherits from Whitman, to my reading, is in the expression of fatherly compassion (instead of the rage of the fathers); yet neither Ginsberg nor Whitman are *fathers*—they are men whose manhood must be achieved in evasion, not only of woman, but of family and children, and in Whitman's case, I think Ginsberg would agree, the homoerotic was not accepted as a basic, obvious factor in the poetry. Regardless of whether Whitman slept with anyone (man, woman, boy or girl), the poetry implies a homoeroticism that remains unstated. Ginsberg's thorny task, then, under the charge he has created for himself, as Whitmanian poet-man, is to achieve compassion (which most anti-homosexual heterosexual males do not) and to manifest his homosexuality in his poetry at large, thereby realizing a spiritual as well as sexual homoeroticism. The difficulty in doing so was previously expressed by Garcia Lorca in his very moving and complicated *Ode to Whitman*. There, a self-loathing tied up with cocksucking is set next to a spiritualized adoration of the blond Whitmanian hero. I am unsure to what extent Ginsberg bridges this dualism (which is loaded with the Williams-Shelley dualism I mentioned before). My reading of the *Collected Poems* leads me to believe that Ginsberg continues to loathe himself throughout his career, and that much of this loathing is tied up with being a man obsessed with assholes, with building into poetry the honesty of what he is actually obsessed with, rather than employing traditional sublimational strategies. In spite of the

playfulness, humor, and suggestions that practiced homosexuality under-
mines man's need to abuse and murder others (thus, in Ginsberg's sense,
a part of his salvational poetry, good for mankind if not womankind), his
presentation of sexuality is programmatic and one-dimensional—"boys"
are urged into the sack in a way that is as pornographic as it would be if a
heterosexual poet were using his poetry to urge "girls" to drop in and ball
him. However, the use of the poem as a poster advertising the poet's
sexual availability takes on a twist when done by a non-heterosexual
poet—it becomes aligned with the necessary aggression on the part of
minority voice entering an arena managed for centuries by the dominant
heterosexual enterprise.

*

The torpid daydreaming that infiltrates the Williamsesque "thing"
world of Palenque and Guanajuato in the relatively long "Siesta in
Xbalba" appears to be a preparation for Ginsberg's "descent" in "Howl,"
written a year later. Xbalba, as Mayan limbo or purgatory, anticipates the
"purgatoried torsos" of the latter poem. Ginsberg's drift south, and his
attraction to a Latin American abyss, enables him to melt down the
one-dimensional hardness of the North American world into images in
"Howl" that are neither merely concrete nor merely abstract. On one
level, Ginsberg was led to Xbalba as part of the Beat adventure, i.e., he
did not go there as Antonin Artaud went to the Tarahumaras twenty years
earlier to place his Western head on an Indian altar and suffer the consequences—or even, for that matter, as Charles Olson, three years before
Ginsberg, had gone to Campeche, to get a feel for a Mayan shard by
holding it in his hand in the same locale where it once had been a
functional part of a human world (as an alternative to looking at a picture
of the shard in a book in a university library). However, Ginsberg did
have the sense to daydream there, and the 13-page "Siesta" hangs, in the
Collected Poems, like the lull before the storm of "Howl." As we get
closer to "Howl" in the book, there is a brief return to Mexico in "Dream
Record: June 8, 1955" in which the ghost of Joan Burroughs (one of the
few women Ginsberg will talk with in the entire Collected) makes an
appearance. On the following page is a 4-line thank-you to the Muses
which, given its placement, anticipates "Howl" more than it refers to
earlier gifts. The rest of that page is white. As one turns the page, "Howl"

suddenly swarms margin to margin before one's eyes. "Hold back the edges of your gowns, Ladies, we are going through hell," writes Williams in his introduction to *Howl*. We know what he means, but it is purgatory, not hell.

*

Ginsberg's mother died in 1956, the year "Howl" was completed. Given the force of the appearance of her death in "Kaddish" (1957–1959), it is reasonable to suggest that one reason Ginsberg is in a visionary panic over the destructiveness of North American society, the way in which it titillates the self and then cold-cocks it, is that, on a very personal level, North America had done the same thing to his mother; and by the time of the writing of "Howl" there was no way even to hope that Naomi Ginsberg would have a redemptive moment again in her life. It is the agony of the son who, when he was twelve, escorted his mother to the asylum (this to be revealed in the opening movement of "Kaddish") that flows through the magnificent first movement of "Howl," and that gives this movement its odd, foggy, numinescent quality that is never really comic, nor really political, nor tragic—but rather rolls all these forces between its palms as a kind of absurd combined object, a chunk of something that hangs between shapelessness and shapeliness.[1] I would propose that the reason the hipsters are "angelheaded" is that on an imaginal level they are Allen Ginsberg "illuminated" by Naomi's spirit poised for departure from this world. By putting it this way, I do not mean to say that "Howl" is *about* Allen and Naomi, but that it does have a quality which makes it so oblique and memorable that it still has a thundering impact today when heard aloud. But it is also a poem which does not yield much thought if one scrutinizes it for a precise vision of a generation; for the activities of the so-called "best minds" erase significance as fast as the Bolero-like strophes can suggest it, and if one eliminates the horde of imaginative adjectives, we have to a great extent the fucked-up kids of any generation "doing their thing," name-dropping the great texts rather than really studying them, moving on a swinging roller-rink band of adventure that will, after four or five years, deposit most of them in a suit, tie, marriage and job.[2] Without the adjectives, "Howl" would be a flat, angry report. It is the electricity created between adjective and noun and the jitterbug of mixed-up and refolded sequences—"the starry dynamo in the machinery of night"—that enable Ginsberg to offer his first map of the interface between American landscape and world culture.

*

"Howl" is Ginsberg's first (and imaginatively the most convincing) demonstration of his desire to consume North America, to devour the crap with the shreds of mostly European and Asiatic culture. If North America is devoured—then what? Not that Ginsberg must present a program for a "new world" to remain valid and valuable as a poet, but the question is a real one given Ginsberg's obsession with salvation, with the light at the end of the North American-Western world tunnel. Given this preoccupation with redemption and immortality, the writing hurtles across the landscape willy-nilly, as if the real act were somehow to get it over with, to bring an apocalypse. In "Howl" the "rush" is an eruption, it works, and the fact that no one gets anywhere is apt, as these "whos" are in purgatory, cleansing/re-dirtying themselves until they drop. This opening up of a North American purgatory allows Ginsberg a great deal of play with word sequence: Nouns are piled up before nouns and made to stutter or creak like adjectives, while at the same time the language is full of associational slide, even slime, with soundings determining sequence (the spill of "b/s" through the Bronx/benzedrine/battered bleak of brain strophe). At the same time, there is a furious Surreal imp crosscutting the meaningfulness of both sound and sense. There is a certain sense in which each strophe spins its wheels, as if by its end it is going to explode into a revelation, but is immediately overwhelmed by another battalion of "whos" dumped by Charon Ginsberg on the bank of another strophe. In the line, "with mother finally *****" (as if the poet had finally passed through and out of the paralysis of his mother's impending death), the first movement of "Howl" lays out a quick definite sketch of its own poesis and sort of drains into the shadows.

*

One of the pleasures in reading through the *Collected Poems* is to find that Ginsberg has written very well at various points throughout his career. The really convincing poems become fewer in the 1970s, but they are there (they can appear not to be there because they present no new technical advances, and have to make their way to the reader's heart through pages increasingly inhabited by "song lyrics"). However, Ginsberg has never written a more solid single page than "Howl II." The zigzag of "Moloch" throughout the movement speeds up the supple gait of the "who" strophes of the first movement, and crowds like a rush of skyscrapers and factories into the reader's frame, which is to say that the poem is kinetically responsible for its argument. The second movement is vulgar and eloquent simultaneously, and goes for its own throat when, in the seventh strophe, Ginsberg for the first time socks himself into the poem (the "I" who saw the best minds of his generation destroyed is now to be presented as one of the flayed ones). "Cocksucker in Moloch!" is an excavation in three words of a condition that I would imagine many homosexual American artists have spent their lifetime suffering. The cry is a sublime torsion of fury, despair, absurdity and brilliant strategic placement of the two key words in balanced alignment. This cry is also the peak of the poem and as we move through the next three strophes, the shadow of repetition and the problem of closure begin to shroud the language. To my reading, the last two strophes reel in a frenzy concerning both Moloch and how to end the section. While the exclamation marks in the final strophe, in context, look like thin plummeting parachutes, the language is losing weight word by word, and the last phrase—"into the street!"—hangs in mid-air, as if a prepositional phrase is called for, and as if this one is Ginsberg's too predictable choice.

*

The litany of fantasies associated with derangement in a mad house in the third movement are not really dada-clever but very close to being cute. The language begins to puff and lose its biliousness and its pointedness with such near-banalities as "resurrect your living Jesus from the superhuman tomb." The momentum of the first two movements is so great that to a certain extent III carries, and in public performance seems finished and successful with "my cottage in the Western night." In a way, III tries to pull off a relationship-oriented redemption ("I am with you . . ." repeated eighteen times), but the relationship itself remains invisible, and in its place we are offered hugging and kissing the United States under the bedsheets. Is this the United States of the first two movements that is being hugged and kissed? Going back over the poem, the direction has been toward an unqualified attack on the sensibility-destroying aspects of North America, and it could have ended by revealing Moloch in

Rockland, the unrelieved pain and despair of "the best minds" who have come to their terminal destruction, wasting away.[3]

*

The other major piece of the 1955–56 eruption, which immediately made Ginsberg part of the meaningful poetic record of the century, is "Sunflower Sutra." This poem shows what he can do with his version of Williamsesque attention to "things," of holding onto an object, quite literally something that one is actively looking at, and drawing its intelligibility out of the naming of its attributes (which Francis Ponge so remarkably does without backdropping the "thing" against futurity).[4] The way of doing this is present in "Howl," but the operatic noise of that poem infolds the syntactical adjustments that are better displayed in "Sunflower Sutra." On one level, it is a sad, elegaic poem laid at the tomb of Blake's "The Sunflower," as well as Ginsberg's most believable use of Blake in his poetry (the most obvious use being the "Contest of Bards"—1977—in which Blake's "prophetic language" is used with bombastic and hollow effect). The nine-adjective paratactic display with which the poem ends foreshadows the landscape scanning in "The Fall of America," in which quick sightings are scooped into a line and allowed to bobble there in such a way that the line appears to have no beginning or end.

*

For anyone in my generation who was starting to write poetry in the late 1950s, Ginsberg seemed to burst onto the scene fully armed, a hero whose destiny was immediately tied up with social cause, the spokesman for a generation. The fact that he was shunned by the English departments, persecuted for obscenity and for dragging the cross of drugs and homosexuality into the livingroom, as it were, of polite American poetry made as much an impression on us as his actual writing did—perhaps more. He seemed to bridge entertainment and literature. I recall taking "Kaddish" up on the roof at a Saturday night party in Bloomington, Indiana, and, with a friend, reading it aloud to the night. "Howl" and "Kaddish" seemed to say that there was no distance—almost no difference—between literature and one's feelings about one's experience. The possibility that the poem was a bold xerox of the poet's lived life has had a lasting many-edged effect on American poetry, and while I do not believe that Ginsberg invented the notion, he has been its messiah. The positive thrust here is that not only is everything material, but all of one's negative life experience can somehow be redeemed by being expressed in art. There is a moral stance in this: that is, I think Ginsberg really believes that if everyone were to "confess out the soul," the world would become a less brutal place. I think I tend to agree with this, but since I also believe that not one person in 10,000 is interested in, or capable of, confessing out his or her soul, I feel that Ginsberg's body of work must be evaluated poetically and not as a program for social redemption.

*

In a 1959 footnote to his 1944 essay, "The Homosexual in Society,"[5] Robert Duncan writes: "Ginsberg (who believes the self is subject to society), Lamantia (who believes the self has authority from God), and McClure (who believes the self is an independent entity) have in common their paroxysms of self-loathing in which the measure of human failure and sickness is thought so true that the measure of human achievement and life is thought false." A reading through the *Collected Poems* leads me to believe that the word "society" is inadequate to express what the self in Ginsberg's writing is subject to. From Neil Cassady to Trungpa, there has been a constant expression of the need to be mastered, to have a new master, a figure who inspires and humiliates. This sense of a master is given cosmic extension in a 1973 four-line poem entitled "Who," in which Ginsberg states that his lifework has been to transmit "to Mankind" the awareness that the "entire Universe" is "manifestation of One Mind." In "Who," Ginsberg claims that his teacher is Blake, and thus "One Mind," in that context, feels less paranoid, more imaginative, than it might read in other Ginsberg contexts. But if it is "One," then there is no choice, and given the extent to which master and society are woven throughout the fabric of all of Ginsberg's poetry, "One Mind" may ultimately be taken as more of an image of imprisonment than of liberation.

*

"Kaddish" seems to be a more thoroughly worked-through poem than "Howl, " and given its presentation of Naomi Ginsberg is at moments very moving. Yet it is a less complete poem than "Howl," and perhaps Ginsberg himself would agree, as "White Shroud" is identified by the poet as a "dream epilogue to Kaddish," suggesting that the Kaddish material is still active. My own difficulties with the poem as printed in the *Collected* have to do with the litany at the end of the first movement (the lines beginning, "Magnificent, mourned no more . . ."), the "Hymmnn" and movements III and IV. The best writing is all of movement II, which in spurt after spurt of quick, edgy prose notation is alive and compelling throughout. I think that I tend to lose interest in Ginsberg's poetry when (with the major exception of "Howl") he works in repetitive patterns, especially when in the "Footnote to Howl" and the "Hymmnn" he appears to be blessing everything that comes to mind. On the other hand, movement IV, with its drilling repetition of "with your eyes" seems to carry its own weight (with the exception of its sentimental last line), perhaps because there is such an abrupt shift from the floating prose rhythms into the line-by-line pressure of the body of Naomi becoming only her eyes and the poet's anguished recollection of what they held. The massive suffering mother-weight is relentlessly sucked down into the garbage disposal of a single eye. Rereading "Kaddish," I was struck by the extent to which Ginsberg's life has been determined by his mother's madness, the extent to which his visionary rants are revisions of her hallucinations, and the extent to which his image of the poet as a combined priest and pariah is fixed by his compassion for and disgust with his mother's predicament and her helpless, ugly body. It appears from the first few pages of the second movement that Allen was the first in the family to escort Naomi to a "rest home" when he was twelve years old, and assuming this is literally true, he must have felt, as a child, in some obscure way responsible for her being there, and remaining in clinics over the years. In a passage two-thirds of the way through this second movement, where Naomi's lower body is described, Ginsberg makes his connection between her vagina and her anus, suggesting that his lifelong obsession in poetry with his own anus, as a kind of vagina, is driven by an extraordinarily unfulfilled and continuing longing for his mother; and on this level, his male "masters" are shrouded mother-strangers. The boulder of Naomi, falling into Ginsberg's pond of poesis, sent out and continues to send out steely ripples to its every shore. In a way, Ginsberg would save Mankind because he was unable to save Naomi.

*

The drug poems of the late 1950s—"Laughing Gas," "Mescaline," "Lysergic Acid" and "Aether"—don't hold up so well. When Ginsberg's

eye leaves the object, i.e., when he starts to think or fantasize, his
language tends to lose the solidity of the thing-oriented line. As an example, one might read "Change" against "Laughing Gas." The former is a
very good piece, humorous as well as politically perceptive, and it works
because Ginsberg keeps his eyes on the coins, with comments congruent
to the description. "Laughing Gas," on the other hand, is a bore, possibly
because it was indeed written when he was on laughing gas, and the drug
kept turning his mind inside out, from abstraction to abstraction, so that at
no point *is* there a point. The more Ginsberg departs from observed
particulars, the more he depends on metaphysical terms—the Great Void,
God, Nirvana, Universe, Beginningless perfection, etc. Such words float
like balloons through the drug poems, and they are accompanied by a
kind of nervous self-conscious chatter, such as the following from "Mescaline:"

> What can I do to Heaven by pounding on Typewriter
> I'm stuck change the record Gregory ah excellent he's doing
>   just that
> and I am too conscious of a million ears
> at present creepy ears, making commerce
> too many pictures in the newspapers
> faded yellowed press clippings
> I'm going away from the poem to be a drak contemplative.

Such poems are often studded with the names of Beat club members, a habit that is felt throughout Ginsberg's poetry. Kerouac,
Burroughs, Snyder and Corso, become a kind of "Ginsberg Saint Company," the right-hand men of his literary presentations of himself. For a
poetry that in other ways attempts to ground itself in compassionate
minority considerations, an odd elitism occurs, the poet surrounded by
his chosen few, not quite disciples but not simply friends either.

*

"Television Was a Baby Crawling Toward That Deathchamber," a
12-page rant from 1961, is more referential than many of Pound's Cantos, and given its "now" centeredness, it uses poetry to force the reader
out of the act of reading the poem into an experience of contemporary
global velocity. But what does the "news" of 1961 *mean* in 1985, ma-
chine-gunned across the page and intershot with Ginsberg's unceasing

insertion of himself *as self?* It is like watching something assemble and destroy itself simultaneously before your eyes, instantly disposable, which yet remains as a pile-driving record of Ginsberg's mind at an instant which was wired into the history vanishing through him. Pieces like "Television" (the strongest of which is "Friday the Thirteenth" from 1970) have the feel of having been written when Ginsberg was "high." If this is so, and if Ginsberg's experience of being high is anything like my own, the difficulty of a reader locking into the poem is partly accounted for: Not only is almost everything interesting with the same intensity and with the same momentary attention span when one is high, but nothing is genuinely interesting, nothing genuinely held to the extent that imagination can offer a shape and "seeing through" to it.

*

My other critical feelings about the poems stressing drug experience have to do with a kind of mental trickery that Ginsberg appears to engage in. As if inspired by Naomi's genuine madness, which he *is* capable of rendering superbly in the second movement of "Kaddish," he flirts with ego-dissolution while at the same time carefully protecting his own ego borders. He can't stand to be sane, but he can't go mad, either, and what becomes a parody of vision is staged with all sorts of metaphysical scenery. The implication is that madness is an intriguing alternative to "square" consciousness, an attitude which from my viewpoint does not respect madness and recognize how horrible it is to be really insane.[6] It is curious that such flirtation crops up in Ginsberg, as probably more than any other poet of his generation he had first-hand experience with insanity, had lived with it, in effect, since he was a little boy. What he may really be after makes a grotesque appearance in "Magic Psalm," where he begs to be violated by "the sex of God" and to have his voice "croaked" "with uglier than reality, a psychic tomato speaking Thy million mouths." Put less figuratively, he is asking to be brainwashed, or rinsed of consciousness by humiliation of his body and destruction of his mind. "Magic Psalm" is a roily, pungent piece of writing and it puts me in the position of admiring the language while disliking the stance.

*

The sixth section of *Collected Poems* ends with two longish pieces, "Angkor Wat," and "The Change: Kyoto-Tokyo Express." They relate to each other in somewhat the same way that "Siesta in Xbalba" relates to "Howl." In "Angkor Wat," a self-pitying preoccupation with salvation and being lost is set in and overwhelms the history and architecture of the ancient Cambodian site, backdropped by the war in Viet Nam. "The Change" is a rush of coiled countermotion, and comes as close to a total purge as I imagine Ginsberg will ever write. Ginsberg has described it in conversation with Ekbert Faas as "a final abandonment of the pursuit of heaven."[7] Given his heavy involvement with Buddhism in the 1970s, I would question that. I am also concerned about a statement Ginsberg makes earlier in his conversation with Faas, when the latter asks if Ginsberg doesn't believe that he must live with his "monsters" permanently. Allen replies: "They are just little *maya* daydreams. Even Buchenwald is a little *maya* daydream." Something that is irreal ("monsters") should not be equated with something that once was real (Buchenwald). To do so is irresponsible and, from the viewpoint of those who suffered real and terrible pain, callous.

*

Section VII (1963–1965) is a kind of lull between "The Change" and "The Fall of America" (Section VIII, by far the longest section, some 200 pages, in the *Collected*). VII is set for the most part in New York City, and has a kind of dailiness to it. The soft loneliness of the writing, with many restatements of early ventured-upon themes, culminates in "Who Be Kind To," a poem I once cried over. I also recall bursting into tears upon hearing the Beatles sing "Hey Jude" at about the same time, and am struck by just how emotionally charged that period was, as if the anguish of Viet Nam played with by drugs and millennial daydreams produced an inner short-circuiting that could bang you out of one mood into its opposite just like that. "Who Be Kind To" is still a touching pleasure to read, and captures the moist sunlit lilt of that period, the giddiness of our hope, backed by skin-crawling LSD experiences, like no other poem of its time.

*

It is fascinating to recall "Howl" while reading through "The Fall of America" section, especially the first 100 pages or so, which map an interstitial reality, the edges of rural and urban landscapes as their character is revealed to Ginsberg via media, principally news information on the

Viet Nam War. The world of "Howl"—"who got busted in their public beards returning through Laredo with a belt of marijuana for New York"—has become "under the bluffs of Oroville, blue cloud September skies, entering U.S. border, red red apples bend their tree boughs propt with sticks." "Howl," in retrospect, appears more inventive, but less serious. The lines in much of "The Fall" are patterned on Whitman's long, cadenced, noun-laden line; one only has to reread Section 15 of "Song of Myself" to see the inspiration, and too, to see Ginsberg's refashioning of the stately Whitman line. Ginsberg's "first thought, best thought" technique speeds up his master's horse-drawn cadences, and his best work with the line occurs in these 100 pages. They are an information-alert, trenchant layout of words which seems to have little grippers holding it, part by part, in place. There is a sense of balanced momentum, quite artful, brisk, often tingling with perceptions. It proves that when Ginsberg is not flopping about in the lather of himself, he can write elegant, sculptured lines, and I think it will be amazing for other readers in the future to set the best of his work against poets who have been judged to be of more *literary* importance. As a brief example, I offer the following typical lines from Galway Kinnell's "The Avenue Bearing the Initial of Christ into the New World," a poem that has been treated with much critical respect and which, like certain passages in "The Fall," is directly off the urban kinetics of New York City:

> That night a wildcat cab whined crosstown on 7th.
> You knew even the traffic lights were made by God,
> The red splashes growing dimmer the farther away
> You looked, and away up 14th, a few green stars;
> And without sequence, and nearly all at once,
> The red lights blinked into green,
> And just before there was one complete Avenue of green,
> The little green stars in the distance blinked.[8]

Ginsberg:

> Down 5th Avenue, brr—the irregular spine
>   of streetlights—
>   traffic lamps all turned red at once—
>   insect lamps blink in dim artery
>   replicated down stone vales to Union Square—

In silence wait to see your home
Cemented asphalt, wire roof-banked,
          canyoned, hived & churched with mortar,
                mortised with art gas—
                passing Ginsberg Machine Co.

In comparison to the Ginsberg, the Kinnell seems flat, and rhythmically self-effacing. It moves into a play with the lights that phases out the jagged weight and particularity of Manhattan. In Ginsberg's lines, each of which is based on a shifting perception, there is a kind of looking and assimilating, and a range of vocabulary that is idiomatic *and* learned. My point in such a juxtaposition is not mainly to criticize the much-lauded Kinnell, but to suggest how Ginsberg's scanning of America, more often than not treated as "notebook writing" by critics, is quite poised, deft and rhetorically ample.

*

In his conversation with Faas, Ginsberg suggests that "first thought, best thought" poetics can "bring the war up into front page, front-brain, picture consciousness," in contrast to "relegating it to third and fourth page."[9] There is an intuitive trust of self in such a motto that would seem to argue with a Ginsberg self dependent on society, master and immortality—but I fear the motto is rickety. First thought, best thought—when? When you are clear, rested, body-alert? Drunk at four AM? On LSD—and at what state of LSD? A lot of the worst, most stupid things we do are "'first thought" oriented, impulsive decisions that pop into our minds and if not examined lead to mindless behavior. And revision? Are Ginsberg's major poems all "first thought, best thought?" I doubt it, and await the facsimile edition of *Howl,* which I hear is to be published in 1986.[10] I believe only in retrospect can one comb out opinions, cliches, redundancies, etc., from *thoughts.* Ginsberg's motto-inspired writing is most convincing in "The Fall of America" when his war research, staying with the news, and knowledge of rural and urban landscapes all seem primed for calligraphic-like jottings (I am thinking of ink and rice-paper calligraphy during which the artist cannot pause for a second in a stroke without blotting or otherwise ruining the line). The writing in "The Fall" implies that the war ricochets off, or is enleaded in, so-called "objective" perceptions—that someone listening to the radio and looking out the window of a car is twisted by the interference not merely of land and war news, but the extent to which especially the urban landscape is plastically pregnant with the wretchedness of what we are doing to the Viet Namese and our own poor. The poems are to contain this schizophrenia, and it would have been stunning to have heard them broadcast as part of the daily news in the late 1960s, for they are an essential part of the news of that era, but news offered with a precise subjectivity that puts the experience of the speaker into it.

*

"Wales Visitation" and its little friend, "Bixby Canyon," are wonderful poems. Has any other American really looked down at the ground and written:

> Skeleton snaketubes & back
> nostrils' seaweed-tail dry-wrinkled
> brown seabulb & rednailed
> cactus blossom-petal tongues—
> Brownpickle saltwater tomato ball
> rubber tail Spaghettied
>   with leafmeat,
> Mucus-softness crown'd Laurel thong-hat
> Father Whale gunk transparent
>   yellowleaf egg-sac sandy
> lotos-petal cast back to cold
>   watersurge.

The thickness of the language here is not really thickness, but a clocklike tuning and turning of the edge of perception as it verges into metaphor, but closing off metaphor while the perception is in process and setting the next "thing" or "noticing" in place. Ginsberg's writing here, and in the Wordsworthian, expansive, but equally beautiful "Wales Visitation," seems to nestle, connected/ disconnected thing to disconnected/connected thing, peas in a pod, piglets at udder.

*

As one plows through Section VIII, the energy of the American "fall" disperses in several directions, mainly two: Ginsberg's grieved turning away from man to the natural landscape, and a set of poems that either address or obliquely evoke the death of Neil Cassady. The Cassady poems are disappointing—the "Elegy for Neil Cassady" is distracted, dispersed, and other mentionings of Cassady are more like memory blips than addresses to his body and his spirit. But Ginsberg had previously written his best "sex" poem about Cassady, and so the failure of the Elegy is in a way understandable. The oddly mistitled "Many Loves" (off the Williams play) is again unique, and presents Cassady's body in a Grant Woods "American Gothic" way. It is a beautiful evocation of the young unsure homosexual Ginsberg's need and almost ineffable gratitude at being *thoroughly* accepted, if only for a moment, by a heterosexual hero. If Naomi Ginsberg gave Allen poetry, in her world-inhabited spectre more grand than a Blakean "Sunflower" voice, Cassady seems to have told him, in gesture, that he was not merely a little creep. Cassady confirmed Ginsberg, and that confirmation faded as Ginsberg matured and went into the world of his own sexual and political concerns. "Many Loves" was withheld from publication until the *Collected*. Before that, "Please Master" was the most striking of the obsessed mouth-asshole -cunt vortices, and a salutary piece of difficulty to have nailed to the hetero bulletin board of North American poetry. Set next to "Many Loves" it reads like a drill pattern. In afterthought, it strikes me that there may be something indeed "military" in being fucked like the mastered one is fucked in this poem, and thus that the "please master" begging refrains are germane. But I still think that "Many Loves" is a larger, more humanly dimensional poem.

*

Section VIII of the *Collected* ends with the "mantric lamentation," "September on Jessore Road," the most effective of the thirty-some rhymed poems in the book. A dozen of these are accompanied by complete or partial musical scores, and they tend to fall either near the beginning of the book or are scattered throughout the final two sections which represent the past decade of Ginsberg's work. The early ones appear to have been written as imitations of Blake's *Songs of Innocence and Experience,* and to have been regarded simply as rhymed verse. Beginning with "September on Jessore Road," the rhymed verse, with irregular internal rhythms, starts to be presented not merely as "songs" in the Blakean sense, but as songs to be sung and accompanied, on stage, by instruments.

I imagine that many readers of the *Collected Poems* will pass through the early rhymed verse as Juvenalia, as I did at first, and be a bit surprised to discover the more or less constant attention to "songs" from 1970 to 1980. However, a bit of research on Ginsberg's sense of his poetics yields the following: He was first inspired in 1947, by hearing Blake's voice "pronounce 'The Sunflower' and 'The Sick Rose,'" which offered him "an illumination of eternal Consciousness." Ginsberg explains: "Since a physiologic ecstatic experience had been catalysed in my body by the physical arrangement of words in so small a poem as *Ah! Sun Flower,* I determined long ago to think of poetry as a kind of machine that had a specific effect when planted inside a human body, an arrangement of picture mental associations that vibrated on the mind bank network; and an arrangement of related sounds & physical mouth movements that altered the habit function of the neural network."[11]

Of the early rhymed pieces, only "The Shrouded Stranger" has any gristle or strangeness to its language. Ginsberg seems in this poem to have made use of the dada ditty "Pull My Daisy," done with Kerouac a bit earlier, which knocked the sentimentality out of a rhymed verse context. He then appears to have abandoned verse and song until the Blake lyrics, and did not start writing his own performance songs until 1971.

Two seem to be of genuine interest: the "Jessore Road" drone and a delightful tub-thumping variation on the well-known Bashō frog-leap haiku. The "Jessore Road" swarms over the reader/hearer with its relentless presentation of starving Hindu refugees. But at times it is so forced as to simply become odd:

> Run home to tents   where elders wait
> Messenger children   with bread from the state
> No bread more today! & no place to squat
> Painful baby, sick shit he has got.

These poems aside, the rest of the performance songs represent the nadir of Ginsberg's poetic output. Most are a combination of sex advertisements in toneless doggerel, soliciting pity for the author's impotence. And they are no better when Ginsberg sings them.

To me, they represent Ginsberg's decision to present his eagerness for teenage boy bodies, tied into his own sexual impotence, as a form of nervy entertainment—instead of facing whatever the core of this situation

is with the same fervor and courage with which he faced other consterna-
tions and turned them into serious, accomplished poetry.

*

Sadly, the songs in the last two sections are the only new things in
the *Collected*. Other than "Old Pond," the only piece of the last ten years'
output that I read with genuine interest was "Mugging." Written in 1974,
it in no sense represents a new drift of attention and energy, but is a fully
written-through piece, which presents with old-fashioned newsreel verisimilitude a slice of Ginsberg's life. Buddhism and the apprenticeship to
Trungpa is there and not there; several poems in the early 1970s are
freighted with Buddhist terminology, but the relationship with the new
master is not really dealt with in the *Collected*. The pervasive tone of the
1970s is carried by the following lines from "Ego Confessions:"

—All empty all for show, all for the sake of Poesy
to set surpassing example of sanity as measure for late genera-
    tions
Exemplify Muse Power to the young avert future suicide
accepting his own lie & the gaps between lies with equal good
    humor
Solitary in worlds full of insects & singing birds all solitary
—who had no subject but himself in many disguises
some outside his own body including empty air-filled space forest
    & cities—

Lines 4 and 6 of what I quote seem so purely Whitmanic that it is
difficult to make anything out of them regarding Ginsberg. The major
piece in the last part of the *Collected* is "Plutonian Ode," which has a
prophetic soar to the language, but the argument is all overcompensation,
with Ginsberg presenting himself as overwhelming the power of Plutonium (in an even more unbelievable way than he had stopped the war in
the "Vortex Sutra"). In line 45, we are told that Plutonium is "doomed"
from having its destiny "spelled." Although a small part of me is touched
by the return of Ginsberg's rippling prophetic language, the argument
itself appears to be psychotic, and I am left with the experience of Allen
Ginsberg as a raving gnat at the same time that the subject of his raving is
doing its thing out in the desert or near our homes.

I think it would be inappropriate to spend much more time here conjecturing about the meaning of the songs, and the unengaging repetition of earlier themes that nearly fill these later years. It may have something to do with Ginsberg having vowed in "The Change" to once and for all have done with his pursuit of heaven and immortality, with its concomitant commitment to save everyone. Perhaps such a manic vision is the true muse of the poetry from 1955 to the late 1960s, a period in which Ginsberg wrote, at times, as powerfully as any poet in the language—with the implication that by giving up an impossible vision he set psychological currents in motion that undermined his writing. There is another possibility too: that his encounter with Buddhism and Trungpa was so overwhelming that it either thwarted much of the poetry, or, as I would prefer to believe, has yet to be plumbed. Ginsberg has now retired from Naropa; perhaps in the next decade, in solitude, he will astound everyone with powerful, cumulative poetry. The poem "White Shroud," which he read at UCLA this past spring, suggests that he has not lost touch with the powers that have moved his most important writing.

*

In conclusion, I would like to suggest a mass-market paperback "Selected Poems" which would represent Allen Ginsberg at his best, a book which might reach the young, non-academic reader, who probably would not even know about the *Collected Poems*.

The Shrouded Stranger [the 1949–1951 version]
The Green Automobile
Siesta in Xbalba
Howl
Sunflower Sutra
Sather Gate Illumination
Many Loves
To Lindsay
To Aunt Rose
American Change
Kaddish
Magic Psalm
Journal Night Thoughts
The Change

Who Be Kind To
"Thru the Vortex West Coast to East" (from Beginning of a
   Poem of these States, through The Old Village Before I Die)
Iron Horse (part II)
Wales Visitation
Please Master
Bixby Canyon
Friday the Thirteenth
Ecologue
September on Jessore Road
Mugging
Old Pond

[September, 1985]

NOTES

1. One of the first intelligent critical responses to *Howl* was by Michael Rumaker in *Black Mountain Review* #7, 1957. It is still worth reading. In regard to the "angelheaded hipsters," Rumaker writes: "But those phrases like 'angelheaded hipsters' when 'hipsters' alone would suffice. Hipsters are not 'angelheaded,' are anything but. The adjective sentimentalizes, implies a mushed 'goodness,' 'innocence,' that no hipster, worthy of the name, would tolerate." Rumaker's main contention is that the poem's focus—anger—is diluted by "sentimentality, bathos, Buddha and hollow talk of eternity."

2. I can say "suit" and "tie" because all of Ginsberg's "best minds" are clearly male: "girls" only make an appearance as the seduced victims of Neil with his Rod of Steel, or as "the snatches of a million girls trembling in the sunset," whatever *that* is.

3. Had the third movement advanced *and* contained the first two movements, I doubt if Ginsberg would have written "Footnote to Howl." Or perhaps he would have found it unnecessary to attach the "Footnote" to the poem. While I disagree with Rumaker that "Howl" would have been stronger had it been sheared of adjectives, I do agree with his complaints about the "Footnote." He writes: "The last section [Footnote] is chaos, the logical conclusion to the build-up. The poem scatters itself, finally, on its own pitiful frenzy. A way has not been found. The poet has not broken through, the poem remains unsaid. Everything is 'holy.' Which is not so. This confusion, this gibberish, is Satan."

4. Regarding "Sunflower Sutra," Ginsberg himself commented (in 1959, in his excellent liner notes to the Fantasy #7006 recording of *Howl and other poems*): "What about poem with rhythmic build-up power equal to 'Howl' without use of repeated

base to sustain it? 'The Sunflower Sutra' (composition time 20 minutes, me at desk scribbling, Kerouac at cottage door waiting for me to finish so we could go off somewhere party) did that, it surprised me, one long Who."

5. Duncan's essay, with the 1959 footnotes, is printed in *Jimmy & Lucy's House of "K,"* #3, January 1985.

6. Ginsberg undoubtedly intends his fascination with madness to be associated with the "madness" of Blake, as well as with the psychotic exuberance of his mother, and he is certainly not the only writer of this period to, in effect, confuse the sanity of genius with alienation, neurosis and paranoia. When N.O. Brown, in *Love's Body*, writes that the boundary between sanity and insanity is a false one, he opens a similar Pandora's Box. The ambivalence regarding madness is powerfully and believably expressed by Antonin Artaud, who indeed *was* mad, in the clinical sense of the word, but who succeeded in speaking through his madness and imaginatively giving it a focus in the last few years of his life.

7. *Toward A New American Poetics: Essays & Interviews,* ed. by Ekbert Faas, Black Sparrow Press, Santa Barbara, 1978, p. 279.

8. *Galway Kinnell / Selected Poems,* New York, 1982, p. 41.

9. *Toward a New American Poetics: Essays & Interviews,* p. 279.

10. (24 August 1987) Since the writing of this essay, the annotated "more than facsimile" version of *Howl* has been published (ed. by Barry Miles, Harper & Row, 1986) and the transcripts and variant versions for the poem suggest that while the central visions of all four sections appear to have been an eruption, and at least sketched out in first drafts, the poem as a whole is in no sense a spontaneous performance, and gained considerably from rewriting and tinkering. Part I has five drafts; part II, eighteen drafts; part III, five drafts; the Footnote (or part IV), seven drafts. I would still argue that the best writing is in part II and it is therefore interesting that this part has by far the most revisions and is the section of the poem least indebted to Ginsberg's "first thought/best thought" poetics, with, however, the following qualification: If we were to change Ginsberg's prescription to "first thought/best thought, followed by a lot of hard work," it might then do two things that do seem to be consistent with Ginsberg's poetry—emphasize the need for a courageous seizing of a perception and moving it to the page without rational/critical scrutiny of its literary acceptability, and acknowledge that the unfolding of "thought on wing" can often be a complex process, in which the nucleus must be scrutinized again and again in order to wrest from it the fullest amplification possible. Inspiration can take place at any point in the process of composition (the traditional Western prejudice is that it takes place in spontaneous inception and gradually peters out as critical/alter ego concerns take over); I have found that inspiration can act as a depth-charge, exploding as an intuitive sensing of significance which only gradually wells up to surface, as it were. Revision may be seen as a way of inducting and admitting the "shock waves."

11. See liner notes to *Allen Ginsberg/William Blake: Songs of Innocence and Experience by William Blake, tuned by Allen Ginsberg* (MGM FTS-3083, 1969).

THE GROTESQUE
ARCHETYPE

Proteus, Poetic Experiment and Apprenticeship

I WAS ASKED TO CONCERN MYSELF in a talk with the experimental in poetry. After I thought, it has to do with transformation—psychic transformation—I fell asleep and awoke at four AM. When I wondered why I had awakened so early, the word "Proteus" appeared in my mind, Proteus the shape-changer, whom I dimly recalled from the fourth book of the *Odyssey*. Menelaus, one of Odysseus' comrades from the siege of Troy, was stuck on an island, and the nymph daughter of Proteus advised him to capture her father, who alone could tell him how to break the calm and secure a breeze. Menelaus and some of his men disguised themselves in sealskins and lay waiting on the shore until midday when Proteus and his seal-flock joined them. Proteus went to sleep among the seals, whereupon Menelaus and his men seized him, and though he turned into a lion, a serpent, a panther, a boar, running water and finally a leafy tree, they held him fast and forced him to prophesy.

As the episode ran through my mind, I realized that my own first desire to change shape, in which I engaged a shape-changer, took place in Kyoto, 1964, when I finished an eight-page poem I had worked on for several months. In the first five pages I had explored my being stranded in the desire to move my life into an articulation that would be my own, and in doing this, I built up a charge that was bursting to realize something I had not known before I began the poem. The last third of the poem is called "The Duende" and opens with my leaving the Ibuki home where

---

This essay was originally written as a paper, at the request of M. L. Rosenthal, and read at New York University in the autumn of 1979; it was published in a longer version in the 1980 edition of the *Spring* annual.

125

my first wife and I lived, walking past the Tsuruginomiya shinto shrine, across the Kamogawa River and on into the entertainment area of Kyoto, which was always nearly unpopulated in the afternoon, where there was a large pleasant coffee shop called Yorunomado ("Night Window"), with classical music and a carp pond. Up to this point, I had been reproducing in the poem a walk I had made for a year and a half, almost daily, to Yorunomado where I would spend four or five hours working on my first drafts of César Vallejo translations. My inability to make any real headway with translating Vallejo had become involved with my disconcerting awareness that in trying to be a poet I had, so far, merely reactivated a lot of my childhood and adolescent stress which, on one hand, I did not feel was "poetic," but on the other, was making such a demand on me that I figured I had to learn to confront it in poetry.

In daily life, my hours sitting in Yorunomado were made up mainly of breaking my head, mentally, against Vallejo's text—not only was his highly experimental Spanish beyond my reading ability, but what he was saying drew me in at the same time that it baffled and repulsed me. As I say, the situation had gone on for some time (at one point my first draft of about seventy poems mysteriously disappeared and I had to start over[1]). In "The Duende, which became the last section of "The Book of Yorunomado," I dramatized the following moment: One day upon opening Vallejo's Poemas humanos, "spine" doubled into book spine and human spine, and there I was, crouched on Vallejo's spine. I followed what seemed to be the direction my own frustrated energies took in this form, and bit into his spine. We became engaged in a terrific struggle which led me, as a consequence, to perform a particular act, resulting in the Caesarean birth of a figure called "Yorunomado." At the time, I had lost the struggle with my Proteus—had not forced him to prophesy—but had succeeded in turning my place of working into a figure of my imagination. Yorunomado became my guide in a ten-year poem project that resulted in the book called Coils[2] which "The Book of Yorunomado" (retitled "Webs of Entry") opens.

Beyond Vallejo resisting my attempt to change him, I had to learn that I was to be changed by him, and be willing to be Protean myself. I had to learn to show no fear of transformation, as did Menelaus.

Now, according to Robert Graves,[3] the Menelaus/Proteus episode is a degenerative version of another myth in which Peleus, a mortal hero who had been chosen to be the husband of the Seal-goddess Thetis, lies in wait for her by the grotto where she takes her midday sleep, knowing that she will resent and resist the marriage because she is an immortal. Once she falls asleep, he seizes hold of her, a struggle ensues, she changes successively into fire, water, a lion and a serpent, but Peleus clings to her resolutely and in the end she yields and they lie locked in passionate embrace.

For Graves, the Seal-goddess Thetis has been masculinized into Proteus, and the goal of oracular answer is considerably less than the goal of intercourse. I feel that the struggle leading to prophesy and the struggle (or rape attempt) leading to intercourse are untangled skeins of a mythologem that is probably even denser, more multi-leveled, especially in our time, when the poet's personal life is splintered through it. Regarding my own circumstances in 1964, the sexual pressure and anxiety that had built up in my marriage undoubtedly contributed to the ferocity with which I "attacked" Vallejo in the poem, and led to the feeling—nothing more— that Thetis was present within the folds of Protean Vallejo but at a depth which at that time I was unable to plumb.

As for Blake's appearance in "The Duende" section: I simply had to acknowledge that the idea of inventing a name for a God ("Yoruno-mado")—in contrast to using a classically defined one—came from his pantheon of Orc, Enitharmon, Los, etc., in his prophetic books. I was reading Blake in the early 1960s and having similar difficulties with him, within one language, as I was having with Vallejo. One aspect of the experimental in Blake was the insight to give names to his Gods or archetypes that were coherent only within the context of his poetry—they have no referential surface to them, while they turn out to have plenty of referential depth.

Let me now set forth my theory of the experimental: The person seeking to be tried by poetry, and thus confirmed or disproved, must invent his own trial figure. For such a figure to be meaningful, it must consist of material from the young poet's lived life, as well as unknown material or a powerful endeavor to reach beyond the known, by engaging that material with an imaginative or created life. The tension between the known and the unknown is imperative. One cannot merely take on Proteus directly, for to do so would be to describe or interpret a struggle that had already taken place in the Greek mind. Yet, if the trial figure is not embedded with archetypal intelligence, the struggle would lack weight. Without such tension, the experimental becomes the perennial nemesis of the avant-garde, being different for the sake of being different, fluff. According to my experience, the truly experimental poet has at core a trial with a figure who is archetypal *and* invented at the same time, and it is this torsion which can give an outer circumference of literary significance to his poetry.

I had read the *Odyssey* several times as a student in the late 1950s, but I do not recall remembering Menelaus and Proteus while I was in Kyoto, so bringing these figures to bear on my poetry is a discovery after the act. However, my experience led me to call the Proteus/Thetis figure the god of the experimental.

My struggle with Vallejo, while it might be said to glisten of Proteus, has different contours: the struggle results in the birth of a third figure, Yorunomado, and it is he, near the end of *Coils,* envisaged as a Sepik Delta New Guinea "head-hunter," who at last prophesies. This occurs in the thick of the title poem when I am trying to contain my mother's death (as a containing wall contains the Indianapolis 500-mile racecars), so that its fluids will not spill out into the relationship with my wife.[4]

I would now like to follow out my relationship to Vallejo as it concerns the experimental. This relationship has spanned more than twenty years; in the mid-seventies I decided that I had apprenticed myself to Vallejo, and that besides achieving accurate translations of his 110 posthumously published poems, my apprenticeship had had another goal: to internalize the transformational process so that it was a gear in my work, not a spar that I was desperately reaching for, as in 1964. For it seems that *until one has worked one's way fully through another's imagination, the extent to which one can experiment is limited.*

Near the end of the poem "Coils," there is still a problem of appearances, of my uncertainty as to who my mother really is, of who I am really desiring, and this is, in Protean imagery, just more shape-changing of the contacted god. This is the way the world is, and it is important to acknowledge it and live within its flashing scales rather than demand it be one thing, and that any deviation from this one thing is a threat to be met by rejection or violence. But for the artist, there is eventually a huge difference between Proteus being inside him or outside him, and the struggle for an ongoing experimentalism may consist in constantly attempting to ingest new figures, and by "new figures" I do not mean merely more gods, but areas of experience outside of literature itself.

As for the pure language of translation, in my case as a translator of Vallejo, Artaud and Césaire, I have felt that it was experimental only in a rather conservative way; I have tried hard, often working with a co-translator, to do versions that are accurate *and* exciting to read. Which is to say that on a strictly linguistic basis, I am not interested in that "improvisational" area between a flexible literal translation and a poem of one's own. That area has in most cases seemed to me to be a limbo, and its product neither a good translation nor a good original poem (although recently rereading Charles Olson's *The Distances,* I was impressed by the way he had made use of the two versions of Rimbaud's "O saisons, ô châteaux" in his "Variations Done for Gerald Van De Wiele," where about halfway through each of the three "variations," Rimbaud's words flare in deftly translated fragmentary phrases, and throw a heightened coloration into what is essentially Olson's poem).

By 1973, having continued to work on Vallejo for more than eleven years, I was excited by the prospect of visiting his tomb in Paris. When I did so, I faced what must be a traditional consternation of sitting on a revered figure's slab and trying to find words in that atmosphere of finality that seem worth sharing with others. As I look at my "At the Tomb of Vallejo" today,[5] it strikes me as more a prayer for transformation than the celebration of transformation that I originally intended it to be. I don't think such makes the poem better or worse, but in the line of thought that I am following, it suggests that I had extricated myself from a need to challenge Vallejo but had not yet been able to summon up the imaginative power to contain him within a poetry that was primarily my own. It was as if I had come out of his forest to a clearing which contained his tomb, bowed and then plunged on into more forest, but with the end now in sight—both of our "ends," as well as the culmination of my apprenticeship.

I mentioned before that new figures for a poet may mean areas of experience outside of literature. When I was a teenager growing up in Indianapolis in the late 1940s and early 1950s, I began listening to jazz as a more promising alternative to neighborhood-teacher piano lessons, in particular bebop, and had the immense good fortune to hear some Bud Powell Trio LPs. The thought that one can vary the tune, *improvise* on the repeated chord structure, made a profound impression mainly because it suggested that I did not have to remain a carbon copy of my family background. I began to experiment timidly with life, and I am certain that the sensations Powell made me feel were the beginning of an improvisational impulse that I have been elaborating since starting to write poetry in 1958.

During the early 1970s, with co-translator José Rubia Barcia, I completed the twelfth through eighteenth drafts of the translations that culminated in *César Vallejo: the Complete Posthumous Poetry,* and began to dream of a big poem that would explore and celebrate apprenticeship. "The Name Encanyoned River" was the result.[6] Looking at that title now, I understand that Proteus' element, water, had given way to the ghost of itself, that the river had become *encanyoned* with Vallejo's name, and that in picking up sensations I associate with rivers—slow, massive push, winding, or meandering, with tributaries or "branch" meanders—I had an open-ended method to work with. The challenge was not to get lost in a single tributary nor to let apprenticeship become a subject locked into itself, but constantly to let the tributaries run out, and then either drop them or run them back into the poem's abiding focus.

Once the translation and "The Name Encanyoned River" were completed, Vallejo seems to have dropped out of at least my conscious writing life. But I had an experience while writing a poem last fall that told me he is still present—though in a very altered form. This poem was the first time I had tried to take Upper Paleolithic cave imagery on directly, and I was moved that Vallejo's ghost made an acute, if brief, appearance at that time.

While reading James Hillman's *The Dream and the Underworld* in the summer of 1978, it began to dawn on me that anthropologists and archeologists had done the same thing with the painted caves that modern man has, according to Hillman, done with his dreams: interpreted them and seen them as a reflection of daylight and temporal activity, thus denying them an autonomous realm, an archetypal place that corresponds with a distinct mythic geography, in short, an underworld that is not merely reflective of an empirical, sensuous world. The same thing has been done to the caves: Hunters, we are told, painted and scratched animals out of an attempt to increase fertility as well as to insure success in the hunt. But when I crawled for four hours in Le Portel and Les Trois Frères, from time to time glimpsing outlines of isolated animals wounded with no hunter figures present, or crouched before a few of the thousands of mysterious signs, or when I stood before what can only be called massive friezes of hundreds of entangled animal outlines occasionally scratched on one great bison outline as if the earth were a thick pelt of animals, and saw at points within this animal labyrinth little half-human animals beginning to appear—more often than not mere dancing bits in the mammal roil across the rock contour—I began to feel that "sympathetic magic" interpretations of the Upper Paleolithic were terribly wrong, that I was witnessing, in the caves (which, thank God, cannot be "picked like flowers" and put behind museum glass) the result of the crisis of Paleolithic people separating the animal out of their thus-to-be human heads; and that such a result was the creation of the underworld, at the beginning of psyche, when Hades was still an animal.

I can best illustrate the appearance of Vallejo's ghost by quoting a passage from his hymn to the Indian earth of Peru, "Telluric and magnetic," following it with the first section of my own poem, "Hades in Manganese."[7] Vallejo's poem draws, and is drawn by, a kind of earth adherence, and my own piece attempts to move from my house in Los Angeles down into the realm of the Upper Paleolithic caves. I felt my poem "cross" Vallejo's in the line, "O dead living depths!," and the juncture in Vallejo seemed to be "Oh human fields!" My sense is that the Vallejo line "enghosted" itself in my own line and made the descent possible. What follows is roughly the first half of "Telluric and magnetic."[8]

Sincere and most Peruvian mechanics
those of the reddish hill!
Theoretical and practical soil!
Intelligent furrows; example: the monolith and its court!
Potato fields, barley fields, lucerne fields, a wonderful thing!
Cultivations which integrate an astonishing hierarchy of tools
and which integrate with wind the lowings,
the waters with their unvoiced antiquity!

Quaternary maizes, with opposite birthdays,
I hear through my feet how they move away,
I smell them return when the earth
clashes with the sky's technique!
Abruptly molecule! Terse atom!

Oh human fields!
Solar and nutritious absence of the sea,

and oceanic feeling about everything!
Oh climates found inside gold, ready!
Oh intellectual field of a cordillera,
with religion, with fields, with baby ducks!
Pachyderms in prose while passing
and in poetry while halting!
Rodents who peer with judicial feeling all around!
Oh my life's patriotic asses!
Vicuna, national and graceful descendant of my ape!
Oh light which is hardly a mirror away from shadow,
which is life with period and, with line, dust
and that is why I revere it, climbing through the idea to my
     skeleton!

Here is the opening section of "Hades in Manganese":

Today I'd like to climb the difference
between what I think I've written and
what I *have* written, to clime being,
to conceive it as a weather
generate and degenerate,
a snake turning in digestion with the low.

But what you hear
are the seams I speak, animal,
the white of our noise
meringues into peaks
neither of us mount—or if we do,
as taxidermists, filling what is over
because we love to see as if alive.

Seam through which I might enter,
wounded animal, stairwayed
intestine in the hide of dream,
Hades, am I
yule, in nightmare
you weigh my heart,
you knock in the pasture at noon,
I still panic
awaking at 3 AM

as if a burglar were in the hall,
one who would desire me, on whose claw
I might slip a ring, for in the soft
cave folds of dream
in conversation you woo, I weigh,
I insert something cold in you,
you meditate me up, I carry
what is left of you, coils
of garden hose, aslant, in my gut . . .

Hades, in manganese, you rocked, an animal,
the form in which I was beginning to
perish, wading in eidola
while I separated you out!
To cross one back line with
another, hybrid, to take from the graft
the loss, the soul now wandering
in time, thus grieving for
what it must invent, an out of time,
an archetype, a non-existing
anthrobeast, rooted and seasonally
loosing its claws in the air!

O dead living depths!
One face cooing to another plungers
that went off, torpedos, in dream,
to spin through a pasture at noon,
sphincter-milled, sheep-impacted,
the lower body attached
to separation, pulling the seam of it along
cold cave stone, the head as
a pollen-loaded feeler tunneling
to ooze a string of eggs
where the rock, strengthening its yes,
returned the crawler to vivid green
sunlight that *was* profundity
now invested with linkage,
the grass invested with linkage,
the whole sky a tainted link,

man a maggot on stilts
desiring to leave elevation at the mouth
to seam unyield to his face.
Tethered, Hades phoned, om
phallos, the metro the zipper
of dread at every branch-off,
the pasture at noon conducted
by the bearmarm below, batoning
sun down word rust scrapper by scraper out.

NOTES

1. I was close to completing a first draft of the translation in March, 1963, when I had the following experience: After working all afternoon in Yorunomado, I cycled over to a pottery manufacturer where I taught English as a foreign language once a week. Whenever I had things to carry on the cycle, I would strap them with a stretch-cord to the platform in back of the seat. That evening, as usual, I did so, and re-strapped the poem-filled notebook, my dictionary and a copy of *Poemas humanos,* when I left the company. It was now dark and the alley poorly lit. I had gone about a hundred yards when I heard a voice, in Japanese, cry out "Hey, you dropped something!" I swerved around—the platform was empty—even the stretch-cord gone. I stopped and retraced my direction on foot. Nothing. I looked for the person who had called out. No one there. While I was walking around in the dark, a large skinny dog began to follow me closely—I was reminded of the Mexican "pariah" dogs and that gave an eerie identity to this dog. Was it Peruvian? Was it—Vallejo? I went back the next morning when it was light, and, of course, there was not a trace of the things I had lost.

2. Versions of this poem have appeared in *Poetry* (Chicago, 1965); *Indiana,* 1969; *Coils,* 1973 and *The Name Encanyoned River,* 1986. It took roughly the same amount of time to get the poem "right" as it took me to complete my apprenticeship to Vallejo.

3. See Chapter 169 of Robert Graves's *The Greek Myths* (New York, 1959).

4. "Coils," in *Coils* (Los Angeles, 1973), pp. 145–146.

5. *The Gull Wall* (Santa Barbara, 1975), pp. 82–83.

6. *The Name Encanyoned River* (Santa Barbara, 1986), pp. 116–120. In the 1968 Moncloa edition of Vallejo's *Obra Poetica Completa,* many hand-corrected type-scripts are reproduced. In a poem entitled "Piensan los Viejos Asnos," Vallejo had crossed out the following line: "le llamaré del margen de su nombre de río encajonado!," which literally would be translated as: "I will call him at the margin of

his name of a steeply-inclined river (or a narrowed river)." I saw "encanyoned" in "encajonado" and reorganized the latter part of Vallejo's phrase to "the name en-canyoned river."

7. *The Name Encanyoned River*, pp. 127–132.

8. *César Vallejo: The Complete Posthumous Poetry* (Los Angeles, 1978), pp. 86–89.

Placements I

For Jerome Rothenberg

Anguish, a door, Le Portel, body bent over jagged rock, in ooze, crawling in dark to trace the button of itself—or to unbutton the obscure cage in which a person and an animal are copulas—or are they delynxing each other? Or are they already subject and predicate in the amniotic cave air watching each other across the word barrier, the flesh?

*

At arm's length the image, my focus the extent of my reach. Where I end the other begins. Is not all art that genuinely moves us done in the "dark" against a "wall"? Olson's whisper (a prayer), "boundary, disappear."

*

I squat in my mother's arch, eating, the black beckons so I go, crawling to I know not where. The terror of crawling within my own shoulder space is exceeded by the instinct that I might fully crawl out of the frame my mother dimensioned me with—but to continue is finally to return, doubled back on my umbilical possibility. It is on the way back that I scratch what might be thought of as the fact that since I ceased being an animal, I have not known what to do with myself.

*

The beginning of the construction of the underworld takes place in Upper Paleolithic caves. To identify this "place under construction," I use the

"Placements I" in a slightly different form appeared in *Hades In Manganese* (Black Sparrow Press, Santa Barbara, 1981); it was reprinted in its present form in *The Name Encanyoned River: Selected Poems 1960–1985* (Black Sparrow Press).

136

later Greek word "Hades," and it is there that the first evidence of psyche that we can relate to occurs. To be in the cave is to be inside an animal—a womb—but to draw there is to seek another kind of birth: an adjustment to the crisis of the animal separating out of the human—or, the Fall. To be inside, to be hidden, to be in Hades—where the human hides in the animal.

*

Since the hidden is bottomless, totality is more invisible than visible. Insistence on a totality in which life is totally visible is the anti-dream. Hades deprived of his depths. Satan attempting to establish a king-dom—or death camp—solely on earth.

*

It took thousands and thousands of years, but we did create the abyss out of a seemingly infinite elastic crisis: therio-expulsion—and we have lived in a state of "animal withdrawal" ever since. The pictures in the abyss that flicker our sleep and waking are the fall-out that shouted us into dot and line and from which we have been throwing up and throwing down ever since. What we project as abyss, and into it, are the guardians, or sides of boundary, the parietal labor to bear Hermes, to give a limit to evasive-ness, to contour meandering, to make connections.

*

As species disappear, the Upper Paleolithic grows more vivid. As living animals disappear, the first outlines become more dear, not as reflections of a day world, but as the primal contours of psyche, the shaping of the underworld, the point at which Hades was an animal. The "new wilder-ness" is thus the spectral realm created by the going out of animal life and the coming in, in our time, of these primary outlines. Our tragedy is to search further and further back for a common non-racial trunk in which the animal is not separated out of the human while we destroy the turf on which we actually stand.

[1978]

A Note on Aimé Césaire

THERE IS A SPECIFIC LIFE force in Aimé Césaire's poetry that arises from an earth that is not only composed of a geological fundament but of the rotted corpses of fallen runaway slaves. Imagine a swamp with stately trees soaring up through the night, trunks swarmed by fog, roots invading a living graveyard of slime and stones. The fog swarming in around these human trunks carries a nauseous mustiness, an odor of despair and spoilage, that goes all the way back to the shores of colonial Africa. The trunks are human, not only because they participate in the principle of growth that courses through Césaire's poetry, but because they identify a soul life that man shares. These are not just vaguely "trees," or even more specifically wild plantains, but a particular kind of wild plantain, indigenous to Martinique, the balisier, which, in Césaire's own words, "has a red florescence at its center that is really shaped like a heart."

To discover a human heart in the center of the botanical world verifies the most profound desire behind Césaire's poetry: to once again place mankind at the heart of the universe. The microcosmic heart in our breasts becomes the place of imagining, and this imagination rhymes with the macrocosmic heart of the world, the sun.

To think of life this way is to believe that within every object dwells an individual spirit or force that governs its existence. Such a concept is extremely ancient, probably much older than the Africa of sources which Césaire discovered as a graduate student in Paris in the 1930s. As an

---

This brief essay was originally read at "Brock Peters interprets Aimé Césaire & Marcus Garvey," a theatrical presentation sponsored by the University of California Press, at the California Institute of Technology Athenaeum, November 19, 1985.

Antillean from Martinique where no one is indigenous, but where to be educated is to have one's identity consumed by models imported from Europe, Césaire began with the greatest disadvantages. His initial move in poetry was to take a step backward as he took a step forward, to ground his work in, as he later put it, "the first days of the species," *as* he assimilated Rimbaud, Mallarmé and French Surrealism. The extent of bridgework in Césaire—this being in the deep past at the same moment he suffers black slavery and anticipates a liberated future—is extraordinary, and it is the main reason that he is difficult and also a great poet. For these forces are not the subjects of poems, but rather, elements in a molten substance, rising to the surface and descending.

If we think of art as the state of imaginative transgression that prompts the desire, the need, for a more profound and ensouled world, we can glimpse the winch about which transgression strains against the prohibitions blacks confront, and understand how Césaire has set this turbine, in time and out of time, in his poetry at large. That his trajectory reaches as far as it does implies an unusual fortitude for overcompensation, and not in a negative way but rather with a magnanimity, in which a heroic imaginal ego is necessary to drive the creative endeavor through the resistance of prohibitions that are present at every turn. A Césaire poem often begins to faint or slacken right before a second wind takes over. This is understandable, because the burden, particularly in the case of *Notebook of a Return to the Native Land,* is that of a parthenogenesis in which the poet must conceive and give birth to himself while exorcising himself from an introjected and white image of the black.

I have participated with Annette Smith in a translation of all of Césaire's poetry because I wanted that slow, slow reading that a six-year multi-drafted translation project affords. I wanted to spoon Césaire, as it were, into all the beds and layers of my own psyche. Having been brought up as a WASP in the Indianapolis of the 1940s, I must never cease making myself conscious of the limitations of my own background and disturbing its control, for imaginatively I know that it is only one glass shard in the mosaic of backgrounds that make up the human experience I am aware of.

In 1978, I tried to explain to Florence Loeb, the daughter of the famous Parisian art dealer, the desire for the prodigal in Césaire's poetry and some of the circumstances under which it takes root. She listened to me and then said something I will never forget: "Césaire uses words like the nouveaux riches spend their money." She meant, of course, that this prodigal son of France, educated and acculturated by France, should cease his showing off, racing his language like roman candles over her head, and return to the fold (to the sheepfold, I might add, to a disappearance among the thousands for whom to have French culture is supposed to be more than enough). To this aristocratic woman, Aimé Césaire's imaginative wealth looked like tinsel. I carried this sinister cartoon of his power around with me for a couple of years. One morning what I wanted to say was a response to Césaire himself:

FOR ÁIME CÉSAIRE

Spend language, then, as the nouveaux riches spend money
invest the air with breath newly gained each moment
hoard only in the poem, be the reader-miser, a new kind of snake
coiled in the coin-flown beggar palm, be political, give it all
        away
one's merkin, be naked to the Africa of the image mine in which
biology is in a tug-of-war with deboned language in a tug-of-war
        with
Auschwitz in a tug-of-war with the immense demand now to
        meet the complex
actual day across the face of which Idi Amin is raining
the poem cannot wipe off the blood
but blood cannot wipe out the poem
black caterpillar
in its mourning leaves, in cortege through the trunk of the high-
        way of
history in a hug-of-war with our inclusion in
the shrapnel-elite garden of Eden.

[1983]

Introduction to *Fracture*

THERE ARE ONLY A HANDFUL of primary incidents in one's life, incidents powerful enough to create the cracks or boundary lines that one will often enter and follow for many years before another crucial event pounds one deeper or reorients one to a new map. As one approaches these events, omens appear everywhere, the world becomes dangerously magical, as if one had called the gods and the gods were now answering.

In the fall of 1980, my wife and I rented a cottage, reached only by a dirt road, near les Eyzies in the French Dordogne. On October 9th, the news of the death of Bill Evans reached me. That afternoon, we picked up a young couple who were hitchhiking in the rain. It turned out that they were staying in the man's parents' summer home a few kilometers away from us. They invited us to look for wild mushrooms with them the following afternoon.

After several hours of tramping around in the woods, we had gathered a couple of pounds of *cèpes*. Crossing a field on the way back to the car, we stopped a farmer on his tractor to inquire if everything we had gathered was edible. While Caryl and the Parisian couple spoke with him (and were informed that more than half of what we had picked were *faux cèpes,* false *cèpes* that when pressed firmly turn bruise blue, and are poisonous), I wandered back to a scene we had passed that fascinated me: Next to several large, mostly eaten Amanita Muscaria, were several caramel-colored field slugs, vibrating on their backs. There was no way to tell if they were in agony or in ecstasy. Evans' death suddenly moved

From *Fracture* (Santa Barbara, Black Sparrow Press, 1983).

in on me, and on the way home, I recalled Diane Arbus' "Jewish Giant" photograph, which in my frame of mind became an image of a gigantic interior slug.

The next morning I wrote "The Death of Bill Evans," and the poem's conclusions disturbed me so much that I decided not to show it to Caryl. I sensed that I was moving toward something that would hurt me, not out of self-destruction, but as if I had been moved "on track" toward a harmed and initiated state. For seven years I had been crying for a vision of Paleolithic Imagination and the construction of the underworld. All this time I had felt protected and safe while crawling around in the caves.

The evening of October 11th we invited the Parisian couple over for dinner, including the edible *cèpes*. Afterward, I drove them home. They invited me in for a glass of prune brandy and informed me that they had a cave on their property.

I explained that I was only interested in caves with prehistoric decorations, but when they insisted, I agreed to see it. A little after midnight, with one flashlight between us, we walked into the woods and descended into a more-or-less vertical cave, perhaps a hundred yards deep, consisting of three chambers and two bottleneck passages.

As I was pulling myself up through the last bottleneck, I felt a sharp sensation in my left ankle, which apparently had got twisted in a crevice, but the sensation was of having been bitten. Once outside, I was limping—the ankle felt sprained. I thought of staying at the people's house all night, but there was no way to contact Caryl and I had felt increasingly uncomfortable with the man. While we were having our brandy, he had pointed out a wood mask that had been lodged in the loft window of a barn facing the house. He said it was a devil's mask, and then went on to talk about how much he hated his father. I was his father's age.

I got into the car and started home. On a wide curve, a cramp shot up through my left calf, apparently stimulated by the injured ankle. I lost control, just for a second, and the car swerved into the ditch at the left (to the right was a fifty-foot ravine that we later found out was the graveyard of several tourist cars per year). Because my foot was pressed in spasm to the floorboard, when I smashed into a boulder in the ditch my ankle broke in three places.

I knew that I would be discovered the following morning by one of the local farmers. Until then, there was nothing to do but sit still and try to make sense out of what had happened. It soon began to pour and lightning crackled about me.

I thought back to when I had begun to write in 1958. Forces were breaking out like diseases, and for years I was beside myself with the midwestern hydra that had been unleashed. The main thing that kept me going was a belief that if I fully worked through the sexism, self-hate, bodilessness, soullessness and suffocated human relationship which encrusted my background, I could excavate a basement. I would have torn down the "House of Eshleman" and laid out a new foundation in its place. I feared that if I did not do this I would be hooked back into the hands of my selfhood by Indiana at the point that I was approaching a "last judgment" in my work. While there are themes and concerns in such books as *Mexico & North, Walks* and *Altars* that have nothing to do with deconstructing a WASP ego, the controlling obsession from 1960 to 1972 was to build a "containing wall" for what it was to be from Indiana.

Then, in 1969, on my back, naked, under the scrutinizing eyes of Dr. Sidney Handelman, clothed, on a chair beside me, I was lured into a baby-like game: he leaned over me making baby faces and sounds, I responded, and soon we were gurgling at each other. A desire to suck his nose broke through my play and I told him so. Gently, he wrapped his forefinger in the edge of the sheet covering my cot and offered it to me. Grateful for even a surrogate, I rolled to my side to take it in my mouth. Suddenly he pulled his finger out of the sheet, shifted back on his chair and reversed his expression. He was now regarding me from a throne of domination. Now in a tentative, contemptuous way, he again offered me the "bandaged nipple." I felt a rustling above my anus, then something rushed up my spine and I struck at him. He just managed to slip his finger out when I locked on the sheet and went wild. In a rage I tore the sheet to shreds before passing out. When I awoke, I felt—and have felt ever since—that I had lost at least ten pounds of dirty linoleum that had been wound about my organs.

A few years ago, when I told this story to an Indian Yogi, he acted, to my surprise, as if it was an ancient Yogic "working." The Yogi told me that the doctor was lucky, that had I bitten into his finger, he would have died—because the doctor had succeeded in bringing "all your poison into your teeth." You were a cobra at that moment, he said, and: you will be protected by that moment for the rest of your life.

As I thought about these things in the ditch, I saw Wilhelm Reich's image of "cosmic superimposition." I then brought the "cobra" experience with Dr. Handelman forward, and saw it as a curving stream of energy moving down from above, with the cave "biting" as a curving

stream moving up from below. It was as if the former experience had
been "answered" by what had just happened, but "answered" felt vague.
The two experiences seemed to have curved into each other and cracked.

I must say that these thoughts were what I was able to distill from
my night in the car. About them swarmed all the little heralds of the
depression that overwhelm us when we feel that we have betrayed ourselves or others. I could hardly bear to think of Caryl, back in the cottage,
frightened and sleepless, not knowing where I was. So the "conjunction"
was taking place on another level too, psychic exaltation matched by
remorse.

The most bewildering aspect of the experience was my inability to
say to myself what the "cracking" meant. I think I now understand it
brought about the "Visions of the Fathers of Lascaux," which I began to
automatically write as we sped down the vast German autobahns several
weeks later. I wrote the first four drafts of this poem, leg in cast, sitting in
the front seat by Caryl as she drove us from city to city, where readings
and lectures had been arranged, for most of November. So the vision I
had cried for arrived, but only after I had been put in my place by the
powers involved.

Several people, including James Hillman, had warned me: You
must be very careful when you are trying to induct prehistoric archetypes,
they had said, and Hillman, in particular, had explained that the reason
for this was that unlike Greek archetypes, which we can today examine as
discrete and complementary structures (puer, senex, anima, animus,
etc.), prehistoric archetypes are highly undifferentiated. This could mean
that such structures as puer and senex, or anima and animus, or all of
them, had not yet separated to take on distinct characteristics in the mind.
After my accident, I began to see prehistoric psychic activity as a
swamp-like churning, in which construction and destruction were twined
forces disguised by each other in such a way that a person seeking to
know them could hardly tell one from another. To enter the prehistoric
cave of one's own mind then, seeking one's mind before birth, as it were,
would be to enter a realm of darkness under the rule of a possibly single
massive core. I envisioned this core as amoebic, as an energy flow and
restricting membrane, that had been activated by the much earlier catastrophic separation between animal and hominid. The membrane would

represent the earlier unity still in agony over being disturbed, while the energy flow would represent the multifoliate desire of differentiation set in motion by the evolutionary branching.

It struck me that archetypal differentiation may spiral out of an earlier core in a way that is parallel to the unraveling of a rope of wisdom. At 20,000 BC it appears as if a figure we awkwardly identify as "the sorcerer" (or sorceress) was the whole rope. Since that time the rope has unraveled to the extent that today its strands are taken up by schools and departments (medicine, psychology, history, magic, art, etc.), and the poet is a single, almost invisible strand at the far edge of communal involvement. The question then becomes: Is it now possible to identify this earlier core, and if so, to glimpse how it has evolved and how we are moved by it still?

In prehistoric art there appears to be several different (though clearly related) modes of imaginal intelligence. One mode is what we generally refer to as "abstract signs," meaning, we do not yet know how to read the meandering lines, dots, tectiforms, claviforms, etc., that *are* a kind of writing which spills across the cave walls in and out of the bodies of beasts. While it is possible to identify a line as a fern or a lance, or to guess that it is "male" as opposed to an oval which is "female," we have really not yet penetrated the vocabulary, and our guesses end up in platitudes about man, hunting and the cycle of the seasons.

Another mode, which to the way we categorize today seems to be in great contrast to the signs, is the exact and realistic animals that appear as singular, non-narrative images for the most part (the friezes at Cougnac and Pech-Merle do not seem to indicate herds but groups that are arbitrary or based on some other combining idea). Superficially, we respond to these images, for one reason because of their astonishing verve and accuracy. The animals Cro-Magnon actually painted represent a small percentage of the kinds of animals he was in contact with. He seldom depicted red deer, his main food supply. And since there are no hunting scenes in Upper Paleolithic art, it seems obvious that he was after something other than hunted animals.

A third mode involves his image of himself as it is confused or clarified with animals and signs. At the periphery of this mode are headless buttock-breast-leg figures that appear to be more in the domain of signs than in that of the realistically depicted animals, or extremely crude human figure depictions that do not appear to be awkward attempts at realism. At the center of this mode there is a hybrid man-animal imagery, often intersected by meandering lines or gouges, that seems to combine the realistic and the abstract; i.e., it is neither, it is a single image that appears to have another image struggling within it, as if it were amoebic, neither one nor two, but a kind of one and a half, on the brink of division. One's first impression when looking at one of these figures in Les Combarelles, Commarque or Le Tuc d'Audoubert, could very well be: How grotesque!

And they are, especially in the sense that the word "grotesque" means "of the cave," and as late as the Renaissance, the Italian phrase "pittura grotesca" referred to "ridiculous faces or figures" found painted on cave walls. I am intrigued, not only by the hybrid wedding of man and animal in these figures, but by the association of this word with the image and the place. It may be that such figures represent the most complex imagining of life that we have available to us today. Based on this hunch, I would like to suggest that they represent an Upper Paleolithic archetype, the *grotesque archetype.* Such an archetype might indicate something basic about the nature of image: that in contrast to the realistic or the abstract, the image represents an ambivalent synthesis in which forces felt as opposites are, to borrow André Breton's term, "exploding/fixed," and that the umbilical cord of the image trails back to a point at which such contrariety was sensed as the struggle of the human to detach itself from the animal.

For is not something grotesque, or monstrous, because it violates evolution? The primal violence carried by a grotesque archetype might be understood this way: Before man, all previous animals had been subject to the evolution of their own substance, i.e., they were *autoplastic,* and their genetic gambling was blind because they played with their own bodies. Man's evolution, on the other hand, is through *alloplastic* experiments with objects outside his own body and is concerned only with the products of his hands, brains and eyes—and not with his body itself. Is it not possible that we shudder before highly mobilized grotesque images because subliminally we know that unrestrained alloplastic invention can lead to nuclear war, and that in the grotesque image we see simultaneously the relatively benign matrix that we abandoned, and the malignant power implicit in the one we entered?

The violence implied by the grotesque archetype is not only negative but also positive: Its violence is that of exuberance, of explosive spontaneity, of those first days of image when the recognizable and the nonrecognizable were veering in and out of conjunction.

These signs and images, painted directly on rock, are not separated from the rest of the world (as a framed, glassed painting on canvas in a guarded museum). Neither are they closed or completed units. Via microphotographic studies we know that they were traced and retraced over periods of time by the fingers of those who had no knowledge of the original painters. Furthermore, there appears to be a full sense of the communal *and* the sacred present in the ambience of the art work itself. While many caves are small and appear to have been decorated quickly by a small group of people who then abandoned them, others appear to be paleolithic "sanctuaries," centers for ritual, initiation and sacrifice. Imagine an underground Notre Dame in which the people themselves could put their fingers into the electrifying sockets of the first outlines of the gods while those very gods were being discovered and while animal (and probably human) sacrifice, rites of passage, commemorations of the dead and rituals to spur generation were going on at the same time!

At 20,000 BC, man was like a small insistent wedge, relative to weather and fauna a mere fleck, but a fleck with a point, a foreign element capable of running a fracture through the entire log, so to speak, at a certain depth of insertion with the grain.

I do not, in this poetry, work off a Renaissance image in which the body of the poem is a strictly completed, finished product, isolated, alone, fenced off from all other poetries, and in which all signs of its unfinished character, its growth and its proliferation, have been eliminated. I have not removed its protruberances and offshoots, smoothed out is convexities or closed off its apertures. I have sought to reveal its inner processes of absorbing and ejection. On a physical plane, the essential images here connect to those parts of the grotesque body in which it outgrows itself. Thus breast, anus, mouth, bowels and genitalia, from a grotesque viewpoint, are still linked to the cosmos, as essential elements in the life of the body and of the earth in the struggle to incorporate death as an aspect of life. These orifices and convexities are also associated with the underworld, with connecting passageways, and with the endless chain of imaginal life.

To a certain extent an archaic and medieval folk sense of the grotesque can be elaborated in poetry today. However, it would be foolish to simply install them in a present body of work, as if their vitalities could represent the world today. One is responsible for the history, the construction and the deconstruction of the images with which one works. The cartoon, an element of the grotesque as early as any other, must also be acknowledged as one of its dimensions, not merely when it means "first sketch" (as in da Vinci) or potent nineteenth-century political satire, but when it occurs as "fabulous beasts" in Greek myth or in the Disney world. It is as if each ambivalence present in any grotesque combined object is capable of generating its own ambivalences, and so on.

Thus while the Nemean lion, the Lernaean hydra and Stymphalian birds appear to be in some way connected to the animals which appear on the walls of the caverns, they are, in a Greek context, fabulous man-hating monsters to be vanquished by Hercules, whose labors become "heroic" to the extent that he accomplishes their destruction. And are not these "fabulous beasts," clearly out of bond with man, in some dim, chilling way, the ancestors of Mickey Mouse and Donald Duck? As if the earlier "making fabulous" turns out to be a way to distort and stretch the beast image to the extent that by the twentieth century it can accommodate an entire cast of North American bourgeois, imperialistic concepts. Since animals, for most people, seem exempt from the vicissitudes of history, what better vehicles to carry (as a dummy carries the ventriloquists' voice) the anxieties of an adult value system that is opposed to sex, growth, primitives and change? Here, in the guise of "innocent" ersatz animals, frolicking about in an aura of "pure entertainment," one finds the atrophy of the already severely constricted Renaissance ideals, finished and isolated bodies now pressed into the service of maintaining the status quo.

We know that North American abundance is to a great and, ultimately, terrifying extent dependent upon the continuing poverty and torture of others in countries we have no direct contact with, but to whom our eyes are pressed via TV news reports, so that a starving mother in Biafra, seated on the side of a cot with a starving infant too weak to even try to suckle her mother's utterly empty breast, poses a complicated set of questions to North American poets: By responding in our writing to such a scene, to what extent do we fulfill our human responsibility to it? To what extent is our response a mere appropriation of materials that mirrors imperialistic ideologies?

Then there is that unbearable sensation of the speeded-up fantasy of one's taxes, via a whirlwind of Pentagon Rube Goldberg manipulations, pouring out the barrel of a flame-thrower with which a seventeen-year-old El Salvadorian soldier is igniting a peasant. As I wrote that last sentence, I was also aware that I had, as a North American, the freedom to write and publish it, "to keep," in Blake's words, "the Divine Vision in a time of trouble." Yet my vision, whatever it is, will certainly be meaningless without the presence of the catastrophes that not only in part define this century, but which this nation continues to conduct "over there" so that it increasingly smells bad "here."

Relative to all others, I am lodged near the peak of a pyramid-shaped dump, and even if poor by local standards, almost at the top when I calculate my conveniences, services and ability to do what I want to do—yet with the unique difficulty that social destiny has offered me: As a white Anglo-Saxon heterosexual male, I must confront the fact that what I represent as a social identity is the great boulder that must be rolled away from the entrance to the cave in which the energies of the minorities throughout the world have been sealed.

Under such circumstances, the first person, the "I," is also the last, and attempts to be true to the material itself, appearing where it is generated, an aspect of the poetic fabric that is similar to the imaginal ego (not *my* ego) in the company of fictive and personal figures of dreaming. The temptation here is to go one way or the other: we live in a time of massive ego reinforcement and massive ego abandonment. Yet the *I* may have become the least egotistic part of the poem. I have read contemporary American poems in which *I,* as a word, did not occur—yet the poem itself was an egotistic fireworks display. While words may lie, the poem itself does not lie. If it turns on its own axis, if its center is polytropic, then a field of centers is present.

It may seem that I have gone back to prehistory to avoid confronting a present that literally affords a human being no place to stand. I have tried to create the visions of the Fathers of Lascaux as a shaping that had "us" in mind, an "us" that we can still find in the art of 17,000 BC. This art is not only with us still, but embodies a perpetual energy capable of contacting a twentieth-century heart off which most contemporary art merely ricochets. Lascaux, then, is a breaking in, a telegram delivered to the French "underground" in 1940, a shamanic paw in whose palm today's marvels and terrors can be read.

The demand that I feel as a poet today is to stand before the deepening shaft of otherness, working to gain insights into early Homo Sapiens consciousness, while registering with as much precise subjectivity as possible the global conflict over which I have no control as well as the imaginative materials over which I have a good deal of selective control, and to do so in a voice that is "personal," in the sense that it does not sound like my predecessors or contemporaries. At the moment when I feel spring may have gone out of the world, I also recognize the ancientness of spring, the chasm in Persephone which deepens to ochre-lined wildflower-strewn Neanderthal burials. We find ourselves at an odd bend in the amplitude and awfulness of life, in which "the voice that is great within us" crumbles into a brother pun, "the voice that is grapeshot within us." Wallace Stevens' "stale grandeur of annhilation" has united with that morbid exhilaration, that leper sperm, which swims in all creation.

[1982]

A Kind of Moisture
on the Wall

Suppose earliest consciousness is worked off the shape of certain earth inevitabilities, that the shape of Cro-Magnon "consciousness" is the contour grid of those specific caves he chose to paint and engrave.

What we call "art" may be a response to the springboard of the womb, to the shapes our minds-to-be were hit with, the tunnels of light/dark, of encroachment, of (false) release, of that move toward EXIT that one so desires, when one is governed by a crawling-ground.

The "irony" of Eden may be that exit is the organic world, the odors of wood, flower and decay that one smells with extraordinary pleasure for a few yards before emerging from a cave.

Yet Cro-Magnon, even with a short life span, was clearly not an infant. The origins of art are not squeezable baby fat, but in a Lawrencian way are very alert to what we call "surroundings." So alert that the trap engraved in a cave wall may have nothing to do with animals but may have been an attempt to trap shadows, or hold them in place, restrain them from infiltrating the world of the living.

The first images may have been *forces put on hold.*

"A Kind of Moisture on the Wall" first appeared in *Hades in Manganese,* and was reprinted in *The Name Encanyoned River.*

(for a bison with a ten-foot hump was not a buffalo; it was the Paleolithic
land equivalent of the great white shark, the supreme defiance)

The bison appearing, its rump say, formed by stalactites, so that by moss
lamp it is without any work by man already present in the rock wall, leads
to the sensation that what is "out there" is inherent.

*

The imagination hiding in rock lived
in concretional vaults for millenniums to be surprised
by a clump of frog-like vamps, pulsating about a pillar,
behind fuming moss, at animal parts of its shape—

they were terrified that giant elk was outside of elk,
was here, in their crawling place—
might elk be inside them?
Might all things be coming to life in all things?

They nailed imagination in place when they engraved
the rest of an elk on the basis of a rump-shaped stalactite.
But what they did not see of the elk—*was* it elk?
Or only elk rump expression on the face or body of something
showing itself momentarily in their fire,
something bigger than the cave,
something slumbering or awakening in the earth?

And the questions? A kind of moisture on the wall.
What was not there might be them.
What is clear: something was in motion that can still be seen,
as clearly today as when the first ones tried to arrest it
by completing the elk outline inside of which
the engraver scratched part of a woman's body with lances
extending from it as if they were thongs to "stitch" her body,
headless, shoulderless, to elk body, as if to decomplete
the finished outline, to question the idea of completion.

A headless shoulderless woman running filled with lances
across the rock of a tautly pinned elk is the sensation of imagination

as it pours through life like hoarfrost, or liquid jade,
the rock wall itself writhes so stilly
that something never to be completed writhes in us,
ringworm intrigues, the tentacular lava of maggot-
lined fables. The moment we touch anything
that touches us the entire human body becomes a pipeline
of inverse fire hydrants wrenching shut the feeling valves,
for to totally connect with even the stain of an image is fearsome,
a cog to cog movement in an enrapt reporter calling up
the abandoned elevators of the lower simian body
derailed in Africa millenniums before, those rotting luncheonettes
visited only by hyenas and ferocious striped worms,
those bleached cabooses individuation pretends
to have left behind but which lurch open onto our brains in dream
to keep us open to the future of an earth
awesome, infinite, coiled in hypnosis.

[1982]

Notes on a Visit
to Le Tuc d'Audoubert

for Robert Bégouën

bundled by Tuc's tight jagged
    corridors, flocks of white
  stone tits, their milk in long
    stone nipply drips, frozen over

    the underground Volp in which
  the enormous guardian eel,
now unknown, lies coiled—

to be impressed (in-pressed?) by this
primordial "theater of cruelty"—
    by its keelhaul sorcery

    Volp mouth—the tongue of the
      river lifting one in—

These "Notes" first appeared in *Fracture;* they were subsequently reprinted in *The Name Encanyoned River*.

to be masticated by Le Tuc d'Audoubert's
   cruel stones—
      the loom of the cave

  Up the oblique chimney by ladder to iron cleats set
in the rock face to the cathole,
on one's stomach
     to *crawl,*   working against
           one, pinning one
as the earth   in, to, it, to
makes one   feel for an instant
feel its traction—   the dread of

WITHERING IN
PLACE

   —pinned in—
  The Meat Server
masticated by the broken
  chariot of the earth

  "fantastic figures"—more beast-
    like here than human—one
horn one ear—   ⎰one large figure
              ⎱one small figure

    as in Lascaux?
(the *grand* and *petit* sorcerer?)

First indications of master/
  apprentice? ("tanist" re. Graves)

the   grotesque   archetype
—   ————   ————

vortex in which the emergent
human and withdrawing animal
    are spun—
        ==

grotesque = movement

(life is grotesque when we catch
      it in quick perceptions—
   at full vent—history
      shaping itself)

the turns/twists of the cave
   reinforce the image turbine—
as does the underground river,

                the cave floats,
            in a sense, in several senses,
                all at once,
            it rests on the river, is penetrated
              by it, was originally made
                by rushing water—
                  the cave
                is *the skeleton of flood*

images on its walls
   participate, thus, as torsion,
in an earlier torsion—

Here one might synthesize:
   1) abstract signs

          initiate movement
          brought to rest in

3) naturalistic figures
   (bison, horses etc)

In between, the friction, are

2) grotesque hybrids

(useful—but irrelevant to systematize forces that must have been felt as flux, as *unplanned,* spontaneous, as were the spots/areas in caves chosen for images—because shadowing or wall contour evoked an animal? Any plan a coincidence—we have no right to systematize an area of experience of which we have only shattered iceberg tips—yet it does seem that "image" occurs at the point that a "naturalistic" ibex is gouged in rock across an "abstract" vulva already gouged there, so that the rudiments of poetry are present at approximately 30,000 BC—)

          image is crossbreeding,
          or the refusal to respect
          the single, individuated body,
          image is that point
          where sight crosses sight—

to be alive as a poet is to be
          in conversation with one's eyes)

What impresses at Tuc is a relationship
between river
          hybrid figures
          and the clay bison—

it is as if the river (the skeleton of water = the cave itself) erupts into image with the hybrid "guardians" (Breuil's guess) and is brought to rest in the terminal chamber with the two bison, i.e., naturalism is a kind of rest—naturalism returns us to a continuous and predictable nature (though there is something unnatural about these bison to be noted later) —takes us out of the discontinuity, the *transgression* (to cite Bataille's slightly too Catholic term) of the grotesque

(though the grotesque, on another level, according to Bakhtin, is deeper continuity, the association of *realms,* kingdoms, fecundation and death, degradation and praise—)

on one hand: bisons-about-to-couple
  assert the generative
  what we today take to be
  the way things are   *(though with ecological pollution,*
                 "generation" leads to mutation,
                 a new "grotesque"!)

*

to be gripped by a womb of stone
to be in the grip of the surge of life
imprisoned in stone

it is enough to make one *sweat one's animal*

(having left the "nuptial hall" of white stone breasts in which one can amply stand—the breasts hang in clusters right over one's head—one must then squirm vertically up the spiral chimney (or use the current iron ladder) to enter the upper level via a cathole into a corridor through which one must crawl on hands and knees—then another longish cathole through which one must crawl on one's belly, squirming through a human-sized tunnel—to a corridor through which one can walk haltingly, stooping, occasionally slithering through vertical catslits and straddling short walls—)

if one were to film one's postures through this entire process, it might look like a St.-Vitus dance of the stages in the life of man, birth channel expulsion to old age, but without chronological order, a jumble of exaggerated and strained positions that correspondingly increase the *image pressure* in one's mind—

while in Le Tuc d'Audoubert I felt the broken horse rear in agony in the cave-like stable of Picasso's *Guernica,*

at times I wanted to leave my feet behind, or to continue headless in the dark, my stomach desired prawn-like legs with grippers, my organs were in the way, something inside of me wanted to be

an armored worm,

one feeler extending out its head,

I swear I sensed the disintegration of the backbone of my mother now buried 12 years,

entangled in a cathole I felt my tongue start to press backward, and the image force was: I wanted to *choke myself out of myself,* to give birth to my own strangulation, and then nurse my strangulation at my own useless male breasts—useless? No, for Le Tuc d'Audoubert unlocks memories that bear on a single face the expressions of both Judith and Holofernes at the moment of beheading, mingled disgust terror delight and awe, one is stimulated to desire to enter cavities within oneself where dead men can be heard talking—

in Le Tuc d'Audoubert I heard something in me whisper me to believe in God

and something else in me whispered that the command was the rasp of a 6000-year-old man who wished to be venerated again—

and if what I am saying here is vague it is because both voices had to sound themselves in the bowels of this most personal and impersonal stone, in which sheets of myself felt themselves corrugated with nipples—as if the anatomy of life could be described, from this perspective, as entwisted tubes of nippled stone through which perpetual and mutual beheadings and birthings were taking place—

*

but all these fantastic images were shooed away the moment I laid eyes on the two bison sculptured out of clay leaned against stuff fallen from the chamber ceiling—

the bison and their "altar" seemed to be squeezed up into view out of the swelling of the chamber floor—

the sense of *culmination* was very severe, the male about to mount the female, but clearly placed several inches behind and above her, not in contact with any part of her body, and he had no member—

if they *were* coupling, and *without* deep cracks in their clay bodies, they would have disappeared into their progeny thousands of years ago, but here they are today still, as if Michelangelo were to have depicted God and man as not touching, but only reaching toward each other, caught in the exhaustion of a yearning for a sparking that has in fact never taken place, so that the weight of all the cisterns in the world is in that yearning, in the weight of that yearning is the real ballast in life, a ballast in which the unborn are coddled like slowly cooking eggs, unborn bison and unborn man, in the crib of a scrotum, a bone scrotum, that jailhouse of generation from which the prisoners yearn to leap onto the taffy machine-like pistons of shaping females—

it is that spot where the leap should occur that Le Tuc d'Audoubert says is VOID, and that unfilled space between two fertile poles here feels like the origin of the abyss, as if in the minds of those who shaped and placed these two bison, fertilization was pulled free, and that freedom from connection is the demon of creation haunting man and woman ever since—

we crawled on hands and knees about this scene, humbled, in single file, lower than the scene, 11 human creatures come, lamps in hand like a glowworm pilgrimage, to worship in circular crawl at one of the births of the abyss—

if I had stayed longer, if I had not with the others disappeared into the organic odors of the Montesquieu-Avantès woods, I am sure that I would have noticed, flittering out of the deep cracks in the bison clay, little wingled things, image babies set free, the Odyssi before Odysseus who still wander the vaults of what we call art seeking new abysses to inscribe with the tuning forks of their wings . . .

[1982]

Seeds of Narrative
in Paleolithic Art

WHEN WE LOOK FOR EVIDENCE of the seeds of narrative, we come upon Neanderthal at 75,000 BC burying his dead in red ochre-lined pits on pine boughs and covering them with wildflowers. By tying up the corpse so that it looks as if it is being buried in foetal position, Neanderthal may have been trying to prevent the formation of a ghost, for the tied-up corpses were often covered with heavy rock slabs. This event could be the earliest narrative seed, yet the only marks Neanderthal made were cup-shaped gouges on the undersides of these burial slabs. While such gougings are evocative of female space, they may be no more "narrative" than a two-year-old child chipping at the wall with a pencil, simply to act on matter, to affect the outside.

It is not until around 30,000 BC that we find evidence for the beginnings of the liberation of autonomous imagination. Much of this evidence comes from south-central France and northern Spain, and was done by people (whose brains were slightly larger than ours) called Cro-Magnon,[1] and consists of finger doodlings in soft clay, sculpture, engravings and paintings in caves as well as incised weapons and tools.

What we call image-making and, consequently, art may have been the result of the crisis of the separation of the hominid from the animal into the distinct though related classes of the human and the animal. Why it resulted in image-making when and where it did probably has much to

This essay was originally presented at the Forms and Functions of the Narrative Conference at USC, in Los Angeles, in 1981; it was subsequently published in *Sulfur* #2, fall, 1981. It was presented, in an abbreviated and altered form, at the Narrative Literature Conference at the University of Michigan, in Ann Arbor, spring, 1987.

161

do with ice-age conditions—an almost total dependence on animals for survival (though Cro-Magnon seldom depicted red deer, his main food source) as well as the effect of severe and prolonged cold on a body that originally evolved under temperate and even tropical conditions. Seemingly suddenly, at around 30,000 BC, these people began to put the animalness that they were losing (or really, had lost), yet were utterly dependent upon, onto cave walls—often in the depths of caves they did not live in, in nearly unreachable places. Consciousness, as I am thinking about it here, seems to be the upswing of a "fall" from the seamless animal web, in which a certain amount of sexual energy was transformed into fantasy energy, and the loss was partially and hauntingly compensated for by dreaming and imagining—processes not directedly related to survival.

Cro-Magnon's main cave-wall obsession was with big herbivores such as bison, horses, mammoths and deer. These animals are sometimes painted as if they had been hung on the cave wall separately, with no relationship to each other—at least in what we could call a narrative sense. Only occasionally do the painted animals seem to interact, e.g., one sniffing another's sex, or two animals copulating. There is one considerable exception to what I say here, the Shaft in Lascaux, and I will come back to it later.

The first images of which we have record appear to be crudely gouged vulvas and possibly phalluses mixed up with animal indications, as well as thousands of seemingly abstract meandering lines and dots— either separate dots, or dots in various formations. As we come forward in time, say up to 15,000 BC, the human image begins to emerge, often in one of three image situations:

1) Person appears to be a satirized, bestialized, distorted phantom (more often than not masked). Such terms, for me, translate back to the fact that it does not at this time recognize itself as human in any finished or even vertical sense. Person was a kind of grotesque merger, an entanglement of seemingly abstract lines and animal attributes, anticipating the worldwide historical tradition of animal-human hybrids (the werewolf, the Minotaur, Roman *grotesca,* Mochican ceramics, etc.).

2) Woman, less often engraved on cave walls than man (and when presented, either engraved in profile with greatly exaggerated buttocks, or sculpted in frontal view, as the figure from Laussel holding up a horn) *is* free-standing sculpture, the so-called "Venuses," small enough to fit in

the hand, whose legs and necks taper (or bulge) into anonymity and whose image force is in obesity, a thick mid-lower body girdle of public delta, buttocks, stomach and breasts.

3) Man begins to appear as a dancing elfin fleck in engraved friezes of wandering lines and animals, and while the shape indicates human being, he is either part animal or garbed in animal, a camouflaged piece of the shattered hominid/animal mosaic.

In almost every case the figure of the human is masked, and often appears to be moving—or, as in the case of the female Venus statuettes, appears to have been tapered to a point so as to be fixable in the ground (several were discovered in such a position in the soil of rock shelters). Two narrative seeds can be gleaned here: the masked, dancing shaman as Coyote or Shiva, the trickster hero of myths all over the world, constantly in transformational motion—in contrast to the fixed, matriarchal figure of "The Great Goddess" who will become the central figure of Mesolithic and Neolithic visions of the womb that is the tomb that is the contrapuntal rhythm of spring and autumn, where the natural and the human are as strands of one cycle twisted upon itself.

Paleolithic space appears to be multi-directional, not only a world of broken interrelation where everything is in association, but also a world that is not partitioned from its material by a frame or some other boundary device. Since there seems to be no evidence for distinguishing sacred space from secular space in Paleolithic imagination, it makes sense to me that paintings were retraced, i.e., participated in again and again by people who were probably in no way related to the original painter.

One could almost say that there is no evidence in Paleolithic art space of the distinctions we make between an exterior and an interior. It seems to be neither inside anything nor outside anything. On the other hand, a sense of boundary appears to be emerging *within* painted or engraved areas. I imagine a Paleolithic frieze as a kind of whirlpool within which the flotsam of inside/outside are spinning toward me. If so, of what did this "shipwreck" consist? In following out the metaphor, I come again to the animal/hominid separation as a catastrophe in the ocean of life, the ramifications of which we have hardly begun to investigate. Inside and outside, in this view, could be seen as the wreckage of an interrelated life vessel.

Eden, which most people regard as a primordial image, from the viewpoint of Paleolithic art is the end of the primordial condition in which what is human and what is animal are bound together. It is possible to follow their separation as it is recorded in imagery. At around 15,000 BC, a figure popularly known as the "dancing sorcerer" was engraved and painted in the "sanctuary" at Les Trois Frères. Wearing the antlers of a stag, an owl mask, wolf ears, bear paws and horsetail, a human appears to be dancing—or is he (he is male, with an animal-like penis) climbing a tree? Is he a shaman—or is he a Covering Shaman, the prototype not only of Shiva but also for the Covering Cherub? The armature of this figure is clearly human, yet his surface is stuccoed with a patchwork of animals. (The word "stuccoed" here comes from Whitman's "I find I incorporate gneiss and coal and long-threaded moss and fruits and grains and esculent roots, / And am stucco'd with quadrupeds and birds all over . . . ," lines which in the context of the Les Trois Frères figure, evoke a human figure in magnetic fusion with other kingdoms.)

As we come forward in time, we can observe the animal anatomy falling away, until with the early Greeks most of the deities are sheerly human-looking, with animals as consorts—or as in the case of some of the chthonian figures, such as the Medusa, with bits of the animal kingdom remaining, like snakes for hair or tusks for teeth. It is possible in the case of the Medusa to imagine the snakes that encircle her face as the winding corridors of a cave, and the tusks, in the center of her face, as the ghost of that dreadful encounter where in total blackness and at times several hundreds of yards from a cave entrance a human met a twelve-foot cave-bear.

By the end of the eighteenth century, in the "civilized" Western world, the "shaman" has lost even a consort relationship with the animal. In William Blake's "Glad Day" painting, the shaman/poet displays himself naked and exultantly free of all animality, his left foot treading on a worm while a bat-winged spirit, symbolizing evil, flies away. The counter-motion to this progression is the animal soul, not only become "fabulous," but increasingly less an ally and more a figure of terror and wrath, pounding on our chests as nightmare, as if what we are is a door locked on separation forever.

Charles Olson's vision of the Odyssey as a dance-drama in which the shaman-hero dances his way through a labyrinth of monsters to be reunited with a human other is a fascinating tie-in of so-called prehistory with history,[2] but such a vision also bears the shadow of Hercules, out of bond with living animals. By tending to depict animals realistically and himself as a hybrid monster, Paleolithic man seems to be in accord with Wallace Stevens' "It is the human that is the alien, / The human that has no cousin in the moon."

While the Shaft in Lascaux has received more attention than any other Paleolithic painting site, it has, since the cave's discovery in 1940, resisted both hunting and shamanistic interpretations. As the final extension of the Passageway and the Apse, the corridor and chamber which branch off the central Rotunda, the 13-foot Shaft represents the "bowels" of Lascaux. Georges Bataille gives an adequate description of the scene:

"Midway down . . . a narrow platform brings one opposite a rock shelf (below which the Shaft continues to plunge) bearing images, on one side, of a rhinoceros and, on the other, of a bison; between them, falling or supine, is a bird-headed man; below him, a bird poised on an upright stick. The infuriated bison's hair literally stands on end, it lashes its tail, intestines spill in thick ropes from a gash in its belly. A spear is painted diagonally across the beast's flank, passing over the place where the wound has been inflicted. The man is naked and ithyphallic: drawn in puerile fashion, he is shown as though just felled by the bison's two projecting horns; the man's arms are flung wide and his four-fingered hands are open."[3]

Bataille then quotes the Abbé Breuil who had written that it is "a painting perhaps commemorating some fatal accident that occurred in the course of a hunt." On the basis of this hunch, Breuil looked for the hunter's body at the foot of the stone rim above the Shaft, but he found nothing—other than some spears at the bottom of the Shaft itself which were dated earlier than the paintings in Lascaux.[4]

In response to Breuil, Bataille comments that the bison could not have been disemboweled by the thrust of the spear (which in the painting is clearly broken off at two-thirds of its length), and while this does not prove the man is not a hunter, it does eliminate him as the cause of the bison's condition. I should add here that since there are no hunting scenes *per se* in Paleolithic art, all things that look like weapons may be symbolic and relate to magic.

Bataille then quotes from H. Kirchner's interpretation. According to the latter, it is not at all a question of a hunting incident. The prostrate man is not dead; rather, he is a shaman in the throes of an ecstatic trance. Kirchner, we are told, has drawn on the idea of "a relationship between Lascaux civilization and the Siberian civilization of our own times." A Siberian scene is cited with the sacrifice of a cow; posts topped by carved birds mark the road to heaven, to which the shaman will guide the sacrificed animal while he is unconscious (the birds being auxiliary spirits without whom the shaman could not undertake his aerial journey).

This interpretation might account for the man's erection (and it also supports S. Giedion's argument that "this bird man is in fact standing upright at the moment of supreme exaltation"[5]), but as Bataille points out, Kirchner's theory overlooks the bison and its wound; "that is to say, is it probable that, in a sacrifice, a bison would be disemboweled? And has not Kirchner's theory forced him to view the rhinoceros as independent of the rest of the scene? However, if one inspects the actual Scene at Lascaux, one quickly discovers the group's unity and similarity in treatment."

The interpretations of other writers seem to be based on fantasies concerning shamanistic rites. Andreas Lommel claims the scene is a battle between shamans, "a fight in which only one of the contestants has assumed the shape of an animal." Weston LaBarre suggests that a bird shaman has come to grief in the underground world of a reindeer shaman. Francois Bordes proposes that a bird-totem hunter was killed by a bison, and a man of the rhinoceros totem painted this picture of revenge: disembowelment by a rhinoceros. William Irwin Thompson states that the bison is "the Great Goddess coming to the shaman in the power vision that sets him apart from ordinary men."[6]

While I have not inspected the Shaft, I have visited Lascaux three times. On my last visit, the guide, Jacques Marsal (one of the original discoverers of the cave, who has dedicated his life to its preservation) mentioned that carbon monoxide accumulates in the Shaft because there is no air circulation. Marsal suggested a dead man may have been depicted there, because the gas would have made it a lethal area.

Let's turn back to the scene and reevaluate what is depicted. None of the cited interpretations take into consideration the six black dots apparently issuing from the rhinoceros' anus—not depicted as falling, as literal dung would, but as floating toward, or in alignment with, the bird on the stick who appears to be watching the dots, and thus on a narrative level connecting the right-hand part of the scene to the left-hand part. The rhinoceros' tail, turned backward, seems to be in acute contrast with the bison's tail, flipped forward. Is it possible that these two animals signify contrasting aspects of a single image?

While the raised bison hair suggests aggression, the animal is hardly charging, or writhing, but appears to be rather stoic, in striking contrast with the bolting, leaping and trotting animals which swarm the Rotunda and Axial Gallery. The bison's front hooves (one of which is split) are modestly drawn back to accommodate (not step on?) the man's oversized feet. The hooves are in geometrical alignment, with the indrawn head aligned, eye to eye, with the man's bird-mask.[7] Might there be a compositional motif to which bison and man are being subordinated? Upper Paleolithic art interpretation has been so dominated by "the hunting hypothesis" and antithetical shaman fantasies that compositional layout has hardly been considered.[8]

Going back to Bataille for a moment: I do not find his "gash" as the source of the spilling intestines (but do want to honor his observation that the spear is laid *across* the bison, not plunged into it, or through it). The spilled intestines, according to Andre Leroi-Gourhan, are "given the shape of concentric ovals," and because of this they may be one of many variations of images of the vulva, which in Upper Paleolithic art can be demonstrated to manifest itself as triangles, rectangles, claviforms and ovals.[9]

Once we begin to notice female aspects of the bison, we may also be struck by the fact that the bison bird-headed man in the scene is, compositionally, a triangle standing on its apex. The horizontal bar is created by flattening out the bison hump and back, and, at the left, by pushing the head down into the chest. The left diagonal is the man's rigid body underlined by his right arm, the head and back of the stick bird and the short hooked object (in hunter interpretations, referred to as a spear-thrower; in shaman interpretations, not discussed). The right diagonal is made by what we have so far referred to as a spear. If one agrees that vulva images are evident, the spear can be read as a penis image. Leroi-Gourhan has offered fairly convincing evidence for an Upper Paleolithic system of gender pairing. The following quote may be relevant to the Shaft scene: "When we consider the variants of the 'arrow' and of the 'wound marks,' we become aware that these graphic markings can be assimilated to variant forms of the male and female signs. In other words, it is highly probable that Paleolithic men were expressing something like 'spear is to penis' as 'wound is to vulva.' To be fully persuaded of this, it is enough to see that the bison in the central panel at Bernifal is marked on its side, not with a 'wound' and 'arrows,' but with an oval vulva in double outline and two pairs of short strokes."[10]

Here I only need to add that the so-called spilled intestines in the Shaft scene could be described in exactly the same words.

Thus if we think of the "intestines" as a variation of a vulva image, and keep in mind the triangular framing, the right-hand aspect of the scene, compositionally, is a small oval vulva tangential to a large triangular vulva, with each diagonal of the triangle—the ithyphallic man and the spear/penis—clearly male. While such a reading does not reduce the painting to abstract or merely geometrical "gender" art, it does interfuse the surface male shaman/hunting ambiguities with strongly feminine rudiments.

The female triangle that I have coaxed out is not a fluke; it is evident in a number of cave frescoes, in particular the Altamira ceiling and the Chamber of the Little Bison in Font-de-Gaume.[11] The imaged vulva is possibly the oldest and most enduring force in creative expression. It first appears with certainty at around 30,000 BC in bas-relief rock-shelter sculpture, and spreads forward through history as the Delta, Holy Door, Yoni Yantra, Virgin-Mother-Crone trinity, etc.[12]

If we allow an ambiguity of interpretation in the right diagonal, i.e., do not insist on a literal spear identification, it is possible to locate it in a slightly different but possibly relevant context: There are numerous depictations of headless or masked figures of women, in profile, with protruding buttocks, slightly leaning forward, as if dancing and super-exposing their buttocks (the Losotho of South Africa still perform such a dance on the occasion of a girl's menarche[13]). Most of such figures in Upper Paleolithic art are marked, or "signed," with a forceful line that traverses the body downward from the rump. Such a line neatly converts a rump-in-profile into a vulva viewed from the front. Such a line may suggest sexual maturity, availability and/or fertility. If we now go back to the Shaft scene, we can see how, in this context, the "spear" turns the bison's rump into a kind of vulva seen upside down.

Given the location of the Shaft scene—at Lascaux's lowest level, in a cul-de-sac often filled with noxious if not lethal gas—we might expect the scene to relate to the lower body. I have mentioned earlier the ways in which the animals' tails contrast, and that rhinoceros and bison may indicate contrasting aspects of a single image. I would now like to suggest that the female-signed bison complex is identified with fecundity, while the rhinoceros, less storied, more naturalistic, and with no prominent sexual identification that I can see, is identified with fecality, and that the two together are a kind of diptych, or synthesis of eroticisms (or an *amphimixis,* to borrow Sandor Ferenczi's coined word from his book, *Thalassa*). The implication of the scene is that permeating magic and hunting, creation and destruction, fecundity and death—potentially all dualisms—is a shuttle, or Double Gate, grounded in genital contrariety (or genital opposition, when retention is stressed at the expense of reception, or vice-versa).

Linking the "panels" of this diptych are the stick bird and the black dots, or seed turds, whose relationship seems to be corroborated elsewhere. Bird and animal excrement are joined ecologically, and humanly, in at least half a dozen spear-throwers, whose carved deer are depicted, in Leroi-Gourhan's words, "with an enormous sausage of excrement issuing from their posterior orifice, with two birds at the end of the sausage, tenderly kissing."[14]

The failure of earlier interpretations to consider, let alone integrate, what appears to be the rhinoceros' excrement, is part of the tragic limitation of Western Christian civilization.[15] Focused on a raised and broken man on a cross, we have lost the perspective offered by a triangle balanced on its apex, a poised life-gate, as it were, pointing down to and cathecting an underworld, which might make us comedically earthy rather than apocalyptically heaven-obsessed.

If Cro-Magnon imaginative space is multidirectional unbroken interrelation without frame or sacred/secular distinction, perhaps the experience displayed in such space is too. Maybe it is time to stop saying that the man in the Shaft is *either* supine/dreaming *or* supine/dead *or* falling *or* standing in exaltation. Maybe the experience concretized here is all those things at once, with the further implication that he is but a strut in female fecundity, and along with his penis/spear the stiffness, or *yang* power, in feminine *yin* suppleness, a kind of visionary resiliency felt in all realms. In this extended sense, the significance of the Shaft scene is not a Rashomon-like situation-tragedy in which "truth" is a never completely interlocking mosaic of contrasting viewpoints, but a significance in which all the associational surfacings fuse into an image capable of bearing the inconsistencies and contradictions that have sapped the power of the interpretational views—

> Fecality wants to be born—
> the fecal nature of the soul offers its berries to this bird
> who will pick life
> from 6 rhinoceros turds, not
> off the ground, but as semaphoric pairs
> in the depths of Lascaux's
> Shaft,
>   at the end of 15,000 years of image we are
> *gathered* here, much more than we now
> suspect, by black manganese turds containing
> the seeds of narrative, or the berries which
> like that bird we must take in our mouths and chew
> to mourn a coalescence, a congruity of all we touch,
> and distill from it the fundamental substance of the soul—
> look, already our torso is a slack empty loop,
> a kind of lariat falling nowhere, at the top of which
> is the bird head we've desperately put on to stop
> conformity to ourselves—already we are a mask
> atop a watery loop of rope, heartless, organless,
> but not sexless, for look, like a gash in motion
> our penis is out, without terminal,
> night-bathing, pronged up as if it could
> match the uterine hunger of Who is that
> hovering above? Looked at
> through a star shower of centuries it may be Madam Death,

her forehead buried in her chest, under
her filthy black beard, lashing her tail as if she could fit
on us, with her uterine loops sounding
like bells under water the labyrinth of our already
organless dream—or is she another like us,
got up in trance, the soul of smallpox, or mange,
or the soul of our itch
to merge with a dug and forestall
the unfolding of this tight bud in which
raised rhino tail is pressed to little bird cheek
inside of which is my head my whole stiff body
a lance against which womb and colon are one mass,
thus kangaroo sac in which the fluid
I am giving off is the fluid I am taking in, my eyes
half-filled green windows, a rolling
sea in the brine emptiness of this Shaft
now rotating rhino to bird to man, as the heart
tinkers with forever in the chance of putting out
while drawing in an intestinal body hard as a diamond,
spirits hurling lances through my body asleep
at the bottom of this Shaft, remaking my body,
giving me the vixen power to insert stones into others,
freeing me from having only wind to pierce, woman to
pierce, bison to wear and that is why
I am talking to you this way, Shaft through death
in which I hurtle both ways, and in that friction
to generate narrative, to make the bison teach me how to dance
their slow swaying dance through which the shadows of
myself begin to emerge, I pin them to signs, to the paths
I am lost between, umbilical hoses, to make this substance,
this showing Emerge, monster to stop
the cascade of separating ends, yet weaving the separations,
splitting the very ends I am mourning never having
been born, to die in the belly of my mother

                                        barren

but for my foetal jungle.

                                        [1981–1987]

NOTES

1. Based on the discovery of Upper Paleolithic skeletons in the Abri du Cro-Magnon (the Cro-Magnon rock shelter), in 1868. Cro-Magnon = Big (or Great) Hole. We are thus Big Hole People, a thought for Western Man to ponder as the Gate of 2000 starts to become visble.

2. For Charles Olson's perceptive notes on the Upper Paleolithic, see *Olson* #10 (Storrs, Connecticut, 1978).

3. All of the quotations from Bataille are from *Lascaux or the Birth of Art* (New York, 1955), pp. 110–140.

4. Breuil himself does not discuss the discovery of the spears. André Leroi-Gourhan does, on p. 315 of *Treasures of Prehistoric Art* (New York, 1967).

5. See S. Giedion's *The Eternal Present: The Beginnings of Art* (New York, 1962), p. 508. Giedion writes: "When I first visited Lascaux in 1949, I asked a local photographer to take a picture of the bird man from the ground of the 'well,' shooting on a plane without tilting the camera or using any artificial expedients. The bird man stood upward in all his strength." While no other observer supports Giedion's contention, there is a photograph in Breuil's *Four Hundred Centuries of Cave Art,* (Paris, 1952), p. 148, shot from the top of the Shaft that represents the scene exactly as Giedion describes it.

6. Andreas Lommel, *The World of the Early Hunters* (London, 1967), p. 128; Weston LeBarre, *The Ghost Dance* (New York, 1972), pp. 417–419; John E. Pfeiffer, *The Creative Explosion* (New York, 1982), p. 31; William Irwin Thompson, *The Time Falling Bodies Take to Light* (New York, 1981), pp. 110–112.

7. In most descriptions of the bird-headed man and the bird on the stick, it is implied that the bird heads are similar, if not identical. According to the photographs I have inspected, they are not. The stick bird's beak is short and curves down, with the bird eye more or less centered in the head. The bird man's "beak" extends straight out from the top of his head, with the eye slightly attached to the stroke that forms the top of his head. It appears that the bottom part of the "beak," the neck, and a brief curve (indicating the beginning of his shoulder), are one stroke. Both "beaks" remain open (which suggests an affinity), and there appears to be an opening in the tail of the stick bird that oddly corresponds with its open beak.

8. An exception to this statement is Max Raphael's fifty-one-page essay which makes up most of his *Prehistoric Cave Paintings* (New York, 1946). At the beginning of his essay, Raphael writes: "It has been said that paleolithic artists were incapable of dominating surfaces or reproducing space: that they could not reproduce individual animals, not groups, and certainly not compositions. The exact opposite of all this is true: we find not only groups, but compositions that occupy the length of an entire cave wall or the surface of a ceiling; we find representations of space, historical paintings, and even the golden section! But we find no primitive art." Raphael's comments anticipate Leroi-Gourhan's research on decorative organization and the placement of particular animals in sixty-four caves (expounded in *Treasures of Prehistoric Art* [New York, 1967]). While Leroi-Gourhan's theories make more

sense to me today than they did a decade ago, there are two major problems in accepting them: 1) His research takes into consideration only about 33% of the French and Spanish sites with pertinent materials; and 2) his statistics for such caves as Les Combarelles and Les Trois Frères are simply inaccurate, simplifying the nearly unidentifiable plethora of forms, near-forms and lines that swarm certain surfaces in these caves. And I should add that my own experience of cave art is that it looks much different on paper than it looks in the caves themselves. On the page, animals can be isolated, or even compositions isolated, so that, given the frame of the photo and the page, something like a historical "painting" results. In the cave itself, there is no beginning or end, no corners, no frames, and the personality of the cave itself affects the way we experience Cro-Magnon's additions to surfaces that often, via their contours, appear to be initiating the art!

9. Leroi-Gourhan, p. 316.

10. Leroi-Gourhan, p. 173.

11. See Chapter III, The Composition of the Magic Battle at Altamira, in Raphael. Also, Part IV, The Space Conception of Prehistory, in Giedion.

12. Barbara G. Walker's *The Woman's Encyclopedia of Myths and Secrets* (New York, 1983) is a valuable source for the layered richness of feminine imagery, much of which has been erased or distorted by Christianity. In regard to the "female triangle," see her entries on "Triangle" and "Trinity" in the *Encyclopedia*.

13. See Chapter 4, The New Maiden and the Eland, in J. David Lewis-Williams' *Believing and Seeing: Symbolic meanings in southern San rock paintings*, (London, 1981).

14. Leroi-Gourhan, p. 64.

15. In earlier versions of this essay, I had used, as epigram, a passage from a letter written by Antonin Artaud to Henri Parisot, from the asylum at Rodez, on October 6, 1945. In elaborating what he calls "the harmonies of the generative tone" of certain poems by Baudelaire, Artaud envisions a "shaft" in which ensouling is involved with fecality and death that relates in an eerie way to the Shaft at Lascaux. Such "harmonies," Artaud writes, "are a shaft in which the uterine hunger of the soul mourns a love that has not been born, in which the fecality of the supernatural body of the soul writhes to death because it has not been born. This century no longer understands fecal poetry, the intestine malady of herself, Madam Death, who since the age of ages has been sounding her dead woman's column, her dead woman's anal column; in the excrement of an abolished survival, the corpse too of her abolished selves, and who for the crime of not having been able to exist, for never having been able to be a creature, had to fall, the better to sound the depths of her own being, into this abyss of foul matter and indeed so pleasantly foul in which the corpse of Madam death, madam fecal uterine, madam anus, hell upon hell of excrement, foments hunger, the fecal destiny of her soul, in the uterus of her own foyer. The soul, say the buried body of being, is that which, focal of the survival of life, falls, fecal as excrement, and is piled up in its excrement." Translation, to which I have made a few changes, is from *Antonin Artaud: Selected Writings*, Tr. by Helen Weaver (New York, 1976).

A Visit from Hart Crane

As I sat adoring Les Eyzies' limestone cliffs, Crane began to speak: "The shark that ate me was not a hammerhead but a self-savaging cruising the hunger-filled waters of North American soul. But you may imagine my light topcoat twisted around a shark, as if it were a Rodin Balzac, wearing my coat as a cloak, on a rise of the ocean floor deep below the *Orizaba* that 1932 noon. *There* is an image for our midwestern souls! To offer it, I had to abandon my work on Hermaphroditus, which involved keeping in constant circulation between 'male' and 'female' poles—the man as double of the woman, the woman as double of the man, a roller-rink my soul glided, never racing to win until it woke into poetry and faced those monsters that thrash our North American souls: the Covering Patriarch and the Cherub of Narcissism, the 'guardians' of that hole between desire and its fulfillment. The Cherub is an infantilization of the soul, helpless crying, abandoned in the grotto the Patriarch 'covers,' in mockery of the cobra spreading over meditating Guatama, his ally and root support from depths in which snake and person are daemonically entangled, where images are winding windows and I am loosed in that pattern Zinsser spoke of . . ."

His voice faded and I momentarily lost him in a geographical confusion: Did Zinsser offer his prophecy to Crane at the point in ocean later recrossed with Peggy Cowley? Somehow "loose yourself within a pattern's mastery or go on to undeserved doom" seemed the locus of Crane's leap, the noon after that day he tried to *lose* Peggy in Havana. They were to meet in a restaurant—Crane (according to Cowley) never showed up. Perhaps some part of him wanted to abandon her there and sail on without her—but she had made her way back on ship. What has this to do with his

174

suicide? For years I thought that after connecting with a woman, Crane discovered he could not *maintain* the connection—that he was doomed in spite of having been given "the independence of my mind and soul again, and perhaps a real wholeness to my body"—doomed again and again to drunkenly seek merger with himself in the figure of an alien man, that in spite of any woman the old pattern would reassert itself. That is why he leapt. In my dream last night, Crane was intact—though only two inches tall, reclining on a glass shelf in what appeared to be the Hart Crane Museum, a homunculus in the muse of my dream, homunculus and muse, a merger.

"No," he spoke again, "I could have continued my work for years, could have been thrashed until old age, lost my ears, even my organs, had not the 'connection,' as you call it, with Cowley, *polarized* my work into clearly male and female opposites. The specter of fulfillment, of gratification, is intolerable, do you know what I mean? Those of us who wind about the never-finished Hermaphroditic body cannot tolerate that sensation of birth that swings like massive vulvular bells through heterosexual intercourse. Its sensation, joyful and corrugated with dread, lifted my tower from a sunless workable gloom into a daylit presence and in that moment it snapped in two. It was my natal daemon, covered with the vermin of our midwestern compulsion to *realize* ourselves in heterosexual intercourse, that drove me before death's altar in that land where more than one gringo has gone *to exercise his skeleton,* that is, to wind it up and let it stroll off at its own speed. I went to the stern trying to understand why I said goodbye to her, or why all my life I had been saying goodbye to that hideous belltower whose breasts in a phallic retort were compacted in the face of things—in the human expression of a snake, in the serpentine look of a man. My man in Havana, my man in Hell, my white serpent father whose breasts I failed to draw forth. I stood by the rail and stared into the filth that had driven and sustained me. Suddenly everything stopped, the waves as well as the ship. I was out of time in the fortress of the Cherub. The ship was perched on one very tall rotten wave and, as if miles below, a dazzling light appeared, a spotlight searching me out as if this were my 'opening night,' as if to die is 'World Premiere.' And then the Cherub of Narcissism was at my ear: 'You're no further along your path than in the instant when you were conceived. You're merely my play, which I restage and recelebrate with limousines and furs.' And the Covering Patriarch hissed: 'It makes no difference if you carry on—we'll only think about you when you're gone.' I hurled myself into this dazzling core, to shatter its lantern mockery, its obsessional pointing out to the night that 'the real show' is bodies winding out those plush caves that psyche is, in fact, to be bled upon . . ."

He paused long enough for me to ask: Your Dionysus, with a Nazarene core, is a full company of bit parts as he flames and sparks at the stake. In what sense is his "target smile" "unmangled?"

"The 'I' must go unpruned and be allowed to elaborate its tendrils. Since I could not 'shoulder the curse of sundered parentage,' I sought a Hermaphroditic grafting. I refused my parents' nature in favor of a vision that included crucifixion *and* pagan multiplicity. Dionysus never *was* mangled—his being takes place in parts, or minute orders, 'divine particulars,' yet 'the bottom of the sea *is* cruel.' For the Protestant, always under curfew, the underworld is infested with criminal elements, thugs of Capone, Manson butt-raped as a child whose later martial hysteria wrote its 'helter-skelter' in living flesh. As a Protestant, I was always on that 'sundered' leash when I went down into the image hive but that was part of my vision too: to wander under Dionysus and to suffer Dionysus in the flesh. Because of this, I allowed my sense of the line to be governed by Tate and Winters. Only the voicings *rising in writing,* I know now, are not estrangements. Winters often visits me in this place. In death his soul has become mellow and most open. I see him wandering a nearby vale, chewing peyote, reading Artaud, his flesh neatly stacked on his skull . . ."

Again he paused, and I caught myself starting to ask: But Hart, how are you?, a question I realized would burden him with human relationship—for he was truly neither well nor ailing—but in my hesitation he vanished, a resonance in the hanging vines, the red geranium pots, the overarching mimosa whose lime- and pink-tipped blossoms swayed *as if*—an "as if" empty enough to enroot the following notion: As poets we are, forever, in Ariadne, divided—divvied up, re-quarried, her fodder, thus her dividend, her divided end, a double *and.* "Whispers antiphonal in azure swing," voicing reversing voicing, ocean reHearsing the casket that has "always" just tumbled out our mouths.

[July 20–21, 1985]
Hotel Centenaire, Les Eyzies

The Bowery of Dreams

AWOKE AT 4 A.M., SLEEPLESS, filled with a grainy rancor, the weight of
the previous day over me. I slit its belly and the unhappiness of my life
was upon me. Why was I misunderstood, mistreated, why were people
out to get me, and why did I even go on fused into Schwerner and Kelly
becoming "religious" in their forties, a shield for the absurdity and the
daily shit around us. Well, I will love this world, as it is, I thought, and
almost laughed out loud at that naive lurch for something here to hang
onto

suddenly I was on the Bowery of Dreams in a throng of human misery
worse than I'd ever seen. A dank almost black long street with abject
figures appearing and disappearing. There was a man in front of me,
limping and hopping along, in a pink coat too little for him, I was afraid
he would lurch into me, and I jumped ahead of him, seeing that his face
was made of vomit. A brown-skinned woman started to beckon me; I
knew she was a whore, and only wanted to seduce me and rip me off. I
said, I will go to your room with you, but I don't want to fuck you. I want
to see your room and for you to tell me about your life.

Then I began to kill snakes. There were lots of them and I was down at
the seashore. They would come swimming in, and I would struggle with
them, and overcome them. I would beat them into kegs, small hard wiry

---

"The Bowery of Dreams" appeared in *Fracture*.

kegs, about the size of a mule turd, but very, very hard. Then I'd take a hammer and smash the keg to bits.

I was in a de Chirico-like building, full of endless stairways slanting across each other, a kind of roller coaster of multiple stairways. On the landing of one, a punk theater was in session. I wasn't interested so turned to go, but bumped into some maggoty punk creature who yelled *I* had bumped into *him*. NO NO I yelled, I just want to get out of here! Then others began to jostle me, and I fought back well until a guy with a torso the size of a VW Beetle slammed into me and sent me reeling down an amazingly long staircase. When I got up, there was an intense auburn moon blazing in the sky which immediately turned into the face of Nat "King" Cole who was furiously mumbling something about his daughter and having brought her here. I threw a long hook out at him which caught in his cheek and pulled it out as if it were tough wood but I could not dislodge it and he piled out of the sky on me, now down in a series of offices, where I knew the jig was up. Cole stood there, holding a gun at my head and I knew I only had several seconds to live

so I shouted at the top of my voice Please Caryl remember me, Please let my poetry live, let my poetry live, over and over until I realized the gun was there but held by no one, and that I was free from no one, then I said to myself "I laughed myself asleep and woke up crying" (as if that explained life) "or did I cry myself asleep and awake laughing?"

I went out then onto a porch by myself. There was a river of snakes flowing around me, sort of lapping and snapping, but I was not afraid of them, and sat there, head in hands, brooding until I realized that Caryl and I were going out with Jerry McGann and his wife to a barbershop for dinner, and entered through the backdoor, into the cleanup area where something was pushing green and purple lettuce through a fissure in the wall. There were plates of stuff sitting around, strange luminous liquids, seaweed like things, but it was not yet time to eat, so we were led into the room where you ate and they cut hair, and sat in a little line by the wall, waiting. JM began to wrestle with me, very playfully, and Caryl finally made us stop. I saw that we had no wine, so I suggested JM and Caryl go across the street for some. They did and I tried to walk around but had on immense showshoes and couldn't move. JM returned alone and said, there is something in the cellar you should see, so I went down into a large cement-floored room, where there was a tub with what looked like a prehistoric frog, all black, putting around, with a white toucan perched, or fitted, on its head. I knew that I was in the Golubs' basement. The frog was quite happy, and said lots of things to me that I did not understand. Then he told me that he became dry when he went through the Golubs' keyhole. I knew then that he had to burrow through all their walls, in one black rod-like motion to reach them. So I went upstairs to visit Leon and Nancy while the frog, which looked to weigh 100 pounds, burrowed through the walls. He was already up there when I arrived, in a gray bathrobe with a cloth over his head. I went back to the basement which was now a street where I met Caryl and told her what happened. She said, we need an umbrella, so I bought a big one, and left it hanging from a pet store awning. I went back to get Caryl, and when we next saw the opened umbrella it was flexing up and down, as if it could not wait to go with us. We looked into the pet store window where a group of raccoons in smoking jackets were begging us to take them home.

I awoke to the feeling that life *was* benign, and that animals and all creatures had lives that human beings had forever not noticed, and that if we only knew how to participate in these very special, marvelous lives, we would not be destroying the earth . . .

[1982]

THE
STEVENS-ARTAUD
RAINBOW

[*from*] An Interview
with Gyula Kodolanyi

CLAYTON ESHLEMAN: Psyche loves to play tricks with our intentions. We invite Psyche, and if she decides to come to our little party, she may come in disguise or in a much different way than we would prefer. A poet sits down to write a poem to his beloved, and immediately is "given" a boot filled with brains. Thus, he is in a situation of potential division and doubt, of being divided from his original intentions, a state Blake referred to as "self-contradiction." One way in which the twentieth century seems so different from the nineteenth is that plans and intentions have become less useful to image-making than what is "thrown up" in the creative process, which can involve a dance or even a duel with the material that Psyche or "subliminal scanning" (the painter Francis Bacon's term) is providing.

What is offered is often so different than what is anticipated, that an artist lacking confidence in the creative process itself will either be stopped completely if at some point the plan does not work out, or will insist on following out a plan that he suddenly has no heart or mind for. But there are exceptions. Artaud, in correspondence with Jacques Rivière, in 1923, had the courage to try to deal directly with this dilemma: that he could not say his mind, that when he would try to say what was on his mind it slipped away before he could contain it in words. Artaud is truer

---

This interview is from a much rewritten transcript of a tape made in Los Angeles with the Hungarian poet and translator Gyula Kodolanyi, in spring, 1985. Portions of it have appeared in *Poetry Flash* (San Francisco, February, 1986), *B-City* (Chicago, 1987), and in Hungarian in *Uj Iras* magazine (Budapest). The entire final version appeared in *Talus* #1 (London, spring, 1987).

to his unique situation at that moment than he is in the poems he is writing. The older Artaud goes with what Psyche offers and makes no distinctions between inner and outer worlds—he goes into the pit of his mind and treats "mental things" as real in a way that the younger Artaud could not have accepted.

GYULA KODOLANYI: Could you describe the goals of Reichian therapy for those who are not familiar with it?

ESHLEMAN: My primary activity was lying on my back, naked, breathing, knees raised, while in conversation with Dr. Sidney Handelman, the therapist. My project was constantly to maintain eye-contact, to breathe deeply and, at the same time, to be in touch as speaker or listener. That particular set of activities was very difficult at first, and the stress involved often hurled me into emotional corners in which background memories, or senses of myself, would come raging or weeping forth. My physical energy became more equally distributed and accessible as the therapy continued.

As you may know, the goal of orthodox Reichian therapy is to enable an "orgasmic reflex" to take place, so that there is a thorough discharge of pent-up frustration, and often a brief blacking-out in the orgasmic moment of intercourse. Handelman was able to determine, he told me, to what extent this "reflex" was being freed by the way my pelvic area moved as I breathed, letting my raised knees open and close, while talking in therapy. At one point I blacked out in a rage. Near the end of the therapy I had a seizure on the New York City subway and crawled home. But I stuck with it, finishing the therapy in about two years, and it has had a basically positive effect on my life ever since. The only thing that I sense was passed over—because of the concentration on physical release—was material of an Oedipal nature.

KODOLANYI: When you speak of orgasm, does this mean only a sexual orgasm, or a more generalized form, a sudden outburst of energy?

ESHLEMAN: I think it is important to respect Reich's term. The "orgastic reflex" relates primarily to the genital area and to a certain peristaltic suppleness that occurs at the point of climax. There is a considerable difference, in my experience, between ejaculation and orgasm. However, your intuition is correct in that the ability to discharge that energy enables a flow of energy to take place during the day in one's relationships with others—but, paradoxically, it does not make life simpler. It makes life more rich and complex, and more complicated at times, because by acting more spontaneously, by letting things move right through, one tends to be quicker in all emotional responses—in anger as well as in enthusiasm, and of course such responses are often taking place in the company of others who are not functioning on the same level.

KODOLANYI: What has the therapy done to your poetry?

ESHLEMAN: The most precious thing in regard to poetry that I have been able to organize out of my Reichian "initiation" is that, to borrow part of a line from Hart Crane, there is an "antiphonal swing" between the orgasmic act and imaginative stimulation. One seems to nourish the other. There is a Hindu word, "maithuna," which I understand as referring to the relaxed but vital fantasy, occasionally hallucinations, that takes place in the half hour or hour after orgasm. Especially, curiously and beautifully, if one continues to lie in one's lover's arms. Orgasm (not ejaculation) seems to release and stimulate what we think of as fantasy or a vivid daydreaming in which, in my own case, I can focus on a subject, or idea, and watch it transform into image after image. All this is in contrast to the probably Christian-inspired sense that men (women are not even considered!) lose something vital in intercourse. There has been an ongoing war for centuries between the custodians of the spirit and the sons and daughters of sexual, soulful, energy. The fear on the part of men of losing their strength and of a subsequent need to elevate and contain their seed, either by abstinence or yoga, is worldwide. Ancient Chinese sages with bulging gigantic foreheads are to be thought of as mentally semen-pregnant, I guess—and that in a society which practiced female foot-binding for more than a thousand years!

KOLODANYI: Could you say more about this "antiphonal swing?"

ESHLEMAN: Among other things, it suggests the alchemical image of the "double pelican," which can be read as the unconscious of one person feeding the consciousness of the other, and vice-versa, so the "swing," as I understand it, involves reciprocity—equal exchange between partners, as well as an interior exchange on the part of an individual between his sexual and creative gratification.

Reich has been criticized for his heterosexual male-oriented genital emphasis, and what appears to be a simplistic equation between orgasmic functionality and a self-regulatory character makeup. I see the situation this way: Reich attempted to excavate several extremely messy middens in the human body and soul, and because of the pressure under which he worked—he was hounded by every society he tried to live in, was ultimately imprisoned in America, an imprisonment that led to his premature death—he left his "work area" in a shambles. But what would you expect? If you were trying to think while someone was shooting at you, do you really believe you could keep rational, or keep the attack pigeon-holed so as to not infect the hull of your thought?

I am not convinced that Reich was fundamentally wrong, and if Reichian therapy had not been nearly ruined by the American FDA investigation and smearing of Reich, his followers might have been able to critique and to build upon his work, as people like James Hillman have critiqued and built on Jung. Unlike Jung, Reich was very socially oriented—he was much more concerned with how to help poor ignorant women stop masturbating with knives than to instruct an elite on "individuation." He had few imaginative theories, and for these reasons, as well as for his sexual aggressivity, he has received less attention from the creative-minded than Jung. And while Jung offers a psychic goldmine, it is one with strings attached.

At the time I sought help in the fall of 1967, in New York City, Freudian analysis had a reputation for ending up in years of talking. Talk, talk, talk, with no fundamental revelations or shifts. My friend the poet Paul Blackburn was in psychoanalysis for many years, and it seemed to have had little effect on his life or art. One day I asked him what he did there. "We talk," he said sadly. I wanted to shout, but did not, "Why don't you talk with ME?" It seemed to me that Freudian analysis tried to come to terms with the present in a completely mental and "family romance" oriented way.

I feel that Reichian therapy, because it sets up a dynamic exchange among emotion, fantasy and physical sensation, and thereby how one lives *through* one's body, is capable of releasing one on a poemic level to be able to imagine and personify the lower body. It can enable one to have an easier relationship with one's entire body, which I feel includes the intermingling of different realms—the coexistence of beautiful, bizarre and repulsive elements—on an imaginative plane.

KODOLANYI: I personally feel that you have a great deal in common with medieval imagination, with the macabre and the hilarious. I know that you love Rabelais. Why is he a contemporary?

ESHLEMAN: I got to a perspective on Rabelais through Mikhail Bakhtin's book, *Rabelais and his World*. Bakhtin explains in his Introduction that what he really wanted to do was to write a history of laughter! He then envisions a form of the grotesque which he calls "grotesque realism." He sees this as generated by medieval folklore, ritual and carnival exuberance, and nominates as its greatest creator-spokesman, Rabelais. What most people think of as the "grotesque" in art is for Bakhtin a degeneration, a Renaissance and subsequently Romantic reaction against Classicism, an attempt to show its underbelly. Bakhtin sees the "grotesque realism" as having its roots in a vision of life in which the body of the individual is not viewed as complete, or finished, but as an aspect or member of a great world body in which the very things that priests and the clergy have found despicable and have satanized are the connective orifices and protruberances that enabled medieval people to participate in a degradational *and* regenerational sense of the world. The key here is laughter, not satire or Baudelaire's "Satanic laughter," but laughter as a renewing force, a lack of fear, an assertion of freedom. Bakhtin's vision of the grotesque has helped me read ice-age imagery, and understand how the hybrid animal/human images engraved on cave walls in 12,000 BC represent an Upper Paleolithic grotesque, or possibly a *grotesque archetype*.

KODOLANYI: Is there any major form of carnivalesque spirit in present-day society? In the Middle Ages and the early Renaissance, you had "high church" religious art—and you had Rabelais. Do we have a similar situation today?

ESHLEMAN: The tension in art between the Classical and the Romantic, between Apollo and Dionysus, tradition and the avant-garde, seems almost eternal. Perhaps it is in its own way a manifestation of a "grotesque archetype," with Dionysus pulling us back toward the animal, and Apollo pushing us toward a world in which there are no animals at all—only people!

Hard to say, when you are embroiled in your own times, just who the Rabelasian figures would be. I have felt that Artaud represents the activated skeleton of Rabelais; and certainly the spirit of a wide-ranging sense of the grotesque is in Joyce, Celine, Miller, Vladimir Holan, early Dali—many of us could make up our own lists in this regard. The spirit is less present in North America than it is in Europe and Latin America, but among my contemporaries I find genuine aspects of it in the poetry of Robert Duncan, Allen Ginsberg and Jerome Rothenberg. A New Guinea head-hunter jumping around with a Wheaties box as head-dress evokes it, as does the Mardi Gras, in spite of its stilted, commercial limitation—and in this sense, Santa Claus and the Easter Bunny are grotesques, as are Donald Duck, Sweet Pea, Alley Oop, Smokey Stover and the horde of comic-strip wraithes that adults plant in children's minds to scamper through their fantasies. You might find more of it in societies that are still kinetically haunted by the weight of Catholic liturgy and ritual, in which there is an obsessive need to transgress at particular times, and to really cut loose and transgress there must be powerful and exciting prohibitions. One of the sad, hapless things about North American life is that there is no imaginative core—no psychic underworld—that enables people to express their fantasies in an astounding, carnivalesque way.

KODOLANYI: I have grown up as a poet by reading and translating American poets. I have been given a great deal by them, and I think they have helped me to break down certain conventions and traditions from which I wanted to free myself ever since I began to write. They have helped me to become more concrete, and less inhibited. Yet I have never been able to reconstruct for myself the network or medium in which the American poet works. For example, I am aware that what you are doing, this personal quest in your poetry, is something that you first have to do for your own sake. This is your own personal quest. On the other hand, a poet is dependent upon an audience. Perhaps I am talking about the obvious, and you don't want to talk about this—it's too obvious. I'm just kind of lamenting, I'm lamenting the fact that, well, you don't really have the kind of audience, as numbers go, that should be there.

ESHLEMAN: I hear you. But there are many facets to this problem. The lack of audience can be viewed, to a certain extent, as a freedom. If one has an audience, one has an obligation, one is responsible for one's performance to a consensus of expectation on the part of those people "out there." One of the few virtues of the absence of an audience is the autonomy to investigate and do what you want to do. I have never consciously cooperated with anyone else's sense of what is appropriate or not appropriate, right or wrong, clever to do or not clever to do, in poetry. Consciously, I have only competed with my own death. Two comments that I happened to read early in my career helped me to make this decision. Blake: "Forget consequences and write." Aimé Césaire: "Put up with me! I won't put up with you." On one level, to date, I have paid through the nose for this decision. On another level, I have come close to doing what I wanted to do, and I am proud of what I have done. If at some point in the 1960s or 1970s I had placed the desire to have an audience over my own desire to explore what I have, to be perfectly frank I think I would now have a tenured sinecure in some university and a compromised body of poetry.

But I should add: I dislike art for art's sake. I work very hard to write what I write as clearly as I can, and I want to communicate—but on my terms. Caryl and I go over everything that I write which looks as if it may be worth publishing, and we do everything we can to narrow the discrepancy between what it looks as if I am saying and what I intend to say.

The psychologist James Hillman told me that when he goes to the Eranos Conference in Switzerland each year to deliver what will be his most important piece of writing for the year, he is really speaking to the chairs, not to the audience. I thought about this for a while, and decided that I agreed with his strategy—to try to address the great dead and invite the living to overhear what is being said. In a poem called "Deeds Done and Suffered by Light," I came up with my own metaphor in this regard: "forget the orchestra / conduct the pit! / Hanged / Ariadne / giving birth in Hades / is the rich, black music in mother's tit."

KODOLANYI: This also means that you can accept a sort of anonymity. In other words, you share Jànos Pilinszky's thoughts when he wrote at the end of his life that he felt that art is going toward a kind of anonymity in the sense that the person, the artist as ego, is becoming less important. If this is true, it is a real service, because the personal hubris is being shed.

ESHLEMAN: Hmm . . .

KODOLANYI: This is what you really mean in some sense.

ESHLEMAN: I don't think what you've just said is directly related to what I was saying.

KODOLANYI: We do not know the names of the artists who carved the medieval cathedrals, though obviously they too, each of them, were very individualized personalities.

ESHLEMAN: You are right in the sense that it is the impersonal art that seems to survive—but wait, your example is cathedrals, religious art—not Rabelais! Or Blake! It strikes me that we have many kinds of survivals, the art of collective effort—pyramids, Tikal—in contrast to an art that is based on an individual's experience, an individual who does not feel that he is going to be redeemed or saved by a force in the cosmos, by a beyond, by a plane that will organize his efforts into its own significance.

On the other hand, I have to listen to your words as an American, I have to hear them partially as your constant amazement that art even exists at all in America! I live in a society that is obsessed with the other on an extremely superficial level. When Sammy Davis, Jr. croons, "I want to be me," he is talking about "me"-ness in a way that has little to do with a genuine sense of ego, let alone self.

KODOLANYI: That would seem to bring us to an interesting question, because Pound, I think, was right when he said that the poetry of significance must reconquer the epic mode. In other words, you have to write a modern epic, and for that you obviously need a self. For lyric poetry, you only need an ego. Pound failed to create a poetic self who is allowed to suffer, to fall, to win and maybe to fall again. This is the problem of the *Cantos* despite many great passages. There is a hubris in Pound—his poetic ego is not allowed, as the heroes of myths are, to suffer and maybe to fall.

ESHLEMAN: Pound never embraced his specter.

KODOLANYI: Never. There is a hubris in Pound's poetic self which excludes compassion and sympathy. I think this must have been one of the recognitions which led you in writing the books of your quest, for your poetic self is allowed to undergo whatever has to be undergone. There is a catharsis, we can feel a compassion. We can feel a sympathy and there is a catharsis.

I'm really talking about two things here. I am partly talking about working on yourself as a person and I am also talking about the importance of having a poetic self which is connected to this personality—which is capable of creating poems that have a meaningful humanity.

ESHLEMAN: In Pound's time I don't think the sense of quest you have generously attributed to my life and work was a priority in poetry. I could be wrong, but I'm under the impression that being an artist then did not set up a challenge to one's background as thematic material to be dealt with directly—background as something to be gone through, worked through as one might bore through a wall, rather than transcending it. For Pound and most of his peers, the strategy was to pole-vault out of America as quickly as possible and end up in European sensibility. Pound never got it through his head, other than in belated quiescent remorse, that he should have stuck his nose back into the nests of prejudice, racism, anti-semitism, sexual repugnance—all those bits that are *ground into* the growing-up adolescent American. By the time Pound was a formed personality, these matters were iron girders in him. He was never able to come to terms with them, not even after the photographs of Dachau; he was still yelling about "kikes" after all the information on the Holocaust was out. I find this unforgivable. It is understandable to me how Pound as a young man would have carried anti-semitic attitudes and jokes around with him, in pretty much the same way that I, possibly you, too, unconsciously spurted dirty jokes. But at a certain point, as an aspect of manhood, you must come to terms with what you are in your mind, and it is overwhelming to me that Pound could not understand something as simple as that we are all god's children, facing the aftermath of Nazism.

I was fortunate in that I came to poetry at a point when a writer like César Vallejo was able to get through to me. The most important things he faced me with were contradictions, contradictions to be looked at. The point at which I determined the contradictions were more valuable than the continuities, let alone the formulas, and it would be a mistake in my case to attempt to transcend or repress my Indiana background, I made a commitment that went like this: I must look back into Indiana and try to go through in poetry what it was to be from Indiana so that I could harrow, or hollow out, that hell. I was convinced that if I did not do so, I would be permanently injured, less than a man, incapable of full manhood, and forever haunted by various paralyzing background attitudes that would continue to manifest themselves and undermine my projects.

KODOLANYI: This is very interesting, because my next question would have been, what did Japan mean to you? You now live in California. Is the ocean there in your poetry? Or the desert? Is Japan there, or is the poetry actually coming from Indiana? Does the poetry always come from Indiana because you see Indiana as the central problem of your poetry, not just personally but communally? Is your mission always to investigate this matter? When you go to another place, do you come to more recognitions about Indiana?

ESHLEMAN: Even though I have spent years exploring the tunnels and cul-de-sacs of my midwestern background, it is still a presence, and probably a goad to write. To a certain extent, I believe that every artist's background is in endless dress rehearsal, and I find, in my own case, that my mother and father continue to appear in dreams and fantasies, but in fascinating disguises and roles, as if they were constantly undergoing sea-change. I find this to be an imaginative grace—not a problem—as my sense of them as an infant did not frame them with mortality, and thus the infantile part of my mind does not know that they are mortal, in a pure sense at times, that they are even dead. And I would not attempt to destroy this "dreaming infant" because he is the force that sees in fleeting moments the stalagmythic instants.

My poetry tends to move forward slowly with large blocks of attention, rather than being subject-oriented responses to daily experiences. Symbols come forth and are adjusted relative to interior shifts as well as translation and research activities. For example, recently I realized that the hallway closet in my childhood home had become the cellar room in the Phi Delta Theta fraternity where with fellow "pledges" I had allowed myself to be humiliated and tortured during "Hell Week" in 1954. Something about me died there, and my soul wandered in limbo until the early 1960s when, in my continuing fantasy of the closet-cave, Vallejo pushed away a boulder that was covering the entrance, and made it possible for me to emerge. There is, I am aware, a certain Christian shape to this fantasy as well; like many other little Protestant boys I identified with Jesus and his fate/rebirth.

However, this symbol continues to remain in formation, for at the point that I could have emerged, I did not and instead went back further into it, taking the daylight/emergence possibility as the sign that the cave was not just a closet-cell but had a vast system of tunnels going further and further back. By 1974, I had begun to see" in this darkness aspects of the Upper Paleolithic cave world, where the personal hallway closet, and the fake Phi Delt underworld, were turned inside out; they became my view of the impersonal, the immense continuum of mankind's first imaginative use of a rock wall in moss-lamp-lit dark.

What I am tracing here has not been a conscious program, and along the way I have certainly been influenced by the cave in literature, in particular Blake's painting known as "The Arlington Court Regeneration," which appears to be Blake's "illustration" of the passage in the thirteenth book of the *Odyssey* describing the magical grotto on the shore of Ithaka. As I hope this example illustrates, I have tried to keep my childhood material active and allow it to graft onto transpersonal, mythological images when there seemed to be a mysterious necessity or appropriateness involved. So on one level, yes, the poetry always comes from Indiana, but with the transformational qualifications and extensions that I have tried to suggest here.

The most important physical move that I made was from Bloomington, Indiana, to Japan, where I lived from 1961 to 1964. I took a job teaching composition and literature to military personnel for one year, and then moved to Kyoto where, over the next two years, I read Blake, translated Vallejo, and began to chip away at the Indiana edifice. The alternative to Japan would have been New York City, and I am very glad that I made the decision that I did. I was not ready at that time to be an "artist," and part of an "artistic scene." When you are brought up as a hick in America and discover art, there is a strong impulsive lure to give more emphasis to being an artist or poet than to painting or writing poetry.

KODOLANYI: You *did* stay on in Japan—for three years. And being a sensitive and open person it must have done things to you.

ESHLEMAN: Kyoto gave me a respect for things, for common objects

made of wood or stone that were a pleasure to hold and to behold. My
first wife and I rented apartments in two traditional Japanese houses,
lived on tatami, shopped in the neighborhood, and had a chance to experience some elements of traditional Japanese culture that by now have
nearly vanished. The Japanese years were on one hand soothing, I would
even say rehabilitating, by our living close to nature in an almost nineteenth-century urban way. On the other hand, the strangeness and isolation created by cultural differences brought me to points of loneliness that
I have never experienced before or after—I learned to be by myself for
long stretches of time, and do my work with no real support system. This
combination of solace and conflict helped ground me, and by the time we
returned to America, in the summer of 1964, I was equipped, and strong
enough on my own, to have a chance at sustaining a life as a serious poet
in America.

KODOLANYI: Your interest in Vallejo and Artaud is interesting to me. We
remember that about fifteen years ago Robert Bly was complaining that as
a result of the dominant logos of Pound, his incredible influence over
American poetry for forty years, several qualities were missing from
American poetry, especially that of surrealism. Now, as I see it, it was
not Bly, but you and some other poets of your generation who brought
this thing back into American poetry.

ESHLEMAN: There has been, from around 1912, an ongoing experimental
tradition in American poetry which was nearly buried in the 1930s and the
1940s by an academic conventionalism more or less "directed" by T. S.
Eliot's poetics and what his followers made of them. After the Second
World War, an experimental vitality revived in all the arts. Pound's
influence does not seem to me to be as monolithic as Bly's comments
imply, and the fact that Pound himself, as well as Williams and Eliot, had
no interest in surrealism does not seem to be *the* factor that kept it from
being assimilated into mainstream American literature. When you say
that several poets in my generation brought it "back" into American
poetry, this is not really true, for surrealism per se has never been a force
in our poetry. While certain poets, such as Zukofsky, Rexroth, Loy, Stein
and Riding, were highly experimental at least in one stage of their careers, none of their work shows much interest in surrealism. In the case of

my own generation, Robert Kelly, David Antin, Jerome Rothenberg and myself were reading with great interest both French and Latin American surrealists in the late 1950s, and I think that all of us, in differing ways, have assimilated qualities associated with surrealism.

KODOLANYI: I was thinking of that part of the psyche that would express itself in a surrealistic mode which was banned at the time from poetry. If you learned to write from Pound, you were not able to let improvisations, and dream imagery, into poetry. I am thinking of Williams, how after he wrote *Kora In Hell* he became a far more tame poet. In that spectacular book, Williams seemed to be in touch with something he never later followed up on.

ESHLEMAN: There has been a marginal orthodox Surrealism here, but since it is so imitative of the French model, it has had little effect on American poetry at large. I imagine, though, that if one took into consideration certain minor figures—like Harry Crosby—and the writing in the American Surrealist-oriented magazines of the 1940s, when Breton was here and actively stimulating European and American exchange, you could find a thread which has continued all the way up to the present. For me, much of the surrealist activity throughout twentieth-century world art has been an attempt to reconnect with what seems to be a larger alternative tradition, that of the grotesque, or "grotesque realism." The most powerful writers to have made use of surrealism, such as Neruda and Vallejo in Spanish, and Artaud, Césaire and Michaux in French, have done so outside of its theories and group regulations, much in reaction to the rigidity inherent in so much of Breton's activities.

I feel that unless you do tie surrealist preoccupations into the historical and prehistorical range of the grotesque, it is generally reactive, an act of contempt, a refusal to participate in what seems to be the current mainstream tendencies. Now of course most of the tendencies are conventional, and especially in American poetry they often represent ego-psychology, a kind of Protestantized arbitrary "imagism," relentlessly dull description—unconscious PR for our materialistic abundance, our muscular gringo eagle with its claws in the backs of our own poor and foreign poor. But just to refuse that does not leave you anywhere! To appropriate bizarre images from the Euro-surreal stockpile can be just as superficial as poems about one's loss of innocence or one's sensitivity. When the white American poet turns away from both of these unsatisfactory tendencies, and looks at the earth he is standing on, he finds an "underworld" that is either the domain of Amerindian peoples, or clogged with the corpse of Capone, a gangster realm in contrast to a fissure into the timeless continuity of the abyss where an Odysseus goes to learn from the dead.

KODOLANYI: So where can the American poet today find those risks and challenges which alone can make poetry important? I am thinking of your statement about resistance in your essay about translating poetry. You were writing there about how you have to seek out the resistance—but resistance is not always easy to find.

ESHLEMAN: I think that each artist must find resistance in his own heart, mind and environment, and find a way to lead himself to figures who are capable of providing imaginative resistance to his own "given" background. The goal is the transformation of both the societal resistance to art and the antagonism of the given life to the creative life, into a resistance in the language itself, a resistance to being seen through, and by that I mean an achieved density and weight so that the reader is provided with a text which stops him rather than merely passes him through words back to the world and life out of which the experience put into the poem came. Autobiographical emphasis in our time has turned much American poetry into a conduit for getting to know the poet himself. This is an understandable consequence of the break-up of classical, New Criticism-inspired writing, but it mainly attests to the underdeveloped psychological being that was under the classical shell. Ego as worm wrapped in classical armor. What happens when this armor falls? I think the answer is John Berryman.

My counter-proposal is that the personal life is not to be abandoned but to be seen as merely a factor in the materials available to imagination. There are points in a poet's life when previously unresolved masses of personal experience enter an imaginative construct, or become images to be worked with. I do not feel they need to be rendered symbolically, or allegorically, or to be atomized so as to force the reader into unending gaps. But I also do not think the personal should be the unscrutinized basis for a poetics. This position, then, would represent a facet of my own resistance in trying to keep my writing from settling (since the early 1970s) on any dominating base.

KODOLANYI: Could you say something about James Hillman, and where he goes beyond Jung—and could you speak about Jung too? I find that Jung is very fascinating for an artist. He is more eclectic than Freud is, and his central idea is not sublimation but individuation. In other words, that one is not substituting something for something, but developing aspects of one's personality which can be followed through—that your life can be a success in some sense.

ESHLEMAN: Hillman seems to me to have assimilated Jung and Freud, and to have attempted to turn psychology away from conceptualization and toward imagination. While he endorses Jung's early attempt to personify the potentially psychotic voices that he heard as "little people," to allow himself to be peopled by his fantasies rather than to reduce or repress them, Hillman has worked to deconstruct the cathedral-like aspects of Jung. Or to put it another way, Hillman has turned his attention away from spirit (and the cast of Protestant values it implies) and attempted to restore the word "soul," that word of words which has almost been sentimentalized out of any genuine meaning by our spirit-dominated culture. Soul, for Hillman, is to be found in the lowlands (in depression) in contrast to the peaks (being on top of it, "peak performance," not losing control), and is an ally of the feminine and the Dionysian. Hillman is pagan in as much as he is polytheistic, and from that viewpoint he has very interesting things to say about materialism, oppositionalism and the underworld. His book *The Dream and the Underworld* was the most thought-provoking text that I found in attempting to gain a perspective on Upper Paleolithic cave art (even though cave art is not even mentioned in that book). He is a poet's psychologist, or I could say, a psychologist who is read and respected by mythology-sensitive poets, such as Robert Duncan and Robert Kelly. I have no active experience with his therapy, so I cannot speak about that, although he does discuss it in a dialogue that the two of us are now writing out as a little book on poetry and psychology. From what I can glimpse, I think that the goal of therapy with Hillman would be to actively and creatively engage, and work with, fantasies, to be in flow with the soul—not necessarily to become a poet or a painter, in a professional sense, but to inhabit an image realm that would be very compatible to that of artists and poets. What Hillman appears to propose as therapeutic activity would be very valuable to offer students, as part of their life training, especially those who are studying the arts. As is, American universities do not teach image or soul—they teach history, technique and appraisal.

[1985]

Response to Mary Kinzie

IT IS HARD TO BELIEVE that Ms. Kinzie is not aware that contemporary poetry includes a number of North American, Latin American and European poets who, over the past fifty years and continuing into the present, have realized in their writing values that she herself espouses yet claims are absent: complex ideas, the real content of inner life, coherence and freshness of perception. The most disturbing aspect of her essay is therefore a willful exclusion and a presentation of insignificant contemporary poems as representative of the state of the art. She seems to believe that it is more important to shake her finger at Linda Gregerson and Catherine Rutan than to engage, for example, Robert Duncan and Jerome Rothenberg. In this way she sentences herself to a present about one millimeter thick, detached not only from the writing of poets now in their sixties and seventies, but from the great and nearby dead whose work, done in the 1930s and 1940s, is part of a living heritage.

She writes: "Not only have we eliminated from the available repertory of literary responses those forms associated with the eighteenth century, formal satire, familiar epistle, georgic, and pastoral, but also those associated with the Middle Ages and Renaissance, allegory, philosophi-

---

This response to Kinzie's "The Rhapsodic Fallacy" (*Salmagundi*, fall, 1984) appeared in *Sulfur* #13, spring 1985. Readers unfamiliar with Kinzie's responses to contemporary poetry can look up her "poetry chronicles" (in which 5 to 10 books are reviewed at the same time) in *American Poetry Review*. It seems clear enough, from the number of books she has written about over the past few years, that she is an omnivorous reader, and aware of the work of poets excluded from consideration in her essay, whose works, had they been included, would have ruined her argument.

199

cal poem, epic, and verse drama and tragedy, until nothing is left for us now but a kind of low lyrical shrub whose roots are quick-forming, but shallow."

If she is lamenting that there are no entertaining stock imitations of these forms, I would respond, so what? What counts is that in variational and improvisational ways, Kenneth Rexroth, Basil Bunting and Robert Kelly have worked the georgic and the pastoral; Antonin Artaud has set satire, erudition and poetry into the familiar epistle; Aimé Césaire has written verse drama; a range of poets including Hugh MacDiarmid, Robert Duncan and Gary Snyder have written long, philosophical poems. As for the epic: what it might meaningfully be has constantly been under scrutiny throughout the century in a number of diverse and original "long poem" forays (Louis Zukofsky's *A* has so many facets that it probably recognizes most of the forms Kinzie mentions).

Kinzie also excludes new forms that have occurred in the breaking up of old forms, especially this century, e.g., the middle-length poem (not a lyric but not an epic, Césaire's *Notebook of A Return to the Native Land* and Vladimir Holan's *A Night With Hamlet* being superb examples, not to mention Rexroth's work in this potential form), and the various revisionings of what a short or a long poem can be (e.g., Cid Corman's very short poems evolving out of his work on Bashō, or Theodore Enslin's extremely long poems that read like marginalia to an otherwise unstated life). Charles Olson was the first, to my knowledge, to reinspect the word "rhapsody" and notice that in Greek it was *rhapsoidia,* "songs stitched together," the technique of epic poetry. It happens that since Whitman's 1855 version of "Song of Myself," the most unique and explored twentieth-century form, the serial poem, is the child of Rhapsodia. The Rhapsodic is far from being a "Fallacy" in twentieth-century world poetry; relative to its roots and older meanings, it is our presiding archetypal pattern!

Kinzie ignores all the poets I have mentioned because her obsession with the past is anchored in hierarchy (high style, versus low style), propriety, literary decorum and order, and in pedagogically *a priori* assumptions about "the truth." Is it possible that she does not realize that we cannot anymore have complex ideas *and* hierarchy, or a coherent inner life *and* literary decorum? She is primarily a rather prissy upholder of outmoded style and taste. Her criticism of an insignificant Ashbery poem is very offensive, for *she* is offended by what she calls Ashbery's "obsessive promiscuity of styles," and after stating that his writing is not only "radioactive," but "dangerously sterile," she concludes that Ashbery is "the passive bard of a period in which the insipid has turned into the heavily toxic." Lurking in such gibberish must be anti-homosexuality, and the fear the self-righteous have at the sight of the high mixing with the low, in short, the intermingling of stratifications and alienations that have to a great extent led the world to its present peril.

It *is* a moral issue, as Kinzie implies, but it is not the one she thinks it is. No alternative model to "The Rhapsodic Fallacy" is needed, simply because the rhapsodic, as technique and sublimation, is not a fallacy. The moral question might be put this way: When will critics like Kinzie, Harold Bloom and Helen Vendler start writing on poetry that knows more than they do? For more than fifty years a new perspective has been assembling. Unfortunately, especially for the young, the poetry of César Vallejo, Aimé Césaire, Charles Olson, Antonin Artaud, Octavio Paz, Robert Duncan, Paul Celan and Vladimir Holan has not been, as it were, cross-indexed, so as to provide the superimposed configuration that it represents. The difficulty in doing so is not, as Kinzie says, because "the steppe is arid and covered with monotonous vegetation," but because twentieth-century world poetry is a rain forest as well as a new wilderness. It takes root, as Césaire has written, in the red flesh of the soil (soil that is at once iron-rich, blood-soaked and haunted by the corpses of "redskins"), but it also takes root in the eyes of Lorca confronting Borges in New York City in the late 1920s with the startling information that the most important figure in North American culture was Mickey Mouse.

I am speaking of a poetry that attempts to be responsible for all an individual writer knows about himself and about his world. It is that simple and that awesome. It is a poetry of wrath rather than instruction, ambivalent about all the major movements of and right before its own time (e.g., in their assimilation of Surrealism, both Artaud and Césaire wrote more fulgurating and enduring poems than any of the Surrealist founders), and it reveals depths and abysses of human nature that only the isolated Blake and elderly Goya, to name two great eighteenth-century "outsiders," depicted. It is Expressionistic *and* Objective as well (think of Olson's attention to the topology of Gloucester, or Césaire's observed Martinican flora). Since this poetry has a critical as well as inspirational relationship to Romanticism, and since much of it carries the shattered lantern glass of previous hermetics in the belly of its lines and is much more concerned with process than with product (= masterpiece), it might be identified as Abstract Romanticism. The most trenchant statement on the burden of such poetry was made by Robert Duncan in the opening paragraphs of his essay "Rites of Participation" (*Caterpillar* 1, 1967).

One reason that the North American poets I mention above are not considered by Kinzie is that the extent of world involvement in their major work is so massive and unrelenting that it cannot be dealt with by standard literary criticism. In the work of Olson and Duncan, as well as several poets of my own generation, "the war within my members," initially sounded by Blake, is out there, at home, in the bloodstream and arguably in the framework of the universe itself. Everyone is implicated —including the critic! What we need is a new kind of critic-reader who is not only willing to take on material that makes her stretch to her last zoa, but also to accept archetypal psychology, insanity, archeology, slavery, anti-semitism and Capitalism as standard and active equipment of literary response.

For Mary Kinzie, a fabulous beast, a kind of Cerebus whose heads are Poe, Baudelaire and Wordsworth, has darkened the aim of poetry into "apotheosis, and ecstatic and unmediated self-consumption in the moment of perception and feeling." To put it rather dully, poets have been concerned with what Kinzie seems to indict since Sappho. *The Divine Comedy,* Blake's long prophetic books and some of the most memorable dramatic moments in Shakespeare define this genre (if it is one). On the other hand, nothing that Kinzie quotes has anything remotely to do with it. Insinuated anxiety, self-indulgence, and violations of surface, the crimes of the unsteady poems trotted out to be heckled, are not apotheosis. Nor do they appear to be damaged by *The Prelude, Les Fleurs du Mal,* or *Eureka!*

Apotheosis, or the deifying/crowning of a god, involves the poet in the strategies of inspiration. Is the source "out there," in aura, in nerves or in a dark transgression in the past—or is the combined figure of the muse, angel and duende made up of all those sources? Apotheosis is the power most sacred to world poetry, from shamanistic incantation and reception to Frank O'Hara overwhelmed with the beauty of Billy Holiday's voice in The Five Spot. Genuine apotheosis is rare and extraordinary (Montale's

"The Orchard" is a fine example), and what we really need is more discussion of it and less sneering at it.

"Ecstatic and unmediated self-consumption" is a peculiar and intriguing charge. In his essay "Revolt Against Poetry," Artaud distinguished between eating his poem and giving his heart to his poem. While in that essay he clearly favored the latter act, his greatest poetry feeds off its own tissue more than it performs sacramental devotions. Poetic autophagy might mean that the body of imagination finds itself good, that all imaginative things are good to consume and transform (Ginsberg's last line of *Howl:* "the absolute heart of the poem . . . good to eat a thousand years"). We all know how limiting and instructive repression and taboo are in the creative process. Apotheosis, in an autophagic sense, might be a state of writerly awareness in which there is nothing to repress, in which all materials are given equal potential poemic status.

Such a state of awareness (as practice in contrast to effect) would in varying degrees be contingent upon the writer's feeling for and understanding of his own physical body, especially in our limbo-less Protestant society, his physical lower body, still the most inaccessible stronghold of material that has been stigmatized as unacceptable to literature. Kinzie pretty clearly indicates the extent to which her ideas about poetry could not accommodate degradation, even the kind that digs a bodily grave for a new birth. Kinzie is set against the "coarse," the "promiscuous" and "the double treatment of words as both ordinary *and* mysterious, clear *and* turbid." It follows that she would find it double-talk to read "ecstatic self-consumption" as self-realization, the imaginative consuming of the generated material upon which the poem has been building. When that which was previously unknown (before the creative process began) is discovered within the labyrinth itself, the Minotaur or specter can be embraced instead of murdered.

Poetry, as a psychological art, is still in its infancy, and young writers who seek to create great poems in the year 2000 would be better off with texts by Bahktin, Ferenczi and Hillman, camped along the Amazon as their workshop, rather than sitting around Argus-eyed, sharpening their defenses in creative writing wards. I, however, fear that the next couple of decades are going to be more populated by schoolmarmish Mary Kinzies than by Blaise Cendrars riding the Transiberian Express. The academic level of Apollonian anxiety appears to feel more and more threatened by the Dionysian rifts and pits that continue to appear in the surface of the century. This means that all of us who believe in a tough, impassioned, critical *and* inspired world-aware poetry that is not meaninglessly avant-garde or conventionally traditional will have to continually speak out for, and seriously defend, a middle ground.

[1985]

A Discussion
with James Hillman
on Psychology and Poetry

CLAYTON ESHLEMAN: I propose that the first things we address are two essays by Jung and what they imply about an opposition between psychology and art. In "On the Relation of Analytical Psychology to Poetry," written in 1922, Jung states that art and psychology cannot be compared. While he acknowledges that they have close connections, and that the connections arise from the fact that the practice of art is a psychological activity, he still wants to keep them separate. He then makes a distinction between intentional and spontaneous art, and set forths these two categories as follows:

Intentional Art	Spontaneous Art
"sentimental"	"naive"
Introverted	Extroverted
A conscious art, one that does not challenge comprehension	An unconscious art, one that is suprapersonal and transcends understanding.

In an essay written in 1929, "Psychology and Literature," Jung more or less maintains these two categories, but expresses them in a terminology more appropriate to his own psychological thinking:

Psychological Art	Visionary Art
Art that nowhere transcends the bounds of psychological understanding.	Art arising from primordial experience, grotesque, demonic, beyond historical and mythological events.

In both essays, Jung clearly shows a preference for the spontane-
ous/visionary category, and he seems to be proposing something incompatible between cogitative, planned activity and inspired, "seized" activity—in fact, in the 1922 essay, he states that "as long as we are caught up
in the process of creation, we neither see nor understand; indeed we ought
not understand, for nothing is more injurious to immediate experience
than cognition."

My experience has been that Jung's oppositional categories are
backed up by the majority of significant twentieth-century poetry. Few
poets would use Jung's terminology, but most would participate in some
form of oppositionalism, whether it is Dionysus *vs*. Apollo, Romantic *vs*.
Classical or experimental *vs*. traditional. The tendency is to believe that
there is a kind of Blakean antinomy between the "prolific" and the "devouring," Devils *vs*. Angels, that is an essential aspect of poetry itself,
and that this "war" is played out from generation to generation, with each
side accusing the other of not really being what they propose to represent.
While it may be that a yin/yang coherence of the new warring with the old
is essential to imaginative movement, the poetic products always seem to
be heavily indebted to one of the two sides.

Rainer Maria Rilke, who would be close to Jung's spontaneous/
visionary category, articulately defends what could be thought of as an
anti-analytical and anti-revisionary position that is dependent upon an
inspirational wind or angel sweeping through the poet. In a 1921 letter, he
wrote: "I believe that as soon as an artist has found the living center of his
activity, nothing is so important for him as to remain in it and never to go
further away from it (for it is also the center of his personality, his world)
than up to the inside wall of what he is quietly and steadily giving forth;
his place is *never,* not even for an instant, alongside the observer and
judge." Now, this observer or judge—is this the doctor, the psychologist,
the man of science?

JAMES HILLMAN: Yes, I think so, but I also think that the notion of the
psychologist as man of science/observer—I think that's where the trouble

---

This discussion is based on an interview with Hillman taped in Dallas, Texas, in 1983; it
was rewritten in 1985, and covers approximately one-third of the taped material. The
complete first quarter portion of the discussion appeared in *Sulfur* #16, spring, 1986.

is. I think that psychologists have fallen into that. They have imagined themselves to be objective, outside critics. Or they have imagined themselves to be interpreters, or commentators, and in the scientific flow, even Freud was there. But the psychologist who is inside his own response is not necessarily outside either, and he is risking, and up against the wall, of his own place, I don't want to say center, but place.

ESHLEMAN: You mean that when Freud is working with Leonardo da Vinci, you think of him as doing primary, creative, imaginative work, even though he is responding to a previous text?

HILLMAN: Yes, and his genre is different, and his writing style is different. It's not effuse, it's not based on rhythm, it's not based on what I would call a poetic genre of writing, but there is poesis going on in it.

ESHLEMAN: Would you go so far as to agree with Jung's statement in regard to what you've just said about Freud? I mean, where he says that as long as we're caught up in the process of creation, we neither see nor understand.

HILLMAN: I would not agree. Because I think Jung is sharing the same viewpoint as Rilke here. And I wouldn't agree with that. I would say that when you're in the midst of the process of—I don't want to use the word "creation" either, it tends to get inflated—but in the midst of writing, or speaking a poem, or whatever, let's just say writing, there is a seeing going on in the hand and in the heart, and in the eye, which is not the kind of seeing that Jung is talking about which is detached outside seeing, but the fingers have an eye in them. E-Y-E. An eye that knows to put down this word and not that word and to cross that out suddenly and to jump to the next thing. That's all seeing. It's not blind. That's again a romantic sense that there's natural creativity and then there's detached scientific observation.

ESHLEMAN: The eyes are in the fingers—meaning, there is an organizing going on that is perhaps not rational in the sense that it would be used in the context of logic. But it is rational or coherent to the creative process itself.

HILLMAN: Absolutely! And I even believe, even in Nietzsche, or in Goethe's *Faust,* which you could say are "spontaneous" in Jung's language, extremely spontaneous, or without guilt, there is a built-in critical learned tradition. It's not absent. Those are not simply effusions. Human consciousness is built into their language, and it isn't even *their* language. It's built into *the* language, perhaps, and their access to language through learning. That's perhaps another side of the issue we're looking at. I mean, it's not some sort of primordial effusion. It's terribly formed as well.

ESHLEMAN: So one way to approach the split is to think that the role of imaginational activity as associated with the poem has been too weighted on the side of the unconscious or of the effusion in which the poet is viewed as this kind of receptacle through whom the power moves, but who has, as it were, no control over the power. And then the psychologist is weighted too far, as he who is in control, he who is, as it were, judging the process, evaluating the process.

HILLMAN: Absolutely. In other words, the discussion has always used the terminology of a certain court model, which splits consciousness from unconsciousness, reason from unreason, creation from criticism, and I think it is, fundamentally, a romantic paradigm. And it puts great weight on access. That the poet is a special person who has access to this beyond. Therefore, the poet is put in the category with the insane, the child, the primitive and, at one time, women. They all had special access to this beyond.

ESHLEMAN: Well, it is a very nifty way of containment. It's a way to applaud and view the poet on Parnassus at the same time that you can definitely say he is irresponsible, and has no real responsible relationship to what he is doing.

* * *

ESHLEMAN: I'd like to keep the Rilke statement before us for a bit longer. It is not clear from his statement about the living center *vs.* the observer and judge, whether he would admit conscious, intentional shaping as a valid part of the creative process. Does he mean that the artist should not judge or observe his work while it is being created, or merely not assume the role of observer/judge when he is not creating? As you may know, Rilke had a deep-seated fear of correction. In 1912, when he was seriously considering Freudian analysis, he wrote to Lou Andreas-Salome: "I rather shun this getting cleared out and, with my nature, could hardly expect anything good of it. Something like a disinfected soul results from it, a monstrosity, alive, corrected in red like the page of a school notebook." While Rilke did not appear to mind if analysis exorcised his "devils"—thinking of them as neurotic habits, I guess, rather than as chthonic powers—he feared that the loss of his angels would mean that he would stop writing altogether.

His desire to stay at what he calls "the living center of his activity" must have involved a lot of observation and judgment. In fact, his concentrated, relentless effort to organize his entire life around his art seems to oppose what would otherwise be considered a highly romantic position. It is as if with great planning and rationality, Rilke built a wall around himself, entered this *temenos,* and then waited, refusing to act creatively unless he was acted upon, "seized," as it were, by one of his angels.

Another point: Freudian analysis in Rilke's day seems to have regarded creativity as being analogous to pathological processes—in fact, while not reductive in the way that Freud can be (seeing images as cover-figures or concealments of basic personal life experience), Jung himself states in the 1922 essay: "The divine frenzy of the artist comes perilously close to a pathological state." If Rilke believed that Freud believed that works of art were an expression of human pathology, he was probably smart to stay away from analysis.

HILLMAN: Now, Clayton, we can't take seriously this "divine frenzy" idea! I know that authority from Plato through Jung argues for it. I know it still appears in notions of the artist as shaman or medicine-man for the tribe, or the artist in league with the devil as in Mann's *Doctor Faustus.* But these words "divine" and "frenzy" have to be unpacked because they come loaded with unconscious Protestant theology, where divine means some glossolaic trance state descending from the Wholly Other (Rudolph Otto), and where "frenzy" means madness, pathology, instead of what it might once have meant when gods were present in the actual world, in Rilke's sense, and not only present in subjective states of possession.

"Divine frenzy," then and now, could mean something far different from Jung's "pathological state." It could mean very close participation with or immersion in actual reality—reality as the radiance of the actual world rather than the descent of inspiration from another world or lifting off to another world. Besides, we have to unpack these words in regard to Jung himself, autobiographically, his anxiety regarding Nietzsche, Dionysus and Wotan. I examined this complex very closely in a paper published in the book I edited called *Facing The Gods,* and you can see in that paper how Jung's division regarding art and psychology parallels his division in himself between personality Number One and personality Number Two. Nietzsche, Dionysus and Wotan as well as the artist, the shaman and the madman are all possibilities of personality Number Two. You see, the entire structure in which Jung casts his life, let's say the narrative of his self-diagnosis, is also the structure he uses to view the artist. Pat Berry worked this out in great length in her study of Jung's buried aesthetics, and we shall have to come back to it with her later. That really is her subject: aesthetics or poetics in relation to psychology.

ESHLEMAN: Let's go on then with Freud and Rilke. There is good evidence that Rilke's masterpiece, the *Duino Elegies,* was begun out of the poet's despair that should he call out for divine aid, no angel would hear him. The entire work opens: "Who if I cried out would hear me among the angels' / hierarchies? and even if one of them pressed me / suddenly against his heart: I would be consumed / in that overwhelming existence." This suggests that if the artist feels that his chosen position, as it were, has abandoned him, he will move to the opposite pole and, like Rilke, set himself on fire by attacking the betraying angel.

All this leads me to believe that we must re-imagine the psychology of cognition, bricolage and inspiration. Perhaps we could begin to do so by asking why Jung insisted on a dichotomy. Was he basing his theories on Classical vs. Romantic "ideals" as manifest in particular works of art, or was he saying something about human sensibility and the extent to which it is creatively limited—that there is something about "us" that experiences creativity as an either/or situation?

After stating that in the process of creation we neither see nor understand, Jung goes ahead to write: ". . . for the purpose of cognitive understanding we must detach ourselves from the creative process and look at it from the outside; only then does it become an image that expresses what we are bound to call 'meaning.'" Clearly, he is referring only to "spontaneous" or "visionary" art here (and by implication relegating *his* other kind of art to a very secondary role). Jung's statement strongly suggests that an artist does not know what his activity signifies while he is doing it. I think this is nearly always partially but *only partially* true—the "muse" of Picasso's "Guernica" was a squad of German bombers (when asked by some German officers, standing before the canvas, "Did you do this?" he is said to have replied, "No, you did"). But I think it is fair to assume that throughout the process of doing the painting, Picasso was aware of the significance of what he was creating—he may not have had an accurate sense as to what extent the world was going to consider it significant, but the fact that its execution was in part a response to a horrible event "out there" creates an immediate field of meaning.

HILLMAN: I think Jung's emphasis on the spontaneous takes aim at those who reduce a poem or painting to an external field of meaning—those German Stuka Bombers. The field of meaning "out there" is always part of the context from which a dream, a poem or anything flows, but that field of meaning is not the cause, or the substance, or the meaning of the dream, poem, etc. Psychology often misses this point in practice. It either literalizes the spontaneous and cuts off an event from any external field of meaning or it literalizes the field of meaning and reduces the event to it. Spontaneous has to be understood not literally, but spontaneous within a specific image or context in which the spontaneity appears. Appears *here,* and only *here,* and not somewhere else.

ESHLEMAN: Jung also places strong emphasis on "the primordial" when he discusses "visionary" art. It is "a primordial vision which surpasses man's understanding . . . it arises from timeless depths; it is foreign and cold, many-sided, demonic and grotesque . . . it suggests the abyss of time separating us from pre-human ages. . . ." I find this definition to be very troublesome; in fact, I do not know how I could accommodate it to most of the poetry I consider to be visionary, because regardless of the extent of the prophetic activity, it is anchored in the anguish of its own times and is, to varying degrees, an imaginative adjustment, or a reaction, against thwarted desire. It appears as if Jung only regarded art of the considerable past when he made his comments about psychology and art, or that there is something inherently distancing in both of his defined artistic categories. To separate the intentional from the spontaneous, or the psychological from the visionary, is to draw a line down the center of much art that participates in all four modes. It seems to be ultimately undermining to the creative process, and in effect subordinates the artist to the observer or judge. Each "type," for Jung, is incomplete, and two incompletes do not add up to a single "whole" artist. It is not only a curious way of exalting and castrating the artist at the same time, but it performs the same kind of elevation/subordination on the work of the psychologist or "judge." His compensation for not being primordially creative is to be seen as a healthy, wise, responsible citizen, empowered with the right to extend or deny significance.

HILLMAN: I seem to be trapped into opposing Jung, yet I can't help feeling annoyed by this word "primordial." Am I hanging on words? Why do I dislike "primordial"—probably because it brings with it all those half-thought-through Darwinian assumptions, cavemen as apemen, developmental history toward the light, and the notion of ourselves as refined, effete, weak-kneed dilettantes making up ineffectual trivia with our minds while deep underneath in the past or in the soul lies grunting primordial truth. This notion of "primordial" leads to an effusionist notion of art, art production based on an altered state of consciousness. Laudanum, absinthe, gin, LSD, cocaine. But what about art as craft, art in cultures where there is no "art" as we call it, where there are only chants made for rituals, objects made for eating, where there is exquisitely complicated dancing, body-painting and masking? These cultures are also "primordial," and yet not merely wild, savage or volcanic. Isn't it told that the people of Bali, for instance, when asked about their "art," reply by saying they don't know what that is; they simply make things as well as they can. No effusion or inspiration here, maybe no novelty either, but at least the everyday and the gods, the ordinary and the beautiful are not divided from each other. So I prefer "primordial" to mean essential or irreducible. So, a painting by Edward Hopper of a gas-station or a cafeteria at night is so exactly irreducible to anything beyond itself, so descriptive of the despairing American soul (which is both its referent and not its referent), that this careful, almost mathematical, image is primordial because it is essential.

* * *

ESHLEMAN: Perhaps we should consider to what extent "access" and "the beyond" are terms that hold up under scrutiny. W. H. Auden has argued that the loss of belief in the eternity of the physical universe, including a loss of belief in the significance and reality of sensory phenomena, have made an artistic vocation more difficult than it used to be. "The beyond" may be a booby prize for those who have lost contact with what is at hand—or as Charles Olson tried to drive home via Heraclitus, "Man is estranged from that with which he is most familiar." It is as if at a certain point in his history man left the thing at hand to quest for immortality, and when that pursuit was revealed to be empty, he was left with the thing at hand, the soul of which had withered from being untended for so long. We now live in a world with a broken beyond and a plastic cup, and one reason that you and I are talking here is because of this. We both seek to lift the essential up through the consumer film and work with it in imagination without vatic inflation.

Because the poet no longer performs a useful function in society, he is to a great extent parked to the side in a playpen where he can dream and say anything. If his writing is entertaining, he is occasionally picked up and carried about in adult arms for a little soul titilation. But the serious poet is not entertaining. He is still involved, as I believe you are, with attempting, through sounding his own adhesion and estrangement, to engage a reader or hearer. Unlike the psychologist, however, his address is more elliptical, harder to get hold of, because he proceeds associationally instead of logically. I think it is a proven fact that an educated person could grasp a good deal of one of Jung's lectures on literature and psychology, but that the same person would be lost on a first or second hearing of *The Wasteland*. On the other hand, your writing in, say, "Blue and the Unio Mentalis" tends to engage associational, or paratactical alignments, so that the argument slides, or moves sideways as it moves forward.

One of the reasons that poets and psychologists have been out of touch with each other is due to the poet's lack of psychological sophistication. From the Romantic viewpoint, such sophistication would be suspect, because the moment of inspiration is absolute and not to be understood by the poet who is to function like a gate (or radio, in Jack Spicer's modern version), through which the poem rushes. I know the thrill, or the bony certainty, of absolute address, and I am tempted, when it occurs, to believe it is the truth, and that it should not be tampered with, regardless of how it looks a week later (awkward, inaccurate, inadequate, etc.), for to think of it as scrutinizable is to regard it as mortal, changeable, capable of error, revisable. I think that, possibly, poets who assert the absolute truth of inspired address do so because they do not want to deal with what other aspects of their mind tell them has occurred at the inspired moment. In that sense, they could be considered psychologically irresponsible.

In his 1929 formulation, Jung puts the poet in an impossible situation: If his writing *is* psychological, meaning if it remains within the bounds of psychological intelligibility, it is, by the way the definition is set up, inferior—a kind of poeticized psychology, versified discourse. If, on the other hand, it is visionary, arising out of "primordial experience which surpasses man's understanding," who can possibly care about it? It may be worshipped by a handful of people who will pass it around like a chunk from outer space, people who adore unintelligibility as an end in itself, and if there are enough "followers, over the years a critical "house" will be built for it, and it will enter the canon as one of the diamonds in the national literary tiara.

I realize that by putting it this way, I am on the verge of saying that because Blake was not understandable to virtually anyone for at least a hundred years after his death, he is solely responsible. Much of Blake now appears to be understandable *and* visionary, so *that* possibility must be kept open—that art which surpasses contemporary understanding can be judged unintelligible for reasons that have little to do with its value. Because it offends taste and style, say, people may claim that it is unintelligible.

HILLMAN: Let's set aside the word psychological for a moment and just talk about the responsibility of the poet. To what is he responsible? Is he not responsible to the poem? Or responsible to receiving, getting out of the way of what Robert Duncan might call "the angels and the demons"? So that he isn't in the way of that, doesn't disturb that, but lets it come through well? Doesn't the poet sense a responsibility in the act of his work?

ESHLEMAN: Getting out of the way of the angels and demons and being responsible to the poem is fine as long as it does not mean a cessation of thinking. To use your image, it means insisting that the angels and demons emerge from the midnight murkiness of the corner of the studio and allow their teeth and messages to be checked out. I believe that there should be a constant critical pressure applied to irrational message. However, if you are arguing that one reason poems fail is because the speaker has foregrounded himself at the expense of imaginational activity, I agree. Then the poem takes on very small grounds and finally becomes only the poet's "scene," e.g., a description of something that he once did—and for him to offer this as his experience is not enough.

HILLMAN: Certainly not enough. But I say it is comparable with ego-psychology. It's comparable with the reduction of the extraordinary that goes on in a dream, and in a life, to my personal experience of it. And psychology, for the most part, today is comparable then with poetry, for the most part—it teaches you to do that. That's what a psychological training is supposed to do, to turn the imaginal richness of the psyche into your own personal account of it. So you lose the archetypal dimension, you lose what you call the imaginational activity. You lose the whole sense of the gods in art in your life. And the focus is on "me," not on the gods. When Rilke keeps turning us back, when he says to get inside your own experience, he doesn't mean it in the subjectivist modern sense of inside your own ego experience. Inside your own experience is focused on the giving back. Because your experience, as I try to say, too, in what I write, is not yours, it is the soul's, and the soul is inherently related to the gods, so that being in the center of your experience is not being in the center of what we commonly call "my" experience. The "my" is sort of *ausgehoben* ("lifted out, removed").

ESHLEMAN: I was talking with Rosemary, the student who picked me up at the [Dallas] airport the other day. She was asking me questions such as, "What is your experience of yourself in the poem?" I made a distinction between the fictive or imaginational "I" and the autobiographical "I," and suggested that the freedom for any "I" to appear in the poem, for there to be a shifting sense of "I" that does not lock into autobiographical frame, was one way to approach the experience of oneself in the poem. The image I offered her, colored by my involvement with Upper Paleolithic cave paintings of animals, went like this: I am in the driver's seat, I initiate the poem as driver, but as the poem gets under way, there is a sense of being outside and almost, to stir the metaphor, of running with

an animal, say, through a field, so while it is clearly C. E. sitting in his
room doing the writing, there is the sense that the less I interfere, in other
words, it is like having this animal bounding . . .

HILLMAN: That's a wonderful image. Wonderful. That's marvelous. And
you don't want to lose touch with the animal by making wrong moves of
your own. So, your self-consciousness is focused on keeping in touch.
Isn't that why one says, right in the middle of writing something, "Oh,
I've lost it. It's gone." By this I mean I've lost touch with that leaping,
bounding (or burrowing)) animal. I do believe this is what we mean when
we say we've lost our concentration. The nose is on a scent, tracking, and
all of a sudden, the track is gone. This keeping on the track, or what's
called concentration, is one focus of self-consciousness. It's a dim
awareness, of honing, of direction, of attentiveness. But it's not *will*. It's
not willing yourself to the track as if it is my personal intention to squeeze
out of myself just what I want to say in this paragraph—although that
kind of self-consciousness can come in too. Sometimes, losing the track
may simply be picking up on a cross scent. Another animal lures the line
of thought into another part of the forest. This feels like a distraction,
dis-track-shun, and just here still another kind of self-consciousness
appears: oscillating between two ways to pursue. Then, there's another
kind of self-consciousness or dim awareness. To do with rhythm or beat.
To do with form. I feel what I am writing is getting too long or wordy.
This kind of focus is on the overall fantasy of the piece as a whole. It is
very much in my mind when I write something—that it not break out of
the dimension of the piece. I think this is the psychological experience of
what Aristotle called *unity*.

[1983-1985]

Vallejo and the Indigenous

IN THE MATURE POETRY of César Vallejo—that poetry written in Europe between 1923 and 1938—there is such an extraordinary assimilation of his background, that his "indigenous influence" is internalized although revealed obliquely. Of the 110 poems that Vallejo appears to have written in Europe, only a handful deal directly with Peru, and in these poems there is no folklore, no political argument, no Quechua or Incan nostalgia —in short, no reliance on the thematic concerns that "third-world" or "minority-voice" poets often utilize to raise before a reader's eyes what has been outcast.

One is tempted to say that when Vallejo physically left Peru in 1923, he also abandoned it as a psychic reservoir of his art. His geographical movement, with Paris as a base, includes Russia and Spain, terminating with his adherence to a socialist art stirred by the Spanish Civil War. Such a viewpoint, however, would miss the most important aspects of Vallejo's European poetry, since for the most part it is not concerned with place, subject matter or theme, and cannot be evaluated on the basis of how many times Peruvian themes appear or do not appear. I would propose that there is an Indian interiority to many of these poems. Their impenetrableness and remoteness is not merely experimental obscurity, but a rendering of sierra "cholo" character, a translation of a personality rooted in Chimu Indian grandmothers and Spanish-Galician-priest grandfathers into poetry that does not explain or even

This paper was written for, and read at, the New Latin American Poetry Conference, Durango, Colorado, October, 1985; it was published in *Sulfur* #15, winter, 1986.

217

address cholo-ness, but embeds its austerity, anxiety and immutability into the Spanish language.

Unfortunately, the indigenous quality I am trying to address is even more complicated than this. By the time the majority of the European poems were written, Vallejo had been in Europe for nearly fifteen years. By the fall of 1937 he had, in effect, passed through Europe, and his poems, which use his own anatomy as studied place, present us with a body that contains the bits and pieces of Western social and religious culture which he had not been able to assimilate. The labor of processing Marxism and Christianity presents him with so many unsolvable problems that it reshapes the way he presents his own dualistic background. On one hand, he is a kind of Congo Nkonde figure, studded with mirrors, nails and hard blades, a Peruvian Nkonde whose magical body juts and glints with European detritus. On the other hand, one can think of his poetry as sculpted stone: running my hands across its contours, I feel a seamless, quiet, ecstatic *anguish*.

His dualistic background seems to be sounded by the two Spanish verbs "estar" and "ser." Vallejo himself pairs these verbs, suggesting that together they indicate a totality of being, with "estar" emphasizing anonymous being, and "ser" emphasizing individuated being. In an attempt to explain Vallejo, one might be tempted to interpret "estar" as passive Indian existence, and "ser" as active European being, but to do so aligns and simplifies two forces that are both static *and* dynamic in this poetry. If they suggest any alignment at all, it is a yin/yang mandala, a kind of animal/human mask, split vertically, with the flesh of one side made translucent in the eye of the other side.

Anonymous being, in Vallejo, is animal being, and he associates a particular category of animals—jackasses, asses and donkeys, all beasts of burden—with Peru itself. He begins one poem: "It was Sunday in the clear ears of my jackass,/ my Peruvian jackass in Peru." His finest thematically indigenous poem, "Telluric and magnetic," is populated with pachyderms, rodents, vicuñas, asses, apes and guinea pigs. While there is a sardonic edge to the image of man as a "gloomy mammal" who "combs his hair," the animal emphasis is on grounded, generational life, a magnetic adherence to biological perpetuation. This is the closest we come to bedrock in Vallejo's poetry, but it is weeping bedrock and therefore unstable.

José Carlos Mariátegui pointed out in 1928 that the fundamental

Indian characteristic of César Vallejo's early poetry is a "nostalgia of exile, of absence." Mariátegui's point is based on poetry written by Vallejo before he left Peru. By the fall of 1937, having been in actual exile for nearly fifteen years, much of which time he lived nomadically out of a suitcase, Vallejo's nostalgic mood had deepened and raised into what might be called the climate of his being. Nostalgia is amplified into sadness, weeping and anguish, none of which directly evoke the Peru of his childhood, or a Peru of a more distant past. This does not mean that Peru is not present. It means that Vallejo is seeking an expression the equal of his own nature's intricacy, that he is blending, beyond racial stratification, his mixed background into a composite image of man.

The crying/sobbing/weeping is especially interesting, as it is one of the most constant currents in these poems, and is rendered more complex-ly than mere loss or frustration. Vallejo speaks of his "beloved organs for crying," he desires to "anoint his body with wept honey," and urges the reader to join him in a banquet that consists of "the flesh of sobbing, the fruit of groaning." Given these positive associations with tears, one is hardly surprised when in a late poem he commands man to "give off rain." Tears, or the body's miraculous liquids, become a kind of fecundation, a way of brimming with the world.

Another current, one that is curiously related to tears and masculine fluids, as well as to the way Vallejo is expressing his Peruvianism, is that of generational consternation, specifically a vexation with his own geni-tality, which appears to be related to the fact that the Vallejos never had any children (Vallejo himself being the youngest of eleven). While I do not want to leave the poetry for ruminations on César Vallejo's yet-to-be-written European biography, I want to point out that I, as well as others, have been told by old friends of the poet who were still alive in Paris in the 1960s and 1970s, that Georgette Vallejo had anywhere from several to more than a dozen abortions. In a remarkable poem, "Today a splinter has entered her . . ." Vallejo seems to be envisioning a moment in which the sexual act transforms itself from sensuality into sheer pain. In other poems, the speaker seems to be meditating in a state of extreme sexual arousal, deriving the poem's content (which is never merely de-scriptive or confessional) from the "pleasure" of this "suffering." One of the fractured motifs that runs through these poems and which seems to agonizingly press the poet up against the meaninglessness of his death, is a stated love for the human family and a consequent nightmare assembly of images coupling masculine sexual desire with complications, morbidity and abortion in the feminine or receptive sphere.

I spent a year in Peru in 1964–65, most of which time I was in Lima. I made two brief trips to the sierra, east of Ica, and in the Huancayo area. While I still have strong feelings for the people I saw and met there, I can't say that I understand something fundamental about their world which would throw a definitive beam into the obscurities of César Vallejo. However, having lived with and retranslated these poems since the early 1960s, I have feelings about the layers of Vallejo's life and the way he manages to keep me active as a reader/translator by particular focuses and deflections. In one of the notebooks from the 1930s, Vallejo remarked that he loved plants for their roots, not for their flowers. My image of the Vallejo plant is one that is rooted in Andean taciturnity. As this plant pushes up through the soil, we are confronted with its struggle to flower, not with the flower itself. In a unique way, the Vallejo plant never does flower, but twists about on itself, a gnarled and branching thing, constricting itself with its own offshoots.

Generation is forced up into view on all levels and held in the poetry in a state of anguished suspension. I think that were Vallejo to have been European or North American he would have chosen one of two other alternatives: either to openly acknowledge the problem and offer an explanation for its cause, or to repress it, to sublimate its awful energy into a literary attitude. I'm suggesting that there is a triple containment in Vallejo's European poetry, based on a humanized Christian trinity, in which the Mother replaces the Holy Ghost. This triple containment consists of tears, stones and the blocked generational drive which is linguistic as well as organic. Triads are everywhere in these poems, such as "my potato and my flesh and my contradiction under the bedsheet."

Over the years I have had the haunting but unverifiable feeling that these poems were loaded with Andean reluctance to communicate, initially with the Peruvian coastal world and ultimately with Europe—moreover, that Vallejo was bearing Indian muteness in his art, and that "indigenous influence" here indicates the translation of "outer" experience into an unceasing internal pregnancy, a relentless bearing within, which is presented without source or realization.

I have spoken of the tears and of Vallejo's sexual morbidity which, I should add, because of the courage involved in expressing it, is moving, and affirmative. The stones are what Vallejo carried with him to Paris, the Andean particles that he could have put in his pocket. The stone is an indication of cosmic instability, for he writes, "do not put your foot on that tiny stone: who knows, it is not a stone, and you'll plunge into empty space, for we are in a totally inknown world." Note that he writes "inconocido" here, not "desconocido," an *in*known, not an *un*known world. He portrays himself as a "black stone" (in black overcoat) on a "white stone," and in the poem compelled by a hunger that is both biological and spiritual, the craving is for:

> A stone to sit down on
> will now be denied to me?
> Not even that stone on which the woman trips who has given
>   birth,
> the mother of the lamb, the cause, the root,
> that one will now be denied to me?
> At least that other one,
> that crouching has passed through my soul!
> At least
> the calcarid or the evil one (humble ocean)
> or the one no longer even worth throwing at man,
> that one give it to me now!

>   At least the one they could have found lying across and alone
>   in an insult,
> that one give it to me now!
> At least the twisted and crowned, on which echoes
> only once the walk of moral rectitude,
> or, at least, that other one, that flung indignified curve,
> will drop by itself,
> acting as a true core,
> that one give it to me now!

In a way, the stone is the unborn child, a lithopaedion of weeping, a consternation in the depth of man that is seldom expressed in art: the consternation of not being able to bring forth life—art as a substitute for offspring. I believe that the trinity of forces I have proposed is a basic configuration in Vallejo's European poetry and that it represents a combined object, too, that each force mirrors the others. Yet they do not add up to an intellectual house of mirrors. They are muscles of the work, as well as clues.

There are a handful of poems that do deal directly with Peru, as if Vallejo continues to keep a siphon into his natal source no matter where he wanders. In one such poem he extols Peruvian miners in a way that makes them seem like archetypal forces emerging each evening from the abyss they deepen each day. Another poem affirms the connections between the speech, labor and physicality of landless Peruvian serfs. The summation piece on Peru is the blistering "Telluric and magnetic," in which Vallejo affirms his allegiance to the biological and zoological combustion of a Peruvian earth that is forever in parthenogenesis, where he catches slopes red-handed becoming slopes. "Telluric and magnetic," in one blow, rivets Vallejo's entire European production to the Andean/Indian aspect of his life, as if at the bottom of his cosmic well the gleams of intelligibility are the eyes of an Indian—or is it a vicuña?—gazing through the blackness. Or to see it another way: as if he is capable of letting the storms of history and personal consternation howl through his poetry because of an inherited Indian endurance that still reverberates with the creation of the earth itself. "Indian later than man and before him!" he shouts near the end of "Telluric and magnetic," thus embracing or surrounding man with Indianness, as well as seeing man as a transitional stage between the primordial and the new, whereby the primordial again appears, recycled and strengthened by the transition.

[1985]

Aimé Césaire's *Lost Body*

THE TEN POEMS OF *Lost Body* interlock thematically in a fugal manner—in fact, their unity of style and tonal similarity makes them read like sections of a single "serial poem." Unlike his first three collections, all of which underwent radical revision, *Lost Body* has seen only minimal changes. Probably composed at the end of the 1940s while Césaire was dividing his time between Fort-de-France and Paris, the collection—or suite—offers the reader a rare opportunity to observe the transitional moment in Aimé Césaire's poetry when the poet's youthful Mercurial fervor is being modified and weighted with the elegaic introspection of maturity.

In coining the word "negritude," Césaire built an ideological structure in which the "nègre" (nigger) could find, not only refuge, but the rafters and supports of a cultural continuity. In *Notebook of a Return to the Native Land,* Césaire argues that the absence of black achievement is compensated for by an earthy, mystical quality that "yields, captivated, to the essence of things." According to the poet, the fact that blacks have not (in the Western sense) invented or explored, and have remained "ignorant of surfaces," implies a potential capable of regenerating an earth that has (and here I am paraphrasing Césaire) become weary with the victories which become the defeats, with the alibis and stumblings of the white world. By the time he wrote *Lost Body,* Césaire seems to have realized

This essay is Section Two of a four-section introduction to *Lost Body:* Poems by Aimé Césaire/Illustrations by Pablo Picasso (New York, Braziller, 1986), co-translated by the author and Annette Smith (who wrote the other three sections of the introduction).

223

that in certain ways the black would remain in exile to himself and, in effect, not enter the house called Negritude which Césaire had built for him. The dynamics underlying this somber revisioning are social as well as psychological.

As a mayor and Deputy to the French National Assembly, Césaire was facing the initial difficulties involved in improving the lives of his black constituents. Perhaps as a result of this, the speaker in "Who Then, Who Then . . ." repeatedly expresses the need for assistance in fulfilling various desires, a clearly more social gesture than is expressed in Césaire's earlier poetry ("The Thoroughbreds," for example), where the speaker destroys and recreates his world by himself. In general, the early fusillades of revolutionary optimism are now giving way to the difficulties of true change. As several poems movingly testify, the tragic roots of being black in a world for the most part governed by whites are deeper and more embedded than the poet of the *Notebook* had calculated.

Psychologically speaking, in *Lost Body* Césaire is struggling with the erosion of his heroic, fiery and phallic aspects, and with the challenge of time, distance, the instability of Eros, as well as with an anguished Saturnian suspicion that his condition cannot be explained by colonialism but is somehow a part of nature itself. While mythological forces are still heroically evoked, they are increasingly battered by the myth-denying present. In both the first and the title poem of *Lost Body,* the word "nigger" limits and severely infects mythological amplification:

In "Word," the speaker commands the "word" (which initially in the poem suggests The Word, or Logos) to keep vibrating within him. At the moment that its waves lasso and rope him to a Vodun center-stake where a shamanic sacrifice ensues, it is also revealed that the "word" is "nigger," and, by implication, the curare on the arrow tips as the quiver of social stigmata associated with "the word nigger" are emptied into him.

And in "Lost Body," the speaker is dissolved and reborn in a predictable Césairean fashion, this time as Omphale—a seer Pythoness who in Greek myth guards the Delphic *omphalus*. However, as this seer seeks contact with the wind, he/she receives not a vision but screams of "nigger nigger nigger from the depths/of the timeless sky."

The requests in "Who Then, Who Then . . ." are responded to at last by a "full-grown girl," who separates the grain of the speaker's shadow from the grains of his clarity while "neatly confusing the accounts." She is to bring into relief Césaire's negative side until now obscured by his intellectual clarity. Ultimately, then, the speaker's "need" is for more attention to the soul and its grim politicized vales in contrast to the spirit's soaring peaks. The brooding, meandering lines of this poem show us how far we have come from the climax of the *Notebook*, where a standing insurrection of slaves wheels the poem up into the stars.

The "full-grown girl" of "Who Then . . ." is the first appearance in *Lost Body* of a shadowy feminine presence that evokes both Isis (gathering the scattered pieces of the "lost body" of Osiris) and perhaps an actual woman. The weight of this presence, however, is linked to the fauna and flora of Martinique as a kind of spirit of the place, increasingly associated with destruction and remorse. In "Elegy," an entropic landscape is paired with a male lover's anguish—for he has discovered that under the surface is not merely, as in the *Notebook,* "a wallow of boars/ . . . your eyes which are a shimmering conglomerate of coccinella," but "the herd of old sufferings" which push their way out of the unconscious like dumb, driven beasts, right into the lovers' embrace and turn it into "DISASTER." Here again, one might recall a passage in the *Notebook,* where Césaire describes the "unexpected sorcery" which would lull his father into "melancholy tenderness or drive to towering flames of anger." This "gnawing persistent ache" now seems to be acknowledged by the poet as a negative force in his own life, as if there are aspects of black anguish that cannot be dispelled by Eros or by imagination.

A sense of abrupt violence permeates *Lost Body*. In "Forloining," a few lines from a folksong describing a cane cutter hacking apart the body of a "long-haired [white?] lady" interrupt the poet's plaintive meditation on his "Distant . . . inattentive-one." And in "Lost Body," the startling nigger screams of the wind inform the speaker that there is madness at the center of his existence. If the wind itself calls him a nigger, then he *is* an eternal fugitive. For a moment, Césaire's body of work buckles with the dilemma that true humanity might only be discovered in madness or apocalypse. The severity of this moment is registered by the wrenching ending where the nigger, although torn apart (by the white devil's hounds), destroys the sky and recreates primal islands in one paroxysmic gesture. Such an ending recalls Hart Crane's great lyric, "Lachrymae Christi," where a Nazarene/Dionysus who is crucified, torn apart and burned at the stake is beseeched to reappear whole. Both poems confront the reader with a radical vision of creativity which is bound up with an assimilation of such destructivity as to render it, in the same moment, sublime and absurd.

"Your Portrait" continues this work of desperate metamorphosis; here the feminine is depicted as a river carrying along the speaker who envisions himself as the uprooted trunk of a poisonous manchineel. As if desiring to lose this aspect of his body in the feminine element, the speaker prays to become liquid himself. In the following poem, "Summons," enrapt with his liquid transformation, Césaire portrays the earth as a wild and beautiful event, once again erotic, and now liberated by Time. The poem ends abruptly with three definitive adjectives stacked one after the other against the left margin: "whole/ native/ solemn." Not only has the "lost body" again been recovered, but these words stand as a summation for Césaire's own personality in his work.

This is the self-assertive peak of *Lost Body*. The last two poems are melancholy, meandering rivers of images, anticipating many of the poems in Césaire's last major collection, *Ferraments* (1960), where evocations of a timeless black "disapora" ring even further changes on the "lost body" theme: the lost collective body as well as the individual body, cast overboard from the slave ships and lost at sea.

In "Lay of Errantry," it is as if the liquid transformation sought in "Your Portrait" has become a style of writing. The sliding, unpunctuated phrase-pulses are riverine in that they collect and carry along countless historical and mythological particles. Here the peristaltic negations and affirmations of *Lost Body* relax in a flow, at once mournful, questioning, self-defining and noble. The poem and collection end with the speaker having reentered Paradise with the flame from the Covering Cherub's flaming sword. The work now, Césaire suggests, is in felling the trees of the Christian Eden, using the gate guardian's sword flame as an ax. Given the phallic associations with tree shafts that pervade Césaire's poetry at large, the final image resounds with atavistic suffering experienced as self-maiming at the core of a reconstruction of Paradise.

[1985]

The Translator's Ego

In his Introduction to my *Selected Poems 1960–1985*, Eliot Weinberger writes: "As for translation: the dissolution of the translator's ego is essential if the foreign poem is to enter the language—a bad translation is the insistent voice of the translator."

My first experience with what I think Weinberger means by "the translator's ego" was with Ben Belitt's translations of Garcia Lorca's *Poet in New York*, in 1959. Belitt appeared to be imposing his own poetic voice onto the Spanish text when, for example, he translated the last line of Lorca's poem "La Aurora," "como recién salidas de un naufragio de sangre" as, "as though lately escaped from a bloody disaster." Lorca's "shipwreck of blood," a powerful direct image that needs no translational revision, had not only been lost but turned into English-English slang—Belitt's "bloody," as in "he's a bloody good bloke," neatly effaced Lorca's "blood." In the case of Belitt's Lorca and Neruda translations, we hear the translator-poet's own mannerisms leaking into and rendering rococo the meaning of the original texts. It is as if Belitt is colonizing the foreign terrain of these poets instead of accommodating himself to the ways in which they differ from his own poetic intentions.

The image of a translator colonizing the foreign terrain of an original text has somber implications, especially in the case of a "first-world" translator working on a "third-world" writer. By adding to, subtracting from and reinterpreting the original, the translator implies that he knows

---

"The Translator's Ego" was originally written for a presentation on translation at Bookworks in San Francisco (February, 1986); it was published as "Addenda to a Note on Apprenticeship" in *Translation Review* #20, 1986.

227

better than the original text knows, that in effect his mind is superior to its mind. The "native text" becomes raw material for the colonizer-translator to educate and re-form in a way that instructs the reader to believe that the foreign poet is aping our literary conventions.

Belitt, of course, is not alone in such activity, although his imposition seems more monolithic and damaging than that of many other translators. When Robert Lowell drops out ten of Rimbaud's twenty-five stanzas in translating "Le bateau ivre," there seems to be a presumption that only two-thirds of one of the greatest poems in the French language is worth carrying over to English. Cid Corman, at times an extraordinarily fine translator, has a tendency to eliminate repetitive phrases and to drop articles. This appears to be a manifestation of his own poetics which have led to the short, terse lyrics he is well known for. I, too, am guilty of ego imposition. For example, in my 1968 translation of Vallejo's poetry, I rendered the line, "pero me busca y busca. Es una historia!" as, "but she looks and looks for me. What a fucking story!"

The Vallejo poem in question here is made up of a series of anguished lamentations on the failure of his wife to connect with him. During the first eight years that I translated Vallejo, I was unable to connect with Georgette Vallejo—by which I mean that she constantly blocked my work with the excuse that no one could properly translate her late husband's poetry. After much effort, by a fluke, Grove Press gained permission to publish the translation. One afternoon I was sitting in Gil Sorrentino's office going over galleys. When I came to the poem in question, I read it to Gil and complained that the last line—at that point rendered, "but she looks and looks for me. What a story!"—lacked punch. By that point, Vallejo's "Es una historia!" was not only loaded with his consternation, but had taken on the symbolic weight of my struggle with the translation and with his widow. My memory is that after a moment's reflection, Sorrentino threw up his hands and exclaimed, "what a fucking story!" and in a giddy moment I said, "that's it!" and added the intensifier to the line. I was wrong to do so, and when José Rubia Barcia and I retranslated the poem six years later, we took it out.

I've gone into a little detail here not to excuse myself but to suggest that a translator's impositions upon his text are not necessarily a worked-out plan to create a new tone or meaning for the original. Were Lowell to be here, he might explain (probably not to our satisfaction) that he left all those stanzas out because he was unable to render them to his satisfaction. Corman might argue that by cutting here and there rather than adhering to the original at every point, he had made a sharper and not really unfaithful version in English.

So, how might a translator work to resist ego imposition or, at worst, translational imperialism? For the fact is, there is no such thing as a literal translation of a poem—denotative choices come up in every line. There is a constant process of interpretation going on, regardless of how faithful one attempts to be to the original.

When the original poet is available for questioning, a certain amount of denotational guesswork can be eliminated. When one is translating the great dead, or out of contact with the author, the only indicators come from the text at large, and the way key words can be identified relative to the author's background. While translating the Martinican Aimé Césaire with Annette Smith, I visited Césaire several times, always with a few pages of specific word questions. Given Césaire's busy schedule, it was never possible to ask him all the questions that came up in translating him, so many tricky decisions had to be made on the basis of the text itself. As an example: Smith and I occasionally came across the word "anse," which can be rendered as "bay/cove/creek," or "[basket] handle." Since Césaire's poetry is very specific to Martinican geography, and since the entire island is pocked with bays and coves (which had led to such place-names as Anse Pilote, or Grande Anse d'Arlet etc), the obvious choice here seemed to be "bay" or "cove" (assuming that the context of a particular poem does not call for a "handle" reading). Yet in the 1969 Berger-Bostock translation of Césaire's *Notebook of a Return to the Native Land*, we find "les Antilles qui ont faim . . . bourgeonnant d'anses frêles . . ." translated as "the hungry Antilles . . . delicately sprouting handles for the market." Not only has the Surrealist Césaire been falsely surrealized, but the translators have backed up their error by adding an explanation to the reader as to what these handles are for. When Smith and I retranslated the *Notebook* in 1976, we rendered these phrases as "the hungry Antilles . . . burgeoning with frail coves . . ."

In the case of Vallejo, I learned not only to check my work with Peruvians and Spanish scholars, but to check their suggestions against each other and against the dictionary. I worked to find word-for-word equivalents, not explanatory phrases. I also respected Vallejo's punctuation, intentional misspellings, line and stanza breaks, and tried to render his obscurity and flatness as well as his clarity and brilliance. An unsympathetic reviewer of Barcia's and my work, John Simon, exclaimed: "Eshleman has tried to render every wart of the original!" Which is, in fact, exactly what we had tried to do—to create in English a non-cosmeticized Vallejo.

As a poet translating another poet, I let my sense of my relationship to Vallejo and his poetry enter my own poetry, so that the translating activity, in the context of an apprenticeship, was envisioned and critiqued as an aspect of my own evolving poetics. Over the years, I constantly tried to skim my own imaginings of Vallejo off the surface of the translations and let them ferment in my own poetry. I came to understand that if a translator does not do this, he runs the risk of building up an imaginal residue in his translation, which, with no outlet of its own, spills into the text.

The thing is: Imagination is always present. We know this when we try to remember and write down a dream upon waking. As we try to remember we forget, and in the flux we reorganize, imagining the dream into a writing that ends up locking the nebulosity of psyche into a fixed grid of print. In a similar way, our imaginations are active as we move one language into another. As we read translationally, we risk revising the original to reinforce our dream of a poetics that might hold its own against alternative poetics.

All the poets I have spent long periods of translation time with —Neruda, Vallejo, Artaud, Césaire, Deguy—have drawn me because I felt that their poetry knew something that my poetry wanted to know. Besides attempting to make accurate, readable versions, I was also involved in a secondary plot, or a sub-text, wanting to shovel some of their psychic coal into my own furnaces.

Since translation is such slow work, requiring multiple rereadings, it can require a more prolonged reading-in-depth than when we read poetry written in our own language. As the translator scuttles back and forth between the original and the rendering he is shaping, a kind of "assimilative space" is opened up in which "influence" may be less contrived and literary than when drawing upon masters of one's own language. The kind of "influence" I have in mind here involves becoming porous to the *character* of the original, and to the various ways in which it resists or does not resist being transformed.

Thus in the case of Vallejo, I do not think of myself as having been influenced, at least not directly, by his Marxism, his Christianity, or by his own indigenous influence which, since he was a Peruvian sierra cholo, gives his writing much of its austerity, anxiety and immutability. No, in Vallejo's case, I believe that it is his capacity for contradiction, and the consequent complexity of viewpoint that has been the fuel. He offered me not merely ideas and stances, but a way of receiving and twisting the blow of the world.

[1986]

Placements II

An Epeira centered in her web, afloat yet anchored between ground and sky. The natural mind of the earth always spinning. Her one "decision," where to start the web. A small male enters, testing, sounding, the thread. At the center of the web, the penetrator is killed.

*

A Japanese Epeira, under whose green, red and yellow abdomen I spider-sat, daily, for a month. One day, finding the web torn, I lamented a death, one that has never ceased to disturb me. The death of anything can contact the anythingness of our own death.

*

After Epeira disappeared, I had a vision during which, at the northwest corner of Nijo Castle, I saw a bright-red human-sized spider working a web up in the night air. The vision was too much for me. I did not have the language, the psychology, to report my own seeing of what I saw. Without Ariadne's thread, the veins, spittoons, claws, colorations and emanations of the goddess's body are opaque, not an image, a grueling picture.

*

At 85,000 BC, a foetally-tied corpse is carried on a pine-bough "raft" to a red ochre-packed pit in the German Neander Valley. Once deposited, the "corpse-raft" is covered with stone slabs. A few slabs have been discovered with cup-shaped indentations gouged in the side facing the corpse. The red-gated pit accepts the bound one—"then closes the Valves of her attention—like Stone." With the power of her red interior, she will wombify the entombed. A belief has persisted in primitive peoples that the soul, or the new-born itself, is a result of the coagulation of menstrual blood. In my spider vision, the green and yellow of Epeira's abdomen disappeared: The visionary spider was all red.

*

At 27,000 BC, 60 cup-shaped indentations were gouged in the form of a spiral in a large stone discovered at La Ferrassie. Red disks indicating vulva-like passage openings in the caves of Chufin and Pech-Merle, and the red vulva symbols in La Pasiega and El Castillo indicate that at the very beginning of image-making, creation magic was related to menstruation. For the Arnhem Land Wawilak Sisters, the Rainbow Serpent is their synchronized menstrual power and its connections to coiling dragons, floodtides and storms.

*

The Wawilak Sisters' story has undergone a structural inversion and is now told in such a way as to help the men justify their having transferred women's mysteries into their own hands. They imitate menstruation and birth in artificial collective bleeding, gashing their arms and genitals, drawing subincisioned boys up between their legs. The women, humbled, go off into the bush to menstruate or give birth, alone. The men have torn apart the Sister web.

*

Let's erase the "Venus of" from the "Venus of Laussel." Let's restore Laussel, figurehead on the prow of the ship Earth, to her place-name identity. Originally colored red, she holds up a 13-notched bison horn, perhaps to link her desire with the animal's force as well as to synchronize her flow with his appearance. There is no bison body—only this horn which she tilts toward her turned head, a Scarlet Woman regarding the bison vortex.

*

Arachne is not Ariadne, although the figures are intertwined: The natural mind of the earth always spinning anticipates the mistress of the labyrinth that the initiate is to traverse. In the labyrinth of the creative life, "the bitter contest of the two natures" can be sublimated from a generational life/death struggle to an orgasmic union with a priestess whose lunar energies are at floodtide.

*

Every artist everywhere participates in Ariadne. The transformation of the "given" life to a "creative" one not only involves entering a dark or "inner" life, but generating as well a resistance substantial enough to test oneself against and to shape the focus of one's work—and, having experienced the bestowal of soul (which is the reality of Ariadne), one must liberate the experience in a creative product, must emerge with more than the claim that something "happened" while "inside."

*

The earliest "pits" or earth-wombs were probably caves in which one to be initiated slept "in magical imitation of the incubatory sleep in the womb." We know that shamanic initiation involved long periods of incubation, pantomimed destruction, burial and rebirth. The incubus was not a perverse Christianized fiend, but an angel brooding on the initiate's body, perhaps in psychic imitation of the digger wasp/caterpillar conjunction. The signs, grotesques and animals in Upper Paleolithic caves may have been painted there as dream allies, left as records of the dream/initiation, or both. The fact that this art is often found in remote and "tight" parts of a cave not only stresses the underground journey, but the criblike congruence between the cave's body and the initiate's body.

*

The Minotaur of the early Cretan myth was named Asterior, synonymous with *aster*, "star." He was "bull and star at the same time," and the ultimate elevation of Dionysus and Ariadne, as a divine couple appearing in unmaimed, fully born, human form in the night sky, suggests that the universe is the labyrinth and in imagination it is possible to be fully human there.

*

On the isle of Naxos, commemorating Ariadne's transformation, Theseus and his fourteen companions danced a Le Tuc d'Audoubert-like swirling dance around a horned altar, which recalls the actual bull horns through which Cretan bull-dancers flipped in a sacred marriage of the sun-king and the moon-goddess. The "horned altar" also evokes the womb's birth cone (and the labyrinth itself is prefigured by the cervix, lined with a branching called the "arbor vitae," or tree of life, where devouring white cells may be imagined to hide and wait like monsters for the Odyssean sperm over whose turbulent voyage the Athenic aspects of woman preside).

*

The horned altar is also the Double Axe, or labrys: bound together by a haft, the crescent-moon blades are a glyph of the labyrinth itself. Think of entering the lower tip of the left-hand crescent and following its curve to the haft, or center, where a change of materials signals an adaptation, through which one must penetrate, and readapt again in order to follow out the curve of the upper right hand crescent. The motion through is serpentine, and in respect to the material, the central confrontation is the movement from iron to wood to iron, organic *vs.* inorganic materials, which Wilhelm Reich layered to build his Orgone Accumulator, a small enclosure into which he invited patients, or initiates, to his vision of a journey, on the peristaltic accordion of the body, from sexual insufficiency to orgastic potency.

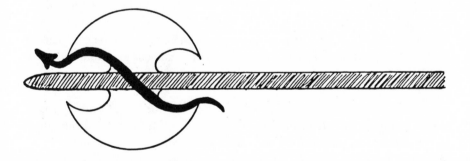

*

As in Arnhem Land, where men took over women's menstrual mysteries and converted them into an attack on the body, there appears to be a takeover signified in the Cretan-Greek complex of myths relating to Ariadne. As Arihagne, the "utterly pure," a spinning hag or sorceress, she enjoyed intercourse with the labyrinth and its grotesque inhabitant. When patriarchal consciousness overwhelmed matriarchal centering, Ariadne became a "maiden to be rescued," who, "falling in love" with the hero Theseus, gave him the "clew" or thread that would enable him to get in and out and, while in, to slaughter the sleeping Minotaur. The labyrinth, without its central being, was thus emptied of animality.

*

In the twentieth century, the burden of the vacated labyrinth involves hairline connections with the myriad cul-de-sacs of the deep past. The myth of Ariadne seems to capture much of Charles Olson's vision of "life turning on a SINGLE CENTER" until a mysterious "contrary will" manifested itself around 1200 BC, and the heroic attempt to "overthrow and dominate external reality" resulted in the migrational waves, or tentacles, that spread out around the planet. Do we in North America live in the bulb of a tentacle end that has, at the point it connects to a body, a slaughtered animal/hominid, whose corpse still fulgurates in our lethal dominational obsessions? Garcia Lorca's great and mysterious essay on the "duende" identifies this imp of the blood, which provokes some of the world's great art, as a struggle with a wound that never closes. Is Lorca therefore caught, whether he knows it or not, in Ariadne's turnstile, responding to a dark power of the blood that thousands of years ago mesmerized and enraged men as it appeared in rhythm with the moon and the tides and, without violence, ceased, only to reappear again and again?

*

In Tantrik sexual magic, the two ingredients of the Great Rite can be *sukra* (semen) and *rakta* (menstrual blood). The sulphurous red ingredient in alchemical goldmaking may have been, in certain instances, this female essence (the *rubedo*, or precious red stone that sweats blood and turns the world to gold, is a conjunction of a whitened queen and a reddened King; such a blending could be seen as a PINKENING). Many images of the labyrinth have not a minotaur but a rose at its center, a sign that a transformation has taken place. Seven days, during her period, the Old King is dissolved, rinsed of himself, his selves, lost in her "bath," her anabasis. The Dionysian initiate who is assimilated into the rose appears with a beard of roses to complement, below, Ariadne's rose-wreath crown.

*

The natural spinning mind of the earth weaves itself in personifications through our humanity. Biological peril is always central, the center, and sublimated by image-making into "scorpion hopscotch," or the imaginative gambling called poetry. It is possible to formulate a perspective that offers a life continuity, from lower life forms, through human biology and sexuality, to the earliest imagings of our situation, which now seems to be bio-tragically connected with our having separated ourselves out of the animal-hominid world in order to pursue that catastrophic miracle called consciousness. If the labyrinth is a Double Axe, one might see it as humanity's anguished attempt to center an unending doubleness that is conjured by the fact that each step "forward" seems to be, at the same moment, a step "backward." And the haft? Phallocentricity which fuses the menstrual/ovulatory cycles into an instrument of inner and outer ceremony that injures but does not restore.

[1985]

"Placements II" has appeared in *Temblor* #3, *Exquisite Corpse* Vol. 4, #3, *Syntaxis* 11, and *12/13* (in Spanish); it was reprinted in *The Name Encanyoned River*. Sources for this reading of Ariadne include: *Dionysus,* by Karl Kerényi; "The Gate & The Center," by Charles Olson (*Origin* #1); *The Gate of Horn,* by G. R. Levy; "Levi-Strauss and the Dragon," by Chris Knight (*Man* #18); *Le Mystère des Cathédrales,* by Fulcanelli; *The Thread of Ariadne,* by Charles F. Herberger; *The Wise Wound,* by Redgrove and Shuttle; *The Woman's Encyclopedia of Myths and Secrets,* ed. Barbara G. Walker; exchanges with James Hillman; the modal legacy of the Cro-Magnon people.

Chapter 7 from Novices

THE ALCHEMIST FULCANELLI: "The picture of the labyrinth i's thus offered to us as emblematic of the whole labour of the Work, with its two major difficulties, one the path which must be taken in order to reach the centre—where the bitter combat of the two natures takes place—the other the way which the artist must follow in order to emerge. It is there that *the thread of Ariadne* becomes necessary for him, if he is not to wander among the winding paths of the task, unable to extricate himself."[1]

ANTON EHRENZWEIG: "Any creative search, whether for a new image or idea, involves the scrutiny of an often astronomical number of possibilities. The correct choice between them cannot be made by a conscious weighing up of each single possibility cropping up during the search; if attempted it would only lead us astray. A creative search resembles a maze with many nodal points. From each of these points many possible pathways radiate in all directions leading to further crossroads where a new network of high- and by-ways comes into view. Each choice is equally crucial for further progress. The choice would be easy if we could command an aerial view of the entire network of nodal points and radiating pathways still lying ahead. This is never the case. If we would map out the entire way ahead, no further search would be needed. As it is, the creative thinker has to make a decision about his route without having the full information needed for his choice. This dilemma belongs to the essence of creativity."[2]

Novices (1987) is a twelve-chapter essay that addresses the initial chaos and the potential coherence involved in making a commitment to poetry. It presents and critiques "Curriculums" by Gary Snyder, W. H. Auden, Robert Graves and Charles Olson, and meditates on the alchemical, psychological and sexual ramifications of making contact with origins; it discusses the labyrinth as possibly the most ancient design of the creative process.

FROM THE 1950 *Webster's New International Dictionary:*
"panopticon (pan + Gr. *optikon,* neut. of *optikos* of or for sight). 1.
A kind of optical instrument, as a combination of a telescope and
microscope. 2. A prison built so radially that the guard at a central
position can see all the prisoners. 3. A place where everything can be
seen; an exhibition room for novelties."

There is an archetypal poem, and its most ancient design is probably
the labyrinth. One suddenly cuts in, leaving the green world for the
apparent stasis and darkness of the cave. The first words of a poem
propose and nose forward toward a confrontation with what the writer is
only partially aware of, or may not be prepared to address until it
emerges, flushed forth by digressions and meanders. Art twists toward
the unknown and seeks to realize something beyond the artist's initial
awareness. What it seeks to know might be described as the unlimited
interiority of its initial impetus. If a "last line," or "conclusion," occurs to
me upon starting to write, I have learned to put it in immediately, so it
does not hang before me, a lure, forcing the writing to constantly skew
itself so that this "last line" continues to make sense as such.

As far as poetry is concerned, "the bitter combat of the two natures"
can be understood as the poet's desire to discover something new or
unique *vs.* the spectral desire of tradition to defeat the new and to continue to assert its own primacy. It is a "bitter" combat because the realization that writing a poem may provide is inevitably partial. The Minotaur
is at best crippled, never slain, and the poet never strides forth from the
labyrinth, heroic and intact. At best he crawls forth, "wounded" as in the
cry of Vallejo in "Intensity and Height"; more often than not, he never
emerges at all. The poet never leaves this combat with a total poem,
because such a poem would confirm that the discrepancy between desire
and the fulfillment of desire had been eliminated. But since my desire is
ultimately to create reality and not merely to observe it, I am bound to be
defeated if reality is at stake in my poem's ambition. As I emerge from
my poem, regardless of what I have realized while in the poem, I am back
in the observable biological continuum, and part of it, part of its absolute
mortality. I suspect that I am always aware of *this* closure, and that it
underwrites (asunderwrites) what I envision while inside the poem.

Harold Bloom's "Six Revisionary Ratios,"[3] which proposes to identify "intra-poetic relationships" among the poets that for Bloom constitute an Anglo-American Romantic tradition, may be most useful to poets themselves as a reading of the stages involved in working through a particular poem. Bloom, of course, intends his "ratios" to challenge current critical attitudes and, as such, his is a book that could only offend poets who are not named as part of the center stage action of Bloom's "tradition," which becomes increasingly arbitrary as it approaches the present. Its argument in which an earlier poet becomes the focus of a struggle on the part of a later poet, who must wrest manna from the former in order to assert himself, is actually depicted by Blake in his vision of his struggle with Milton in "Milton: A Poem." My idea here is to regard this "struggle" in the context of Fulcanelli's and Ehrenzweig's images of the labyrinth as a symbol of the creative process, in which much more than literary combat takes place. The nodes, or advance positions, that send out radial possibilities everywhichway, are charged with the poet's personal life as well as the context of his times, to mention two considerable influential powers that lie outside Bloom's sense of influence.

Here are Bloom's Six Ratios, followed by the key word he focuses them with:

1. Clinamen, or Swerve
2. Tessera, or Completion
3. Kenosis, or Emptying
4. Daemonization, or Counter-Sublime
5. Askesis, or Curtailment
6. Apophrades, or Holding Open to the Dead

Is it possible that these terms double Fulcanelli's three-beat rhythm of the labyrinth, offering a more complex and asymmetrical sense of the contractions and expansions involved in solving the burden many but not all poems take on?

The poet Swerves into the poem by redirecting his attention from the utilitarian world to one in which "precise subjectivity"[4] is constantly at stake. Or think of the poet as a falling angel who refuses at the last moment to continue to fall and become one of the fallen (= unimaginative man, the literal-minded, one for whom the objective world is the real world). He Swerves, beating his wings up, up, up, and enters a new space.

The Swerve into imaginative space and the first few words or lines determine mode, tone, direction and some of the difficulties to be undertaken. Once all of this is in place the poem runs the risk of lapsing into a conventional handling of its direction, in effect Completing itself before it has gotten underway (as a joke poorly told may telegraph its punchline and thus be "over" way before the actual punchline falls). While the taking on of direction is necessary, if the direction takes its theme or subject matter for granted, the reader has "heard it before," and the poem no longer belongs to itself. Thus the initial move toward Completion must be redirected, or complexed, in order to build up steam, or availability to the unknown that is beyond the poem's initial knowing. Such a move is a contractive one, and would be the Emptying, or willingness to introduce contradiction and/or obscurity via sound-oriented or associational veers.

Emptying makes it possible for the poem to have space for the other or the otherness that can be the most single compelling moment in composition. Daemonization (in contrast to demonization) is the admitting of unconscious material into the composition-in-process, the point at which the poet weds himself, consciousness and unconsciousness fuse—the poet is the world, no separation between his skin and everything else. The eagle of inspiration has sunk its talons into the poet's shoulders and he is borne aloft. There are many ways to approach this moment: in Blake it would be the moment in which the authors in eternity communicate to mortal secretary William. In D. H. Lawrence, the moment that the wind does blow through him (Lawrence states the archetypal daemon plea in: "Not I, not I, but the wind that blows through me!"[5]). Garcia Lorca, weary of hearing critics and conventional poets prattle about the Muse and the angel, borrowed from the world of Flamenco dancing the figure of the "duende," which translates into English rather poorly as "imp." It is a figure of the blood for Lorca,[6] an uprushing or seizure, in which the dancer or poet is momentarily possessed, or incubated (as if by a dream incubus, who lays a psychic egg in the dreamer's body as she fucks him, and "steals" his semen).

Daemonization is perilous because as such it cannot complete the poem (when we are stoned, daemons seem to rush through us, but when we try to articulate their message-sensations, we have nothing—if not less than nothing, for the Daemon of Marijuana loves to gobble up imaginative potential, eating the poem on the spot that had we not gotten stoned might have been *written* the following day). Curtailment is similar to Emptying, in that both are experienced as severe, contractive moments—however, Curtailment is more complex, because the poem has taken on much more burden and possibly unmanageable material than earlier. If the poet does not successfully separate himself from the Daemon's embrace or claws, one result is that inspiration turns into ego-inflation (nearly always just around the corner in Whitman or Ginsberg). In Curtailment (Bloom's Ratio term, Askesis, is based. on "ascetic"), the poet must cut into his own beanstalk, bringing the drama tumbling down or seeing into the meaning of the action in Giant Castle through a narrowing, densifying perception. Or to put it another way: In Curtailment, I step outside the poem and in a sense become my own critic, looking for loose ends, ego-inflations that have gotten into the Daemonization, gaps to be plugged—while at the same time I must stay with the shape of the energy recast by the Daemonization.

Bloom's Apophrades is a marvelous image. The dead, the great dead, return to inhabit our houses—life returns to before that fall in which a Swerve was a possibility. The dead return—the poem is over, *the way things are* overwhelms metaphor. The poet, like a streaker now, shows himself to the dead, a phantomic act the dead could care little about. The dead return, life returns to its deadliness, its obliviousness to poetry. Our poems end because at Curtailment we know we cannot escape the product of the poem if we are to have art at all; we know we cannot sustain the poem against the desire of the dead to reinhabit the *temenos* they believed they inhabited in their own time. In a great closure (Wallace Stevens' "Each person completely touches us/ With what he is and as he is/ In the stale grandeur of annihilation."[7]) there is a shadowed Daemonization, an embrace at the edge of here and not-here.

The dead are now back in our houses. We are outside, outsiders to the poem, peripheral, schizophrenic, caught up in the physical need to reconnect. Every completed poem collects its rejected children, bundles them into its immense laundry basket and takes off. Image of its huge ass, in peasant shoes, hurrying away from Van Gogh's corn field.

[1987]

NOTES

1.   Fulcanelli: Master Alchemist, *Le Mystère des Cathédrales* (London, 1974), p. 48. On the following page, Fulcanelli offers an alchemical definition of Ariadne.

2. Anton Ehrenzweig, *The Hidden Order of Art* (Berkeley, 1971), pp. 35–37. Ehrenzweig's drawing of "the maze (serial structure) on p. 36, reminds me of shattered glass more than of the concentrically infolding/outfolding labyrinth. See also Van Gogh's "The Starry Night," with its two milky flows of light, one curling down to tuck into the other curling up—a figure Wilhelm Reich identified as "Cosmic Superimposition." The so-called "serial poem" (Whitman's "Song of Myself," Jack Spicer's "Books") attempts to make use of nodal discontinuities, viewing sections as corresponding rather than connecting.

3. Harold Bloom, *The Anxiety of Influence* (New York, 1973), pp. 14–15. The novice must decide to what extent Bloom's highly exclusionary study (in which only several twentieth-century American poets appear in a context that presents them as representing the end of an essentially English literary tradition) is a projection of his own anxious desire to be with poets, one of them, a poet himself. Is it possible that in failing to realize himself as a poet, he envisions the end of a great tradition in its own time, and appoints himself as the eagle-surveyor on a crag overlooking a battlefield of his own construction that stretches narrowly back to Milton?

4. Robert Kelly's phrase, which appears in his own context later in *Novices*.

5. *The Complete Poems of D. H. Lawrence*, Vol. 1 (New York, 1964), p. 250.

6. "Theory and Function of the Duende," *Lorca*, The Penguin Poets (London, 1960). See Robert Duncan's novice encounter with Lorca elaborated in the 1972 Preface to *Caesar's Gate*. For distinctions between "daemon" and "demon," see James Hillman's *The Dream and the Underworld* (New York, 1979), especially the "Barriers" section, which considers Materialism, Oppositionalism and Christianism. Emily Dickinson's #754, written around 1863, is as severe a description as I know of of Daemonization and the extent to which its possession can become a life possession, a living out of an alien other's commands. Lawrence emphasizes unconscious message over the poet's willing; in Dickinson's visionary description, the poet is seen as a tool (a gun), at the trigger-mercy of an owner-duende who can fire her at whim (see Susan Howe's thoughtful and differing consideration of this poem in *My Emily Dickinson* [Berkeley, 1985]):

> My Life had stood—a Loaded Gun—
> In Corners—till a Day
> The Owner passed—identified—
> And carried Me away—
>
> And now We roam in Sovreign Woods—
> And now We hunt the Doe—
> And every time I speak for Him—
> The Mountains straight reply—
>
> And do I smile, such cordial light
> Upon the Valley glow—
> It is as a Vesuvian face
> Had let it's pleasure through—

And when at Night—Our good Day done—
I guard My Master's Head—
'Tis better than the Eider-Duck's
Deep Pillow—to have shared—

To foe of His—I'm deadly foe—
None stir the second time—
On whom I lay a Yellow Eye—
Or an emphatic Thumb—

Though I than He—may longer live
He longer must—than I—
For I have but the power to kill,
Without—the power to die—

7.   Wallace Stevens, *The Collected Poems* (New York, 1957), p. 505.

The Stevens-Artaud Rainbow

THE RANGE OF POSSIBILITIES within which the American poet now works can be suggested by a spectrum with Stevens at one pole, and his antithesis, the French poet Antonin Artaud, at the other. If we think of Stevens as an aspect of the archetypal hermit still wandering through nature holding his lantern out before him, then Artaud—incarcerated for years in asylums and subjected to more than seventy electroshock treatments—is the inscape of the same image, the actual hermit worked over by the century, whose lantern in his stomach is in pieces.

Most American poets today are neither aristocratic, reactionary vice-presidents of insurance companies, nor diagnosed autistic coprophiliacs. However, our burden, I believe, is to discover in ourselves the Stevens in Artaud, and the Artaud in Stevens—to produce a poetry in a nuclear lethal world that is researched and experimental, unstable and brimming, a resource for others that does not play false the rips in all the assumed continuities that may have stabilized poetry in the past.

An overview of the past forty years might be this: The conflict between the traditional and the experimental which produced the heady atmosphere of the late 1950s and the 1960s became more conservative *and* more radical in the 1970s. If, on one hand, we think of Robert Lowell as the most powerful traditional poet of the earlier period, we can see how his disciples, modifying confessional anguish to hyper-sensitive self-description, have become the poet-teachers in the university writing programs that have turned poetry into a middle-class profession. If, on the

This essay appeared in *Margins* magazine (London, 1988).

245

other hand, we posit Charles Olson as the most dimensional experimental poet of the earlier period, we can see how his attempt to unbind thinking has helped generate the "Language Poetry" of the past decade, so haunted by instability and the inadequacies of traditional narration that much of it reads like white noise. Easy communication and the refusal to communicate at all now seem to caricature the fluid elegance of a Stevens and the enraged attempt of an Artaud to say the unsayable. Regarding this polarity, it does not matter that Artaud is not American. Translation has made all poets everywhere neighbors.

If in this essay I tend to foreground the experimental in contrast to the traditional, it is because for years canon-making textbooks and literary criticism have ignored the many kinds of experimental poetry, thus falsifying the most precious aspect of twentieth-century American poetry: its diversity.

As a young poet in the early 1960s, I felt that an experimental front had established itself, not as a new "academy," but as a flexible, communal proposal: American poetry had to be informationally acute, historically and prehistorically curious and psychically bold—or accept the fate of being the minor, decorative art used as "filler" in the pages of *The New Yorker* and *Atlantic Monthly*.

The conventional poetry of the time had split in two directions: As exemplified by the poetry of Richard Wilbur, it was formally anecdotal, dressed up in rhymed verse; as represented by the "Confessional" poets, it was autobiographical gossip shocking to polite society, rendered as "free verse." While the poetry of Wilbur and Sylvia Plath, say, looked different on the page, the poetic assumptions were quite similar: Development was predictable, as in a joke or story, implying that life itself was made up of self-contained, explainable units.

In contrast, the poetry that was exciting me argued that experience was discontinuous, the mind unstable and sexuality of all sorts a power to be confronted in the poem itself. This was the point at which many of the previously outcast minorities—women, blacks, Indians, gays and lesbians—began to invade the essentially WASP stronghold of American poetry. Their appearance (and its subsequent permutations) argued that the so-called stability of mainstream verse was based on massive exclusion. Thus, while such words as "discontinuous" and "unstable" had, from a conventional viewpoint, a negative meaning, in the light of the invading minorities I did not see them this way: Rather, such terms seemed to be true to what life really was—they helped put me in touch with my own personality, which I experienced as fragmentary, volatile, anguished and fulgurating.

Robert Duncan's title for his first major collection, *The Opening of the Field* (1960), proposed a multiple reading of the word "field." Together with the obvious natural site of primal events, it suggested via the terminology of physics that the poet was both a source and a conductor, and that the poem itself was a kind of "middle-man" for transmitting forces. In contrast to the linear Wilburesque presentation of the poem as a pretty gift in a ribbon-work of "pictures" (as opposed to images), the poem was, according to Duncan's ally, Charles Olson, "energy transferred from where the poet got it, by the way of the poem itself, all the way over to the reader." Rather than a shape into which content was poured, as water into a glass, the poem was a spill of water, its contents determining its form, each poem responsible to the energy it tapped in the process of being written out.

Olson was particularly valuable for the amount of world and self he was engaging in his epic-in-progress, *The Maximus Poems*. Not only could he make me feel the psychic and material contours of Gloucester, but because he was able to envision this eastern American port as a "divine particle" in currents of Western civilization and migration that went back to Mesapotamia, he indicated that ancient history, geography and geology—in effect, the congruence of man and earth—were part of poetry's responsibilities. In regard to the self, the point was not to repress it, or limit it as a deified ego. Rather, as Olson put it, in a crucial passage from his epic:

It is not I,
even if the life appeared
biographical. The only interesting thing
is if one can be
an image
of man, "The nobleness, and the arete."

An artist's lifework is a sentence under constant reformulation that death interrupts. Completed poems, completed books, may be more like points of emphasis, or points at which the meaning in that sentence veers, than discrete units. Olson, who died in 1970, with *The Maximus Poems* uncompleted, is a unique figure of his time for the extent to which he was able to pack into his talk and his writing a mind in ceaseless inquiry which preferred the probe to the synthesis. At the same time, he opened a Pandora's box of poetic problems, for the amount of material he attempted to handle threatened, on one hand, to jam the machinery with informational overload and, on the other, to render it abstract by Olson's hyper-active multiple-viewpointing. And underlying these disturbances is the central problem that undermined both Hart Crane's *The Bridge* and Olson's rapport with Gloucester in the *Maximus* sequence: If in a materialistic society "bridge" and "city" are only commercial entities, how can the poet believe in them and offer them a figurative presence in his writing?

Well, he must—and he can't. And I think it is this problem that has built an adversarial element into much of the best poetry written this century. What Americans appear to have inherited from tribal societies (where the material is fused with the metaphysical) never quite meshes with what is under our noses, and it builds in us a divisive obsession with *things*. We feel estranged from things because as commercial entities they have no psychic "shine." However, they make up much of our reality, and to evade them is almost inevitably to look back to Europe, or under the surface of America for an indigenous integrity which, on scrutiny, does not belong to most of us. While the famous admonition of William Carlos Williams—"No ideas, but in things"—evokes an adherence to specifically American reality, it also carries as a kind of backwash the sterile indication that here ideas are bound up with utilitarian products.

In the past, especially in the deep past, it seems that the belief in an overworld and an underworld gave volume and significance to a middle- or earthworld. Not only do American poets lack a given realm of God or gods, but more importantly, I believe, they lack a psychic underworld. To say "underworld" in America merely evokes Al Capone and his empty Chicago vault—not Tiresias in conversation with Odysseus. Most of us inherit the Christianized version of the underworld: hell—a furnace of torture and damnation, rather than a realm of journey and exchange.

One reason why Olson pushed further and further back in human history in *The Maximus Poems* was because of his inability to ground his epic in American reality. He went back as far as the Neolithic; perhaps he should have gone further, to the Upper Paleolithic, where the underworld appears to have been first conceived. For in the "light" of Chernobyl, we must find the deep past relevant. At the same time, we must find the present relevant!

We do not want to be taken in by the apocalyptic fervor of the late 1960s which must have been in part a desperate attempt to overwhelm what had been building in people since Auschwitz and Hiroshima: that the tumblers had been set not for an Edenic return, or an advance into Aquarius, but for world destruction. For if there is no future and therefore no serviceable past, the present might resemble a flux of instantaneously equal alternatives, slipping forward from second to second, with each second, or sentence, supplanting the last. Modern painting and the writings of Gertrude Stein prefigured atomic consciousness; the abstract interiors of John Ashbery and the wrecked phrases of Charles Bernstein (poems which resemble an endless string of rear-ended Laurel and Hardy autos) picked up on the vibrations of the 1970s and became the avant-garde of that decade.

Bernstein and other "Language Poets" represent a new strategy for resistance to and accommodation of the American present. The accommodation is in how his poetry imitates the frenzied particle flow of our times, restricting content to buds of noticings that flicker like a grid of flashing lights or disappear like snowflakes. The resistance is in his refusal to allow himself to be read with the gamut of sentimental response that characterizes middle-class identification with art. His internalized, non-referential punning forces the reader into the jungle-gym of syntax, and insists upon reader-participation to the extent that it is the reader who must organize what is traditionally called "meaning" in the poem. The extent to which Bernstein's poetry is a perceptive "reading" of our age, and to what extent it is a Dadaesque contempt for outworn modes, remain open to question.

The difficulty in believing in the poem, for an American, is not a recent phenomenon. The awful discrepancy that Crane sensed between his vision of the Brooklyn Bridge and what it represented in American culture increases as one comes forward in time. While at work on his epic in 1926, Crane wrote to Waldo Frank: "The bridge as a symbol today has no significance beyond an economical approach to shorter hours, quicker lunches, behaviorism and toothpicks. And inasmuch as the bridge is a symbol of all such poetry as I am interested in writing, it is my present fancy that a year from now I'll be more contented working in an office than before. Rimbaud was the last great poet that our civilization will see—he let off all the great cannon crackers in Valhalla's parapets, the sun has set theatrically several times since while Laforgue, Eliot and others of that kidney have whimpered fastidiously. *Everybody* writes poetry now—and 'poets' for the first time are about to receive official social and economic recognition in America. It's really all the fashion, but a dead bore to anticipate. If only American were half as worthy today to be spoken of as Whitman spoke of it fifty years ago there might be something for me to say—not that Whitman received or required any tangible proof of his intimations, but that time has shown how increasingly lonely and ineffectual his confidence stands."

The university creative writing programs, uncannily prefigured in Crane's words to Frank, may ultimately be documented as a child of the slump in reading ability that goes back to the hands that reached out of a TV screen in the early 1950s and have held the American public in full-Nelson, facing the screen, ever since. Over the past several decades it has increasingly dawned on literature students that it is more fascinating and rewarding to try to write poetry than to read Chaucer. Unfortunately, meaningful writing is contingent upon assimilative reading as well as upon a passionate interest in one's experience. The problem posed by the remarkably similar 300 creative writing programs across the country (worked out as BA, MA, or MFA degrees) is two-fold: because nearly all of these programs are "studio-" or workshop-oriented, students end up competing with each other rather than with the great dead—and the emphasis is on turning out teacher-poets (who will immediately be plowed back into the system) instead of poets.

Without the mountain of the other to climb, the young writer stagnates in an atmosphere filled with peer anxiety and a need for immediate reinforcement. The product is generally verse that is talky, likeable and principally about the author's "sensitivity." It is also, alas, anonymous, and free of the tension and concentration that shapes the best poetry. One of the mysteries in poetry today is determining how one of these poems is chosen for publication over another.

Perhaps the greatest weakness of the creative writing programs is that they tend to obscure that period traditionally known as apprenticeship, in which the poet-to-be (or not-to-be) incubates himself, drawing nourishment from a dead or living master. Concomitant to such an apprenticeship is a survey of the master's values, an evaluation of the repercussions of his viewpoint, with a strong hunch on the apprentice's part that gaps and errors will be discovered, thus enabling him ultimately to birth himself out of what he will turn into the master's dry crysallis. Rilke's secretarial relationship with Rodin, or Olson's exhaustive study of Melville, are milestones of apprenticeship in the art of poetry.

Writing significant poetry today is more complexly adversarial than in the past. It is no longer a matter of the Dionysian *vs.* the Apollonian, the experimental *vs.* the traditional, the legendary oppositions which have for the most part divided poets against themselves. I began this essay by suggesting that Stevens and Artaud—both great poets in my estimation—represented a genuine range of poetic diversity. In no sense did I mean to imply that one must choose between them (or worse, the writers that crowd together in that gray area—Middle C—between the extremes). No, I evoked Stevens and Artaud to suggest that fulfillment and antagonism—in effect, all oppositions—are to be accommodated in the writing process.

I see no need to eliminate a narrative context in which a self (personal or transpersonal) is struggling with its fate. However, if such a self is conscious of the extent to which it is a fleck in the global network, "free" and "imprisoned" as an American citizen, and at the center of a panopticon that includes an ecological deathrow as well as a cosmic library, then poetry is seen both as a synthesis *and* a melee. And I do not mean this thematically: I mean a process of writing which involves a ceaseless shifting of gears, backward, forward and crabwards at the same time, a kind of poetry that faces what America is doing right now to Nicaragua and at the same moment does not sweep aside the pleasures of physical existence.

Such writing has been occurring here since the end of the Second World War. I am thinking of the "grand collage" that the poet Robert Duncan has been building since the late 1940s in which, to quote Duncan, "the very form of man has no longer the isolation of a superior paradigm but is involved in its morphology in the cooperative design of all living things, in the life of everyone, everywhere." I am thinking of Allen Ginsberg whose lifelong attempt in art has been to show reality with a simultaneous force similar to that with which Krishna reveals himself to Arjuna in the *Bhagavadgita;* of the elegant and dissonant "chance" configurations in the poetry of Jackson Mac Low; of Jerome Rothenberg's chorused lines in which Martin Buber, Marcel Duchamp, Gertrude Stein and Sitting Bull kick together; and of the eerie vibrations in Clark Coolidge's prose and poetry where noise and information twist and fray.

Do all of these poets have any single thing in common? I would say yes, but it is not a movement or a single thematic tendency. It is a furious combination of so many themes and tendencies, an appetite to not play false the fantastic diversity and terrible monoculturation every seeker is aware of today. As a way to pinpoint the configuration that all these intersecting works evoke, I would bring forth the Russian scholar Mikhail Bakhtin's phrase, "grotesque realism," and rephrase it as an "American Grotesque."

Bakhtin coined the phrase in his book *Rabelais and his World* to identify the carnivalesque degradation and regeneration that in his view represented, via Rabelais' writing, the high point in the history of the Grotesque. Such a phrase implies a plural, unfixed, tragicomedic view of life, and the Grotesque itself stretches back to the Upper Paleolithic decorated grottos (which give us the origin of the word), and comes forward through Romanticism and Surrealism to the present. "American Grotesque" places the Bakhtinian phrase in present-day American reality and might be a concept elastic enough to identify and honor certain poets' attempts to deal with our annihilational atmosphere, the extent to which we are participating in a world collage, a mortal planet, and information-channeling that drives us wild to try to get everything in, or at least a sense of everything, as each word, mostly ignorant of our desires, inches forth on the page. An American Grotesque would show how our societal and military might have infected and honed perhaps the oldest tradition in art.

In 1980, Gary Snyder wrote to me, "The '50s–'80s was the discovery of the depths of Far Eastern religious thought for Occidentals. The '90s should be the period of the beginning of the discovery of the actual shape of early Homo Sapiens consciousness: for both Occidental and Oriental seekers. A profound new step. Knowing more of the Paleolithic imagination is to know the 'Paleo Ecology' of our own minds. Planetwide human mental health in the twenty-first century may depend on arriving at these understandings. For it is in the deep mind that wilderness and the unconsciousness become one, and in some half-understood but very profound way, our relation to the outer ecologies seems conditioned by our inner ecologies. This is a metaphor, but it is also literal."

If we inject the veering present with Snyder's vision and at the same time keep our eyes on the grotesque surface of society and its sustenant grotesque abyss, might we have an imaginal grid so charged that it is capable of providing an adversarial resistance to negation and despair? In 1982 I realized that Wallace Stevens' "the voice that is great within us" had split at its center into "the voice that is grapeshot within us," and that his "stale grandeur of annhilation" had united with that morbid exhilaration, the leper sperm, that swims in all creation. I now propose that American poets regard their own lives in a context that not only includes these negations, but the words of Stevens' dark brother, Antonin Artaud: "The great total dimension is to become, as a simple man, strong as all infinity."

[1986]

APPENDIX

1965. "The Book of Eternal Death," a serial prose poem. Unpublished.

1966. "Letter to César Calvo Concerning the Inauguration of a Monument to César Vallejo"; and "Bud Powell, 1925–1966," *Indiana* (Los Angeles, Black Sparrow Press).

1969–1972. "Heaven-Bands," a journal. Unpublished.

1971. *Bearings* (Santa Barbara, Capricorn Press).

1972. *The Sanjo Bridge, Sparrow #2* (Los Angeles, Black Sparrow Press).

1975. "Letter on Perloff," *Contemporary Literature* (a response to Marjorie Perloff's "The Corn-Porn Lyric: Poetry 1972–1973," *Contemporary Literature,* 1974); "Adhesive Love," *The Gull Wall* (Los Angeles, Black Sparrow Press).

1977. *On Mules Sent from Chavin* (Swansea, England, Galloping Dog Press); "The Lorca Working," *Boundary 2,* Jack Spicer issue (New York).

1978. "Satanas" and "Joseph," *What She Means* (Los Angeles, Black Sparrow Press); "Vallejo 1978," *Montamora #4* (New York).

1979–1986. Books reviewed by CE in the *Los Angeles Times Sunday Book Review: Kill the Messenger,* by Robert Kelly (4/27/80); *Walt Whitman, A Life,* by Justin Kaplan (12/7/80); *Shadow Train,* by John Ashbery (6/7/81); *Selected Poems,* by Czeslaw Milosz (7/5/81); *William Carlos Williams: A New World Naked,* by Paul

Mariani (12/30/81); *The Magician's Feast Letters,* by Diane Wakoski (7/18/82); *The Life of John Berryman,* by John Haffenden (10/10/82); *Corpse and Mirror,* by John Yau (8/7/83); *The Other Side of the River,* by Charles Wright (8/19/84); *Selected Poems,* by Philip Levine (9/10/84); *Otherwise,* by Eugenio Montale (2/24/85); *Selected Poems* of Kenneth Rexroth (3/31/85).

1981. "Tartaros" and "Narration Hanging from the Cusp of the Eighties," *Hades in Manganese* (Los Angeles, Black Sparrow Press). Also, a review of *Great Slave Lake Suite* by Leland Hickman, *Poetry News* (Los Angeles).

1982. "Modern Poetic Polarities," an essay in the *Los Angeles Times Sunday Book Review,* February 7th.

1984. "Open Letter to George Butterick," *The Exquisite Corpse* magazine, Jan/Feb (Baton Rouge, Louisiana), a response to Butterick's review of *Fracture* which appeared in the same magazine in December, 1983; "Translation as Transformational Reading: Vallejo, Artaud, Césaire," *American Poetry* 1/3 (Jefferson, North Carolina).

1986. "Dedication," *The Name Encanyoned River: Selected Poems 1960–1985* (Los Angeles, Black Sparrow Press).

1987. Response to "Is there, currently, an American Poetry?", *American Poetry* 4/2 (Jefferson, North Carolina); "Introduction" to *Parallel Voyages,* by Paul Blackburn (Tuscon, Arizona, Sun/Gemini).

There is also an "Index to *Caterpillar* Magazine," by Jeanne Somers, in *Credences* (Buffalo, New York, spring, 1985).

INDEX